MULTI-PARADIGM
DESIGN FOR C++

MULTI-PARADIGM
DESIGN FOR C++

James O. Coplien

ADDISON-WESLEY

An imprint of Addison Wesley Longman, Inc.

Reading, Massachusetts • Harlow, England • Menlo Park, California
Berkeley, California • Don Mills, Ontario • Sydney
Bonn • Amsterdam • Tokyo • Mexico City

Many of the designations used by manufacturers and sellers to distinguish their products are claimed as trademarks. Where those designations appear in this book and Addison-Wesley was aware of a trademark claim, the designations have been printed in initial caps or all caps.

The author and publishers have taken care in the preparation of this book, but make no expressed or implied warranty of any kind and assume no responsibility for errors or omissions. No liability is assumed for incidental or consequential damages in connection with or arising out of the use of the information or programs contained herein.

The publisher offers discounts on this book when ordered in quantity for special sales. For more information, please contact:

U.S. Corporate and Government Sales
(800) 382-3419
corpsales@pearsontechgroup.com

For sales outside of the U.S., please contact:

International Sales
(317) 581-3793
international@pearsontechgroup.com

Visit Addison-Wesley on the Web: www.awprofessional.com

Library of Congress Cataloging-in-Publication Data

Coplien, James O.
     Multi-paradigm design for C++ / James O. Coplien.
          p.   cm.
     Includes bibliographical references and index.
     ISBN 0-201-82467-1
     1. C++ (Computer program language)   I. Title.
QA76.73.C153C675   1998
005. 13'3--dc21   98-36336
                                                        CIP

ISBN 0-201-82467-1
Text printed on recycled and acid-free paper.
3 4 5 6 7 8 9 10 11 12—MA—0706050403
Third printing, April 2003

To Dennis and Tom,
who taught me everything I know

J. J.

Contents

Preface

I have rarely invested as much energy in any endeavor as in naming this book. As the manuscript evolved, its title evolved to emphasize one or two concepts at any given time from the set of basic elements *Domain, Engineering, Multi-Paradigm, Analysis, Design, Programming,* and *C++*. The publisher was afraid that the unfamiliar term "domain engineering" would fail to engage the target market. One of the reviewers, Tim Budd, was concerned about confusion between his use of "multi-paradigm" and the way the term is used in this book. I was concerned about using terms such as "analysis" because of my desire to put the book into the hands of everyday programmers, whose problems it strives to address. Tim Budd graciously offered that our discipline is diverse enough to accommodate a broad spectrum of definitions for "multi-paradigm," and I insisted on a title that emphasized the role of the programmer and not that of the methodologist. That led to a happy convergence on the current title, *Multi-Paradigm Design for C++*.

I never considered titles containing the words *pattern, object, CORBA, component,* or *Java*. Multi-paradigm design tries to dig deeper than any single technology or technique to address fundamental questions of software abstraction and design. What is a paradigm? What is the relationship between analysis, design, and implementation? These questions go to the foundations of abstraction that underlie the basic paradigms of programming.

One of the most basic questions is, what is abstraction? Abstraction is one of the key tools of software design; it is necessary for managing the immense and ever-growing complexity of computer systems. The common answer to this question usually has something to do with objects, thereby reflecting the large body of literature and tools that have emerged over the past decade or two to support object-oriented techniques. But this response ignores common design structures that programmers use every day and that are not object-oriented: templates, families of overloaded functions, modules, generic functions, and others. Such use is particularly common in the C++ community, though it is by no means unique to that community.

There are principles of abstraction common to all of these techniques. Each technique is a different way of grouping abstractions according to properties they share, including regularities in the way individual entities vary from each other. To some, commonality captures the recurring external properties of a system that are germane to its domain. To others, commonality helps regularize implicit structure that analysis uncovers in the recurring solutions for a domain. Multiparadigm design honors both perspectives. For example, the technique called *object-oriented design* groups objects into classes that characterize the common structure and behaviors of those objects. It groups classes into hierarchies or graphs that reflect commonality in structure and behavior, while at the same time allowing for regular variations in structure and in the algorithms that implement a given behavior. One can describe templates using a different characterization of commonality and variation. Commonality and variation provide a broad, simple model of abstraction, broader than objects and classes and broad enough to handle most design and programming techniques.

Commonality and variation aren't new to software design models. Parnas's concept of software families [Parnas1976] goes back at least two decades. Families are collections of software elements related by their commonalities, with individual family members differentiated by their variations. The design ideas that have emerged from software families have often found expression in widely accepted programming languages; good examples are modules, classes and objects, and generic constructs. The work of Lai and Weiss on environments for application-specific languages takes this idea to its limits [Weiss1999]. The so-called analysis activities that focus on the discovery of software families and the so-called coding activities that focus on how to express these abstractions have always been closely intertwined. Multi-paradigm design explicitly recognizes the close tie between language, design, and domain structure and the way they express commonality and variation.

We discover software families in an activity called *domain analysis*, which is another field with a long history [Neighbors1980]. Software reuse was the original goal of domain analysis, and this goal fits nicely with software families. Multi-paradigm design explicitly focuses on issues that are important for reuse. To help the designer think about adapting software to a spectrum of anticipated markets, multi-paradigm design explicitly separates commonalities—assumptions that don't change—from variabilities—assumptions that do change. We strive for *domain* analysis, not just analysis. We design *families* of abstractions, not just abstractions. Done well, this approach to design leads in the long term to easier maintenance (if we predict the variabilities well) and to a more resilient architecture (we don't have to dig up the foundations every time we make a change). Of course, multi-paradigm development is just one tool that helps support the technical end of reuse. Effective reuse can happen only in the larger context of organizational issues, marketing issues, and software economics.

We use these foundations of commonality and variation to formalize the concept of *paradigm*. A paradigm, as the term is popularly used in contemporary software design, is a way of organizing system abstractions around properties of commonality and variation. The object paradigm organizes systems around abstractions based on commonality in structure and behavior and variation in structure and algorithm. The template paradigm is based on structural commonality across family members, with variations explicitly factored out into template parameters. Overloaded functions form families whose members share the same name and semantics, and in which each family member is differentiated by its formal parameter types.

C++ is a programming language that supports multiple paradigms: classes, overloaded functions, templates, modules, ordinary procedural programming, and others. Bjarne Stroustrup, the creator of C++, intended it that way. Most programmers use the C++ features that go beyond objects (though some abuse them to excess and others force designs into an object-oriented mold when they should be using more natural expressions of design provided by other language features). The powerful template code of John Barton and Lee Nackman [Barton1994] is perhaps the height of tasteful multi-paradigm design.

Even though Stroustrup designated C++ as a multi-paradigm language, there have been no serious attempts to create a design method suited to the richness of C++ features. And though C++ provides a particularly rich and crisp example of multi-paradigm programming, the opportunity for multi-paradigm development generalizes to other programming languages. There is a gap between the current design literature and the intended use of C++ features that is reflected in current practice. This book bridges that gap, using simple notations and vocabulary to help developers combine multiple paradigms instructively.

During a lecture I gave at DePaul University in September 1995, the department chair, Dr. Helmut Epp, suggested the term *meta-design* for this work because its first concern is to identify design techniques suitable to the domain for which software is being developed. That is a useful perspective on the approach taken in this book and in fact describes how most developers approach design. One must first decide what paradigms to use; then one can apply the rules and tools of each paradigm for the system partitions well-suited to their use. This concern is the domain not only of the system architect and designer, but also of the everyday programmer.

Deciding what paradigm to use is one matter; having tools to express the abstractions of a given paradigm is another. We can analyze the application domain using principles of commonality and variation to divide it into subdomains, each of which may be suitable for design under a specific paradigm. This partitioning occurs during a development phase commonly called *analysis*. However, it is better thought of as an early phase of *design* because it tries to create abstractions that the implementation technology can express. Not all implementation tools (programming languages and other tools such as application generators) can express all paradigms. For this reason, it's important to do a domain analysis not only of the application domain, but also of the solution domain. Multi-paradigm design makes this an explicit activity. Solution domain analysis is another facet of the "meta-design" nature of multi-paradigm design.

There are many things this book is not. It is not a comprehensive design method, software development life cycle model, or turn-the-crank approach to design. Most good new designs are variants of old designs that have worked; it's rare that we face completely new or unique software problems. It would be inappropriate and a waste of time to apply the notations and techniques of this book to every module in a new system. But we should be armed to face new problems when they arise so that we can discover the structure in them and carry that understanding into design and implementation. Furthermore, the notations and techniques of multi-paradigm design provide a uniform way to document designs that augment object-oriented techniques with other paradigms.

Multi-paradigm design is a craft that is neither fully an art nor fully a rigorous discipline. This book presents notations, diagrams, and design models to support the developer's thought process. As is true with all such formalisms, there is always the temptation to get caught up in them for their own sake. Multi-paradigm design is a collection of activities that produce an architecture, and architecture is about relationships between pieces. But architecture is also about utility and aesthetics—properties of good software that elude most methods. Good taste has a key place here, and I don't intend the techniques to fuel automated design or coding. Good taste comes in part from experience and in part from good insight. For that reason, this isn't an entry-level book, either. Readers should have a year or two of experience using C++ doing object-oriented (at least) programming in a substantial system.

Used with common sense, these techniques complement good human judgment and experience. If you find that by applying these techniques, you arrive at a design you neither like nor understand, then don't use the design. The techniques are a tool, not a mandate. But all readers should take one thing away from this book: The object paradigm, or any other paradigm, is just one of a set of useful paradigms, and design must express structures more broadly than any single paradigm can.

The Book's Organization

Each chapter builds on the ones before it to build new concepts and increase the reader's understanding of domain engineering and multi-paradigm techniques. Most readers will read chapters sequentially and return to specific chapters as reference material.

Chapter 1 through 7 are the foundational chapters that lay the groundwork for domain engineering.

- Chapter 1 introduces vocabulary, motivates the need for multi-paradigm design, and lays high-level foundations for domain engineering.

- Chapter 2 and Chapter 3 cover commonality and variability analysis, respectively. The two concepts are used together in application, but each is presented in its own right both for simplicity of presentation and to emphasize its language subtleties. Chapter 3 introduces the central concepts of positive and negative variability, themes that are important to clean designs and to understanding how domain engineering interacts with commonly used design patterns.

- Chapter 4 explains how to use domain analysis to find abstractions in the application domain; it builds on the techniques of the preceding chapters.

- Chapter 5 demonstrates how the principles of domain engineering can be used as a basis for the abstraction techniques of the object paradigm.

- Chapter 6 is an important chapter, both because it applies "analysis" techniques in an unconventional way—to characterize the *solution* domain—and because it places C++ constructs in a formal framework that form the basis of commonality and variability analysis.

- Chapter 7 ties together all of the preceding chapters into a coherent framework for thinking about design. It introduces a taxonomy of design problems that have varying degrees of structural complexity. It also presents a high-level set of activities that guide good design and that could be the basis for a method based on domain engineering and multi-paradigm design techniques. The chapter deals with the simple case in which each domain can be developed largely independently of others in a single paradigm.

- Chapter 8 goes a step further, investigating structurally complex designs in which simple divide-and-conquer techniques don't prevail. It presents examples of such recursive, structurally complex designs and presents heuristics for "breaking the recursion."

- Chapter 9 is an addendum that shows the relationship between popular design patterns and domain engineering. The parallels will surprise many readers, and provide new insights into both patterns and domain engineering, as well as the relationship between them. Though the chapter isn't central to understanding domain engineering, it is crucial to understanding contemporary design practices that incorporate patterns together with objects and other paradigms, with or without domain engineering.

Domain names appear in a typeface that looks like this: *TEXT BUFFER.* Pattern names appear in a typeface that appears like this: TEMPLATE METHOD. Member function, class names, and code examples appear in a typeface that looks like this: `Code Example`.

Class diagrams in the book follow the Unified Modeling Language (UML) notation [Fowler+1997].

Acknowledgments

Many thanks to all of those who, through their dialogues, comments, and feedback, improved the quality of the manuscript. Just van den Broecke, Frank Buschmann, Paul Chisholm, Russell Corfman, David Cuka, Cay Horstmann, Andrew Klein, Andrew Koenig, Stan Lippman, Tom Lyons, Lee Nackman, Brett Schuchert, Larry Schutte, Herb Sutter, Steve Vinoski, and David Weiss all provided review comments at many levels, from the highest level of conceptual murkiness to the smallest C++ detail. I appreciate them very much for their efforts. I also want to thank my tireless and patient editor, Debbie Lafferty, who also worked with me on my first book. She has been a true joy to work with. Special thanks also go to Jacqelyn Young, my production editor; to Laura Michaels, the book's copy editor; and to Kim Arney, the book's compositor. Discussions with Lalita Jagadeesan inspired me to create useful examples. A special thanks to Tom Stone, the acquisition editor, for his early advice to me and his early enthusiasm about this book inside Addison-Wesley. A special thanks to Andrew Klein for help with the UML diagrams. And last, a special thanks to my Bell Labs management and colleagues, especially to David Weiss, for sharing their work with me and providing support and encouragement.

CHAPTER 1   *Introduction: The Need for Multiple Paradigms*

This introduction motivates multiple paradigms in software development. It ties domain engineering and multi-paradigm design to the state of the art, prior art, and emerging themes related to object-oriented design. It also introduces important vocabulary for the chapters that follow: software families, commonality, and variability.

1.1 Domain Engineering and Multiple Paradigms

Contemporary software seems to equate design with objects. The object paradigm has given us powerful new tools to capture the common abstractions of many application domains, and object-oriented design has become a ubiquitous tool. To implement these designs, C++ is still the language of choice at this writing. Yet not all that is in C++ is object-oriented, and most implementations take advantage of C++ features that are not object-oriented. This suggests that most designs in fact have a nontrivial component that is not object-oriented. Given that most projects use object-oriented design methods, where do these non-object-oriented structures come from?

These questions go to the heart of software design. The first purpose of design is to meet business needs, which are usually dominated by user expectations. Success is predicated on a good understanding

1

of the business, or domain, for which the system is being built. But design has other purposes as well. For example, design should lead to an implementation that is understandable and easy to build (to paraphrase Einstein, as easy to build as possible, but not more so). Also, design should strive to build systems that can be evolved over time and adapted to new markets and applications.

All of these design goals are actually different outcomes of the same basic principles. Most relate to the structure of a business and how it evolves. Our understanding of the business increases the likelihood of our meeting the customer's needs. It also lays a foundation for a system structure and a design vocabulary that helps express and shape the design. And by understanding the broad, stable aspects of the business, we can design structures that evolve well.

Domain engineering is a software design discipline that focuses on the abstractions of a business (a *domain*) with the intent of reusing designs and artifacts. Reuse is one of several good outputs of good design, and the same design techniques that lead to good reuse also lead to extensibility and maintainability over time.

Multi-paradigm design embraces many of the goals of the object paradigm, but the goals differ in scope. The object paradigm also focuses on extensibility and reuse. It does this by separating the common, stable parts of a design from the variable, uncertain parts of a design. To oversimplify a bit, one can find the stable, invariant behaviors and data in base classes (particularly in abstract base classes) with the variations factored into derived classes. This works well if the design can be factored into common/stable parts and variable/uncertain parts along the lines of behavior and data structure. But there may be other useful ways of separating what is common from what is variable. For example, we may want to select between a short and a long in an otherwise identical data structure; this is a suitable application for C++ templates—nothing object-oriented about that. Function overloading, function templates, and other C++ language features express other kinds of commonalities and variations that are broader than the object paradigm. Domain engineering covers all of these considerations.

Design is the structural aspect of the process of problem-solving, with activities to abstract, partition, and model the system so that the designer can understand it. Object-oriented design helps us "find the objects" by using business rules of thumb, principles of coupling, cohesion, and subtyping, and an informed allocation of responsibilities to objects. How do we build the design abstractions and implementation modules in a world that isn't purely object-oriented? First, it's important to recognize that we're no longer dealing with a single paradigm but with multiple paradigms, each with its own rules for abstracting, partitioning, and modeling. Second, it's useful to understand that most software paradigms—certainly those supported by C++—can be characterized in terms of the more general design concerns of commonality and variation. We call this *domain analysis*. Domain analysis builds a model (not *the* model, just *a* model) of the business. We can draw on this model to build the solution structure. The first focus of design is to understand the commonalities and variabilities for the components of this model.

Domain analysis uncovers groupings of abstractions and artifacts that are tied together by their commonalities—and perhaps by the similar nature of their variabilities. Such groupings are called *families*. While object-oriented design is an exercise in "finding the objects," domain analysis is an exercise in "finding the families." Note that object-oriented design is a special case of finding families: Classes are families of objects, and class hierarchies are families of classes. We group them together because of what they have in common. We can use criteria other than those germane to the object paradigm to find other important families that are not object-oriented—hence the importance of multi-paradigm design.

The second focus of design is on how to match those commonalities and variations to implementation technology structures such as classes, functions, templates, class hierarchies, and data structures. This is called *application engineering*, and it is what comes to mind when most people hear the word "design." If we understand the kinds of commonalities and variabilities that can be expressed by specific paradigms, then application engineering can use the results of domain analysis to select the most suitable paradigms for the system architecture and implementation.

This book presents a framework of formalisms, ideas, and simple notations that can support such a design process. It takes a broad view of design based on the analysis of the domain, thus producing an implementation engineered for the domain. I call the technique *multi-paradigm design*, a specific approach to domain engineering that builds on a small but rich collection of paradigms supported by the C++ programming language. The techniques generalize to other programming languages, particularly those with expressive-type systems, and to other implementation technologies. The emphasis on C++ here is in the interest of focus and pragmatism.

In summary, domain analysis is a set of techniques for identifying software families, and application engineering is a set of techniques for implementing and managing software families. Domain analysis and application engineering together form a discipline called *domain engineering*. Multi-paradigm design is a form of domain engineering, whereby domain analysis applies both to the application and solution domains. In multi-paradigm design, application engineering builds on existing tools and paradigms.

Multi-paradigm design and domain engineering revisit the first principles of abstraction and design to broaden the solution space beyond objects. This broadening has implications for design, architecture, and implementation. The next section builds a vocabulary around these basic concepts in light of the principles of commonality and variation. With those concepts in hand, we can appreciate most principles of multi-paradigm design in a straightforward way.

1.2 Design, Analysis, Domains, and Families: Term Definitions

Design, in the software engineering tradition, refers to the activities that take place between analysis and implementation. *Analysis* is the activity that elicits user needs and wants. Before these terms were adopted by software, they carried broader meanings. Multi-paradigm design appeals to the broader sense of these words. This section introduces key words of the multi-paradigm design and domain engineering vocabulary.

In domain engineering, analysis goes beyond the application analysis that elicits a given customer's needs. We must also assess what's in our toolbox. We must consider the limitations and assets of the tools and techniques at our disposal and use them to the best advantage of the designer and customer. For example, when does the designer consider whether to use UNIX libraries or MFC (Microsoft Foundation Classes)? This may seem like an implementation decision, but often it is a factor in market requirements. It is clearly a decision that shapes the architecture and functionality of the final product. This *analysis* must take place before we can transform its results into an implementation. It certainly precedes "design" for any traditional definition of design, that is, the process of deriving an implementation structure from needs. But just as design can continue through the end of implementation, so can this analysis continue as long as there are design activities. Ongoing development may yield insights about the selection of tools, techniques, and paradigms.

1.2.1 Analysis

In multi-paradigm design, we talk about *application analysis* and *solution analysis*. Application analysis is the "traditional" analysis of the problem space. Solution analysis borrows the abstracting tools and formalisms of application analysis and applies them to the *solution* space. Understanding both sides of the development equation helps us to use the right tool for the right job and raises the likelihood of success. Designers should assess the contents of the project toolbox even during application analysis.

Usually the term "analysis" means "understanding the problem." The term "object-oriented analysis" has come into increasingly common usage, thereby suggesting that the design principles of the object paradigm provide good tools to codify the problem. Unfortunately, the use of any design paradigm during analysis prejudices the implementation to use that paradigm, even when another paradigm might in fact provide a better partitioning. One approach to this dilemma is to avoid contaminating analysis with any of the prejudices of design. However, that leads to an analysis that doesn't foresee straightforward implementations that use available tools. Multi-paradigm design solves this dilemma by considering *all* implementation paradigms during analysis. More precisely, the analysis considers basic principles of abstraction and partitioning that underlie most software design paradigms. We don't do partitioning during analysis; that would require a paradigm that provided the partitioning rules. Analysis gathers the information to support the choice of one or more paradigms.

1.2.2 Design

Design is an activity that gives structure to the solution to a given problem. It starts with a problem and ends with a solution. Here, "problem" means a mismatch between the current state and the desired state, a definition broad enough to include bug fixes and enhancements. Design must struggle with pragmatics—the constraints imposed by the business and by real-world considerations such as tractability. In software, as in building design and in some mechanical engineering disciplines, the solution—the output of design—includes an *architecture* and an implementation.

We still view design as the activity that takes us from a needs statement to an implementation, but we broaden its scope. Because analysis scrutinizes both the application and the solution, it is, in part, a design activity. Because multi-paradigm design considers implementation tools to be like the expressive constructs of a programming language, it touches on many implementation issues. Design and analysis are deeply entangled in this model. This perspective smooths the transition from the application structure to the solution structure. It helps avoid the "phase shift" that happens after data-flow diagrams in structured techniques, while avoiding the false hope that the solution structure will match the problem structure. This is a common pitfall of early object-oriented techniques that presume that analysis classes map directly onto C++ classes.

1.2.3   Architecture

Architecture is the primary output of design. It is the articulation of the things of interest in the system and the relationships between those things. "Things" may be objects, tuples, processes, and other individually comprehensible chunks that figure prominently in the designer's vocabulary and toolbox. For example, in a finite-state machine (FSM), these "things" include states, transitions, transition actions, messages, and the machines themselves. The context-free word "thing" is preferable to "abstraction" because the pieces may not be abstract at all, but rather concrete and complete. Such "things" may be logical architectural artifacts that lack physical continuity in the source or in memory: An example of this is a process, which comprises procedures scattered all over a program.

We usually associate the informal term *structure* with architecture. System structure emerges from the building blocks we put into it and how we put them together. Both the selection of the blocks and their arrangement follow the desiderata and constraints of the problem statement. The architecture helps us understand that the design process addresses the problem. Multi-paradigm design helps us choose building blocks well-suited to the available solution structures and guides the synthesis of those blocks into a complete system.

An architecture usually corresponds to a *domain*, an area of interest for which a system is being built. A domain may be hierarchical, which means that architectural models may also be hierarchical.

1.2.4 Domains

A *domain* is an area of specialization or interest. We talk about the *application domain*—the body of knowledge that is of interest to users. Because it is of interest to users, it is hopefully of interest to us. We break down application domains into *application subdomains*—we divide and conquer. We talk about the *solution domain*, which is of central interest to the implementors but of only superficial interest to system users. Any given design may deal with multiple solution domains at once, for example, C++ constructs, patterns, and maybe state machines and parser-generators.

1.2.5 Families and Commonality Analysis

Most advances in software design, and certainly those that have found their way into programming languages, have been tied to new ways of forming or using abstractions. Abstraction deals with the general case without reference to the details of any particular instance. When we think abstractly, we *emphasize what is common while suppressing detail*. A good software abstraction requires that we understand the problem well enough in all of its breadth to know what is *common* across related items of interest and to know what details *vary* from item to item. The items of interest are collectively called a *family*, and families—rather than individual applications—are the scope of architecture and design. We can use the commonality/variability model regardless of whether family members are modules, classes, functions, processes, or types; it works for any paradigm. Commonality and variability are at the heart of most design techniques.

Domains often (but not always) comprise families. A family is a collection of things (such as objects, functions, classes) that we group together because they share *common* properties. *Commonality analysis* is the activity we use to form and elaborate families; that is the focus of Chapter 2.

For example, there are many sorting algorithms one might use in a business application. One usually ignores the differences between these algorithms during design. What matters are the preconditions and postconditions common to *all* sorting algorithms. We simply don't care about the steps within the algorithm. A specific program may use several different sorting algorithms, each tuned for a different time/space trade-off. At some point, the designer must choose from among the available implementations.

The same is true if we are using an abstraction like `Stack`, which can be implemented using an unlimited number of data structures and algorithms. At design time, the designer cares only that `Stack` supports all operations needed by a given family of applications and—usually with some foresight—defers the proper implementation of those operations. A given program may use several different kinds of stacks—`Stack<int>` may be implemented much differently than `Stack<Message>`—but all `Stack`s have *common behavior*.

During low-level design and implementation, the designer starts to care about the differences between different kinds of `Stack`s. The programming language should provide a convenient way to capture commonalities but be flexible enough to express variabilities. Each kind of `Stack` has a unique data structure and unique algorithms. For example, `Stack<int>` may use a simple vector, while `Stack<Message>` may use a linked list of head cells, each of which contains a pointer to a `Message` instance. `Stack`s *vary* in *internal structure*. They also *vary* in the *algorithms* that manipulate those structures.

Some domains do not form families; they are no more than areas of focus or interest. Consider OVERLOAD MANAGEMENT as a domain in a real-time transaction processing system design. OVERLOAD MANAGEMENT takes over the allocation of system resources, such as memory and real time, when the system is offered more work than it can handle in real time. The designer may establish overload strategies once at the beginning of the system's life cycle. There may be one overload design that fits an entire product line unchanged. The code for overload may never change (except for bug fixes) over the product's life. But we still want to treat it as a domain, as a discipline worthy of focus in its own right.

"Good" domains (the ones we can easily manage) usually correspond to subsystems or system modules. Some domains cross modules, particularly in complex systems (see more about complexity in Section 1.6). Again, OVERLOAD MANAGEMENT is an example of a domain that may touch many pieces of code in a system. This means that it interferes with other domains; as it changes, other domains may need to track it. Such interactions complicate the design. We address those interactions in Chapter 8.

1.2.6   Dimensions of Abstraction

Software design space is multidimensional, with multiple dimensions, or "axes," of design: a procedural axis, a data structure axis, an axis of compliant behaviors, and others. Each design technique picks its own favorite axes of commonality and variability and uses those to formulate abstractions. The object paradigm focuses on families of abstract data types that share a common interface, though internal implementations may freely vary. Instead of dwelling on a single combination of commonality and variability, as in most paradigms, multi-paradigm design focuses more on commonality and variability in their own right.

Multi-paradigm design uses characteristic dimensions of design called *dimensions of commonality*. Important commonality dimensions include structure, behavior, and algorithm. Specific combinations of commonalities and variabilities correspond to *commonality categories*, which will be more formally introduced in Section 2.3 and elaborated on throughout this book.

1.2.7   Precise Abstraction

"Abstract" and "general" do not imply "vague" or "ambiguous." On the contrary, a good abstraction should be described with precision. For example, we can define the abstraction File in terms of concrete responsibilities (such as reading or writing sequences of characters) or in terms of verifiable properties (a file must have *size > m + n* characters for a read of *n* characters to succeed, if the current file position is at index *m*). Though the description is abstract in the sense that it prescribes only behavior and general in the sense that it accommodates many implementations, it is not vague or ambiguous. We throw away the details that are not common to all cases, but we certainly retain those that characterize the abstraction!

1.2.8   Implementation and Engineering

After architecture, the implementation is the second output of design. *Implementation* means actual code—not just diagrams or formalisms.

Many contemporary methods view design as a phase intermediate to architecture and coding, instead of viewing architecture and coding as products of design. But from a more practical point of view, we can't separate design from either architecture or implementation. If design is the activity that gives structure to the solution, and if architecture is about structure, isn't "design" a good term for the activity that produces it? And much of code is about structure as well. Why shouldn't that be "design" as well? If you look at how real programmers work, you'll find they don't really delineate architecture, design, and implementation in most application domains, regardless of whether the official house method says they should or not. (How many times have you completed the coding before holding the review for your design document?) Object-oriented designers gain insight into the allocation of responsibilities to classes by coding them up. Empirical research on the software design process reveals that most developers have at least partially coded solutions in hand at the time of their design review and that design decisions continue into the last throes of coding [Cain+1996].

Multi-paradigm design looks ahead to implementation constraints and opportunities instead of leaving them to "the implementor" as if implementation were something that followed design. If design is to produce a solution, its output must be usable. This is where the *engineering* part comes in. Engineering solves a problem or class of problems by building on proven techniques, on scientific principles, and on the ingenious thinking of the problem solver. It is never done without an eye to implementation; it is very practical. Domain engineering as a whole raises problem-solving from an activity focused on individual problems to an activity that addresses families of problems, that is, commonly recurring problems of design. Multi-paradigm design, a specific form of domain engineering, unifies the abstraction techniques and vocabulary used throughout the development process. The application engineering component of multi-paradigm design isn't deferred until late in the process; rather its formalisms are an important component of domain analysis activities.

1.3 Beyond Objects

Many readers will say, "I am already using object-oriented design techniques, and though there are occasional problems, things tend to work out somehow. Why should I put those techniques aside and look at multi-paradigm design? After all, C++ is an object-oriented language, isn't it?"

One hidden danger of this objection is that the term "object-oriented" has become a synonym for "good." Multi-paradigm design offers formalisms that can be used to describe the object paradigm with more precision than is acknowledged in casual use. Furthermore, it demonstrates the relevance of those formalisms to important software objectives such as decoupling and cohesion, abstraction, and evolution.

In today's market, you can find the "object" label attached to every paradigm imaginable. That leads to hybrid design environments that build on an attachment to the past, usually supported by a desire to build on investments (people, tools, embedded software, and even reputations) in old methods and technologies. And most of these environments are just called "object-oriented." One liability of such combined methods is that they obscure some of the central principles of object-oriented design, substituting principles from other methods in their place. These confused combinations of design techniques can lead to architectural disaster. One common failure mode is to use structured analysis to build an initial design around system data structures and then implement using responsibility-driven design. A common result of this technique is that cohesion of the original data models breaks down and objects are forced more and more to expose their internal data structure. Maintenance becomes difficult, the overall structure weakens, and it takes tremendous energy to keep the system viable.

But pure objects aren't the answer, either. Perfectly good paradigms have been marginalized by object-oriented hype. The tone in contemporary development shops is that no one would be caught dead using procedural decomposition, even for a batch sorting routine—objects must somehow be crafted into the solution. That leads to designs in which square pegs have been forced into round holes.

It has always been a good idea to mix multiple paradigms tastefully, and great software designers have long kept several tools in their toolbox. Peter Wegner once remarked that the object paradigm is itself a hybrid that builds on the paradigms that preceded it, among them modularity, abstract data types, procedures, and data structures. C++ goes further to support procedural, modular, object-based, object-oriented, and generic programming on an equal footing. Mixing paradigms is admittedly hard, just as it is difficult to tastefully mix several architectural schools in a single building. There are few widely understood formalisms, guidelines, methods, or rules of thumb for mixing paradigms, so the mixing is driven by ad hoc and political considerations. This is an especially important issue in C++ programming projects that tend to mix C and object-oriented development cultures.

This book motivates the need for multiple paradigms and lays the foundation for a semi-formal treatment of multi-paradigm development. It provides vocabulary and notations that might be used either as the basis for a reusable design method or as heuristic adjuncts to existing (for example, object-oriented) methods on a case-by-case basis. The book introduces a form of analysis based on commonality and variability, intuitive concepts that already underlie most design methods. Much of object-oriented design falls out naturally from commonality and variability analysis; class hierarchies are one way of tying together members of a software family. The relationship between objects and commonality analysis is the topic of Chapter 5. But there are families that are not best implemented or thought of as class hierarchies. And there are techniques that address fine points of object-oriented design that go beyond the goals of domain engineering and multi-paradigm design. Those techniques complement multi-paradigm design well.

1.4 Commonality and Variability Analysis

Commonality and variability analyses form the fundamental underpinnings of design, since they are the essence of how the human mind forms abstractions. Good abstraction techniques address software complexity and help the designer elicit and organize domain knowledge. The two problems of complexity and problem definition are among the predominant challenges facing contemporary practical software development. We will define the concept of "paradigm" itself in terms of commonality and variation.

Commonality and variation are simple concepts that underlie most of the principles of this book. Each chapter will both use and elaborate the basics of commonality and variation. We have already seen their use to identify and describe software families. They also describe major design structures, as will be discussed in Section 2.1. They lead to structures that are likely to evolve gracefully, as will be described in Section 2.6. They help capture, structure, and codify the domain vocabulary, as we discover in Section 4.3. They are really the foundations of what we have known as object-oriented analysis all along, as we discuss in Section 5.1. In fact, commonality and variability analysis are powerful generalizations of many design techniques. They cover most of the abstraction techniques that C++ inherits from the past two or three decades of programming language development.

1.5 Software Families

One way we abstract is by grouping similar entities or concepts. If we group steps of an algorithm by their relationship to each other, we call the abstractions *procedures*. If we group related responsibilities of an encapsulated collection of related data, we call the abstractions *classes*.

We can group by many criteria that we don't find in any popular paradigm. In the interest of abstraction, we take commonality where we can find it. These commonalities fall along many dimensions: structure, algorithm, semantics, name, inputs and outputs, binding time, default values—almost anything that causes us to group things together. In this book, we call these groupings *families*, following the FAST (*F*amily-oriented *A*bstraction, *S*pecification, and *T*ranslation) terminology of Weiss [Weiss1999]. The concept of software families has even earlier roots in Dijkstra [Dijkstra1968] and Parnas [Parnas1976; 1978]. Parnas characterizes families as groups of items that are strongly related by their commonalities, where commonalities are more important than the variations between family members [Parnas1976].

Weiss has elaborated and extended Parnas's work. A family is simply a collection of system parts (or even concepts such as processes, which aren't contiguous parts) or abstractions that we treat together because they are more alike than they are different. Because family members have so much in common, we can usually treat them all the same. We explicitly characterize their differences, called *variabilities*, to distinguish individual family members. This characterization of families brings inheritance hierarchies to mind for C++ practitioners. However, it's an equally valid characterization of templates, overloaded functions, and most other C++ language features that express design structure.

Commonality and variability shape families. We can draw an analogy with biological families whose genetic makeups are the foundation of common and distinguishing characteristics. Families are defined by their genetic commonality, and family members are distinguished by their genetic variations. Weiss notes that one could think of the variabilities as generating a family tree based on the order in which decisions are made during design.

Families of programs are made up of families of parts. A differential equation solving program will likely contain a family of differential equation packages (families of algorithms). A telecommunications system will contain families of software for different kinds of lines and trunks. A compiler may have a family of code generators for different kinds of optimization, for different target platforms, and to support a spectrum of debugging facilities.

Many software families are naturally expressed by existing programming language constructs. Classes in an inheritance hierarchy form a family, with a progenitor class at its root and mutant classes in the branches and leaves. Their common behavior (presuming a subtyping hierarchy) is the basic gene set. Each class may alter the characteristics it inherits (a curiously suitable word) from its parents. We may have a base class called `LogFile`, with derived classes `RemoteLogFile`, `SummarizingLogFile`, and `ScavengingLogFile`.

But some family groupings don't fit naturally into object-oriented or procedural structures. There are many computer science constructs that express commonality and variability but which are not programming language constructs. The vocabulary of databases is rich with such expression. Processes, tasks, and threads form families of sorts in the operating system arena. Network protocols are families of messages. Even within programming languages, we find rules, tasks, exceptions, patterns, and many other groupings. These loom important in everyday design.

Commonality defines the shared context that is invariant across abstractions of the application. Once we discover commonality, it becomes uninteresting; we agree to it and put it behind us, and we discuss it no further. Variabilities capture the more interesting properties that distinguish abstractions in a domain. It's important both to uncover variabilities in analysis and to provide a way for the implementation to express them. In FAST, the commonality is implicit in the application-oriented language (in the compiler and its environment), while the variability is explicitly expressed in language constructs.

We can make a direct analogy to object-oriented programming languages, whose programs group abstractions by commonality in signature. Class hierarchies form families; new classes need to capture only how they differ from the other family members. The user of any of those classes can take their commonality for granted and use their instances interchangeably.

1.6 Multi-Paradigm Design

Multi-paradigm design is a domain analysis technique that features concurrent analyses of the application and solution domains. The goal is to find solution domain constructs that most naturally express the structure of the application domain. We want to look for a match between commonalities and variabilities of the solution domain with those of the application domain to understand what solution techniques to apply to which parts of the problem. To support this, multi-paradigm design offers techniques to build taxonomies of solution domain constructs. The taxonomies describe the kinds of commonalities and variabilities that are germane to each of several paradigms, along with the C++ language features that express those paradigms. Designers can use those taxonomies to fit the appropriate solution constructs to the commonalities and variabilities produced by application domain analysis.

1.6.1   The Language: C++

The paradigms of "multi-paradigm" in this book are those expressed by the C++ programming language. This is an unambitious use of the word "paradigm," which usually implies the functional, database, and rule-based paradigms that reach far beyond the boundaries of C++. "Paradigm" is nonetheless an appropriate term, and the technique generalizes to formal structures beyond those supported by C++ or any other programming language. It generalizes beyond the object paradigm, which itself is often viewed as somehow being more general than other techniques. Chapter 6 presents a taxonomy of the C++ solution domain, the result of a domain analysis of C++ itself.

Multi-paradigm design helps the designer align natural application domain commonalities with those offered by a programming language.

In this book, we focus on C++ as that programming language. The object paradigm expresses just one of the many kinds of commonalities and variabilities available to a fluent C++ programmer. Multi-paradigm design attempts to bring out other features of the programming language, just where it makes sense to do so, so that programs can better express a good design partitioning.

Paradigms that are beyond the scope of C++ per se aren't directly addressed in this book, though multi-paradigm design principles generalize to other solution domain tools. Databases and scheduling abstractions—both undeniably important—are beyond the scope of this book. An excellent database book is the classic *Introduction to Database Systems* [Date1986], while excellent foundations for parallelism can be found in *Object-Oriented System Development* [DeChampeaux+1993].

1.6.2   Dealing with Complex Families

It is important to recognize that software families are not simply descriptions of disjoint sets or subsets of application entities. As in biology, families overlap. And just as families intermarry and have members that mix genetic characteristics from multiple parents, so we find rich and complex associations in software architecture. There are many interesting partitionings of any complex system, and many complex systems can best be understood using multiple, simultaneous, independent views. Each view addresses a particular set of concerns for a particular observer: performance, resource use, message flow, and so on. For example, a telecommunications system might have software families for billing, for individually marketable features like call waiting, for diagnostics, for initialization, for fault tolerance, for auditing, and for many others. It is rare that these families form disjoint subsets of code. Rather, they are interwoven into a multi-paradigm system.

Families, or views of a system, must be chosen, mixed, and managed carefully, and accommodating multiple, simultaneous views is difficult. But when multiple views are absent, important semantics of system architecture are often omitted. This has been one of the great downfalls of most software design techniques and practice. Early object-oriented designs tended to miss the importance of use cases; these were finally given just stature in the work of Jacobson, et al. [Jacobson+1992]. It seems that every paradigm has drawn attention to its own partitioning criteria only by belittling others, a marketing and political dynamic that works against embracing multiple paradigms in a single project. It is particularly important to be able to mix paradigms in complex systems. Complexity is proportional to the number of distinct, simultaneously meaningful views of a system. That is, complexity is proportional to the number of overlapping families within the system. It is unlikely that we can reduce any complex system to a single class hierarchy without making the base class— which characterizes the domain semantics of the hierarchy as a whole—largely devoid of any domain semantics. This shows up in systems that gratuitously use class `Object` as the common base.

At the next level of sophistication, the designer can partition the system into *class categories* [Booch1994], subsystems with a class hierarchy at their core. This turns out to be less than ideal because of the potential coupling between hierarchies. Such coupling often comes from abstractions of process, while the class hierarchies capture abstractions of structure. For example, consider a design with separate hierarchies for the GUI (graphical user interface) and for application objects. Where does one put the code that manages interactions between the program and the user? It is a process consideration that does not belong wholly in one hierarchy or the other. Such code could be allocated to its own class category, but doing that would create a complex pattern of coupling between the hierarchies. A pattern like model-view-controller (MVC) gives this system view first-class standing without creating a separate, physically distinct hierarchy for the domain. MVC captures the dependencies between the domains. Such dependencies won't always surface as patterns, and we need more general design mechanisms to deal with interactions between domains.

The object community has struggled with this problem. As the object discipline matured, increasingly rich mechanisms came on the scene to address this issue: multiple inheritance in the early 1980s, the separation of type and class in the 1990s, the popularization of role-based modeling in the mid- to late-1990s, and design patterns in the same time period. We have come a long way from the original Cartesian divide-and-conquer models of inheritance at the roots of object-oriented programming.

Whereas most domain engineering techniques equate domains with modules, subsystems, libraries, or other self-contained constructs, multi-paradigm design supports the interweaving of multiple domains. Multi-paradigm design deals with families delineated by structure, names and semantics (including the semantics of inputs and outputs), behavior, algorithm, binding time, granularity, and state. Most methods build on these very principles, though most methods use a few high-level formal structuring concepts (such as objects or modules) instead of the more general (and lower-level) concepts of multi-paradigm design. Multi-paradigm design describes domain interactions in terms of these more general concepts.

1.6.3   Incorporating Patterns

Chapter 9 explores the relationship between software patterns and multi-paradigm design. Designers can combine structural patterns with multi-paradigm design techniques, and Chapter 9 will demonstrate that many structural patterns (such as TEMPLATE METHOD and STRATEGY [Gamma1995]) are just special cases of multi-paradigm design techniques. Other patterns are outside the scope of multi-paradigm design and offer design leverage that can't easily be attained with a method or semi-formal approach like multi-paradigm design. Such patterns complement multi-paradigm design well.

1.7 Multi-Paradigm Development and Programming Language

Many analysis techniques focus only on the application, or "problem," domain. By distancing themselves from solution "details," these methods claim to be more abstract. They also claim applicability across a wide variety of programming languages. For example, some methodologists claim it is possible to do analysis and even design under the object paradigm, while implementing in any technology of choice. Such an approach may stagger to success in a greenfield system, but it leaves many difficulties for long-term maintenance.

Language guides, constrains, supports, and expresses how we partition an application and how we manipulate it and give it form. As a trivial example, a homogeneous List in Smalltalk would have one closed form in code to serve all possible types of contained elements, thereby dealing with different types of contained elements at run time.

The same implementation in C++ would probably use templates to generate one copy of code for each family member. The implementation technology must be reckoned with.

Multi-paradigm design investigates commonality and variability in both the application and solution domains. We use commonality and variability analysis in both domains and align the two analyses to derive the solution structure. This is a bit different than the FAST approach, which derives the implementation technology from the domain analysis.

1.7.1 Application-Oriented Languages in FAST

The original FAST method of Weiss et al. [Campbell+1990] took an enlightened view of the application and solution domains and their relationship to each other. The key to a good analysis is to gather the design knowledge that relates to commonalities and hide it as a "design secret" so that it doesn't clutter the code that developers use to express the design. Ideally, the programming language itself should hide all of the commonalities of the domain whose implementation it expresses so that the programmer can focus on expressing the variabilities.

For example, a spreadsheet language hides the common mechanisms for automatically updating value cells. This is logic that is common to most cells and which doesn't vary from application to application. However, most spreadsheet languages offer rich constructs to express the values and structures that vary across applications.

In the original FAST method, Weiss uses commonality and variability analysis to characterize families of software artifacts or abstractions. Instead of leaving the programming language to chance, FAST builds a structured vocabulary of family members as the basis for a custom programming language for each domain. The language expresses variations in family members; family commonalities are presumed to hold for all abstractions in the domain being analyzed. There is a translator for the language that produces family members from specifications, thereby taking advantage of the shared commonality. This language and its associated supporting tools form an application engineering environment for the domain. The FAST method is a refinement of early work by Campbell, Faulk, and Weiss on synthesis processes [Campbell+1990]. It focuses on application engineering environments that most often employ application-oriented languages (AOLs), which are also called "little languages" [Bentley1988] or application-specific languages.

For example, one might use the FAST technique to analyze a protocol and then use the analysis results to guide the creation of an AOL that succinctly expresses solutions in the protocol's domain of application. The FAST technique analyzes the application (problem) domain as the source of constraints for the structure of the solution domain. There is little consideration for constraints that come from the solution domain itself. Solution domain constraints become important if there is a goal to reuse solution domain technology instead of to customize a new application engineering environment for each domain.

Some domains benefit enough from AOLs to justify the cost of a customized application engineering environment. AOLs make it easier to rapidly generate solutions within the domain. Some support formal analyses (such as for freedom from deadlock in the protocol domain example) and substantial optimizations that are difficult with general-purpose languages. When these factors dominate project needs, it can be cost-effective in the long term to develop an AOL and the application engineering environment to support it. Projects facing such decisions can benefit from a cost-benefit analysis for each domain being considered. For a first cut, the decision can be made for each domain independently.

One downside to the application engineering environment approach is the cost both of initial construction and of long-term maintenance of the tools, processes, and support staff, particularly if the cost can't be broadly spread across several projects. Another downside is its lack of guidance for translation from analysis to the programming language. The success of a language (such as an AOL, but for general-purpose languages as well) requires the designer to be skilled both in the application domain and in language design. Even with a good language designer on staff, good languages are notoriously difficult to design and good language design could (or should) take months. One might address this problem by doing an object-oriented analysis of the completed commonality and variability analyses to find cues for the solution domain language, as has been done in unpublished work by Weiss and his colleagues.

Multi-paradigm design steps back from any single paradigm to generalize this process. Furthermore, it focuses on reusing existing solution domain constructs where possible. This is why the analysis of activities of multi-paradigm design take into account both the problem domain and the solution domain.

1.7.2   Domain Analysis and the C++ Programming Language

Weiss's principles underlie most of the precepts of this book. We part company only at the point of choosing a programming language. Multi-paradigm design does not derive the structure of a custom programming language from the application domain analysis. Rather, it extracts the structure from a rich, general-purpose programming language such as C++ and matches it to the needs of the application domain. It uses that structure to guide design with more regularity than with the original synthesis process but with more flexibility than with the FAST process alone.

The techniques of commonality and variability analysis are broader than any programming language. We could have chosen any language that can directly express recurring design structures without relying on convention. The advanced or innovative designer can adapt the techniques of this book to such programming languages by modulating the models developed in Chapter 6 and applying them to the remaining analyses in the book. Indeed, much of the material in this book has little to do with C++ or with programming language, particularly in the early chapters.

So why C++? No doubt, the popularity of C++ will be a factor in how broadly the techniques of this book are applied. This was an important consideration relative to the "little languages" used in application engineering environments, which almost always serve a small and local clientele and which enjoy the support of a local wizard. But more to the point, C++ supports multiple paradigms well. C++ has templates, overloaded functions, inheritance, and virtual functions—a rich collection of facilities to express a broad spectrum of patterns of commonality and variability. In C++, we can write a single List template—one set of source—that can maintain lists of any kinds of objects. We can do the same thing in Smalltalk, though the mechanisms that make the same genericity possible are implemented in a much different way. All other language debates aside, one advantage of C++ is that it directly expresses the intent of the analysis in a way that Smalltalk can do only by convention.

The application engineering component of the FAST method goes beyond commonalities and variabilities of any single general-purpose language. Its application engineering advocates customized languages that can capture the commonalities and express the variabilities of specific domains—the language helps the developer focus on properties that vary. The background commonality provides a context that the programmer can presume to hold true across a domain. FAST favors development cultures that need simple, expressive languages and environments to go with them. As described previously, a good language and environment come at considerable expense, and they can address only limited domains well. C++ is a true general-purpose language that rises to the complexity of domains that are inaccessible to "little languages" and that enjoys popular support. These advantages of a general-purpose language sometimes outweigh the advantages of AOLs, in spite of the complexity and other liabilities of C++.

The same principle that encourages us to draw on multiple paradigms within C++ also encourages us to employ multiple design strategies at a higher level. Some domains are sufficiently rich that a mixture of little languages and C++ is the best solution. One might use multi-paradigm development to build a C++ class library that serves as a foundation for an AOL. Another approach is to partition a domain, using C++ for some sub-domains and little languages for others; the two parts would communicate through an architectural interface. Compiler writers often use **yacc** in this fashion. Common sense and experience usually suggest one or more of these approaches.

1.7.3   Polymorphism

Polymorphism is behind each of the paradigms that C++ supports. The term *polymorphism* has entered mainstream technical jargon through the object paradigm, to whose advocates it means roughly run-time operator lookup. Virtual functions support that sense of C++ polymorphism. But overloading, templates, inheritance, and even type conversion are forms of polymorphism as well. We will revisit this in depth in Section 6.9. The etymology of "polymorphism" translates literally to "many forms." If there are many forms of a thing, that implies some commonality by which the variability of forms is established or judged. Commonality establishes a framework in which polymorphism can make sense, and variability characterizes the polymorphism itself.

For example, if we are using polymorphism in a shape-drawing graphics package, the variabilities are the drawing algorithms and data structures for different kinds of shapes. But all shapes have something in common. They all share some data structure (such as their location, border, and fill colors), and they all share some behavior (they can all be moved, reshaped, created, and deleted). It's the commonalities that make them shapes; it's the variabilities that make them *kinds of shapes.* Polymorphism takes advantage of this balance of commonality and variability. The result is an abstraction (an abstract base class) that characterizes the entire family.

Of course, we needn't confine ourselves to an object-oriented example. All sets have things in common: They can all have things inserted into them, and they may all share algorithms and data structures. But a set of integers is different from a set of windows. This is because the logic that inserts new elements uses different algorithms to determine if the new element is the same as any element already in the set (you can't replicate elements in a set). This, too, is polymorphism. There are many forms of sets that share most properties in common, but each kind of set varies from others in subtle ways. We can capture those differences using templates, which are another form of polymorphism. A single abstraction (a template) characterizes the entire family.

1.8 Commonality Analysis: Other Perspectives

Multi-paradigm design draws on related techniques from the legacy of computer software design. A few of them are discussed in the following sections. These analogies help tie together multi-paradigm design with broader design models. Examining multi-paradigm design from multiple viewpoints also offers insight on why its principles work and why they are important.

1.8.1   Policy and Mechanism

Separation of policy and mechanism underlies many long-standing software engineering principles, and we can think of multi-paradigm design in these terms. To a first order of approximation, the market doesn't care about the mechanisms used to implement its policies as long as the policies are carried out. Most of the time, mechanism answers the question, "*How* is functionality implemented?" while policy asks, "*What* is being implemented?"

The mechanisms of a business domain often remain stable over time, while the policies shift with market needs, regulations, and other external influences. Because mechanisms are stable and because they are of secondary interest to the system customer (they rarely appear in requirements), we want to bury mechanisms where the user can't see them. This hiding of the secrets of implementation behind a class interface is an often-heralded goal of the object paradigm. This idea isn't new to objects, of course. It was an early principle of modular design. The end user shouldn't see the mechanisms, but the user should be able to manipulate those parts of the design that correspond to the policies of the business domain. That's the fundamental spirit of Parnas's information hiding. In many good systems, commonality captures mechanism and variability captures policy.

In multi-paradigm design, we express variabilities—policies—and hide commonalities—which are often mechanisms—by using the programming language of choice (in this book, C++). We build a framework for each application domain and bury domain commonalities inside of it. The framework has external "hooks" that the programmer can manipulate or extend to tune the framework for a specific application. These "hooks" can be expressed as C++ abstract base classes (the programmer provides a derived class), templates (the programmer provides template parameters), and overloaded function families (the programmer can extend the family or can call existing functions). They also can be expressed through other language features. A general approach like this keeps the design flexible.

1.8.2   Variability over Time versus Variability over Space

We can adopt two different perspectives during analysis: focusing on changes over time or focusing on variations within a family. We can think of variations in a family as occurring in "space," as different configurations that coexist in time for different customers or markets. These two approaches have separate but related goals.

By focusing on commonalities in a family of abstractions for a product or product line, we increase architectural abstraction. We reduce development effort—this is reuse at its best. We might notice that there are several different window system technologies and designs around their parameters of variation. Doing that allows us to deploy a family of systems in which each member of the family incorporates a different window technology. This is the strategy most commonly associated with the term *domain analysis.*

By focusing on what will remain common over time, we try to lower maintenance cost. We try to predict how the domain will change. Better yet, we try to predict how it *won't* change, cast that as a commonality, and capture it in the system's structure. Variabilities should express what changes over time. A test of a good design is to anticipate market changes over the lifetime of the system and to predict how badly they upset commonality assumptions. Predicting wrong can be expensive and can lead to those all-too-familiar situations in which a small requirement change leads to a large development effort. History is often a good predictor of the future: What has remained stable in the past often remains stable in the future.

Commonalities in space often unfold as though they were commonalities over time. In time, system designers may adjust the parameters of variation to select different family members one by one in successive releases. The project may also introduce family members that were unforeseen in the initial design. In a good design, these newcomers can take advantage of the foresight of a good commonality analysis because the commonality analysis tries to predict change, whether over time or in space.

In multi-paradigm design, as in any process that uses domain analysis, the designer must be careful to anticipate variabilities in "space" as well as changes over time. The test of time is usually the stronger test of the two. One can generalize from existing applications in mature domains, and those generalizations point to commonalities that will meet the test of time (remember, the past predicts the future). In new domains, it's more important to project commonalities and variabilities in time.

1.8.3 Late Binding

Gregor Kiczales notes that you want to bind all decisions as late as possible so that you can give customers control over system evolution [Kiczales1994]. Deferred binding is an important part of the object paradigm and a key part of the kind of "polymorphism" that object-oriented programmers hold dear.[1] We want to use the available facilities of the programming language and other implementation technologies to align domain variabilities with language constructs that support change with a minimum of ripple effect.

Prediction is always difficult, and we can't foresee all of the ways in which a system will change. Providers and users sometimes must change not only the system policies but its mechanisms as well. Using the principles of FAST, we try to bury the mechanisms where the user doesn't have to bother with them. Can we make *everything* easily changeable?

Kiczales feels that's why meta-object protocols are so important: They make it possible to reprogram the contract between the programmer and the system. C++ has no facilities for evolving its object model directly; analogous functionality comes from idioms [Coplien1992] and patterns [Gamma1995].

We might achieve a broader range of flexibility by doing a commonality analysis on the commonality analysis itself, looking for opportunities to regularize multiple domains. Following Kiczales's lead ("if you can't conquer, divide, and try a meta-object protocol"), we might have more success in the solution domain than in the problem domain. That might lead to another "language" that captures the meta-object protocol. While we find this issue resolved in symbolic programming languages, we must simulate reflection in C++ using the kinds of conventions mentioned previously (in particular, see [Coplien1992], Chapters 8 and 9). This takes us much in the direction of design patterns (Chapter 9), which encode recurring structures that express semantics not easily encapsulated in objects. Patterns provide a vocabulary that raises the level of the contract between programmer and system, much as the meta-object programming constructs of Smalltalk and CLOS do.

It's also noteworthy that Kiczales's nascent but promising concept of *aspects* [Kiczales1997] corresponds closely to the concept of "domain" as that term is used in domain engineering, and certainly as it is used in this book.

Multi-paradigm design doesn't aspire to such reflective solutions; this is largely an issue of practicality and scope. The pattern tie-ins in

---

[1.]   For more on the relationship between multi-paradigm design and polymorphism, see Section 6.9.

Chapter 9 are limited to structural commonalities and variabilities that are simple extensions of C++ constructs.

1.9 Summary

Choosing a design method is a crucial software development decision. While the object paradigm is currently in vogue, we must generalize beyond objects alone and look for opportunities to apply other paradigms. Not everything in nature or business is best seen as an object. We can use commonality and variability analysis to look for the dimensions of commonality and variability in both our application and solution domains. The dimensions shape families of abstraction.

To get started with multi-paradigm design, we now move on to describe analysis. The next chapter describes how to build the underpinnings of a rudimentary "language" for the application domain: a domain dictionary, which captures the families of interest. Later, we will explore C++ for the families it expresses most naturally. The goal is to find a natural match between the structure of an application domain family and a suitable solution structure. To the degree we succeed, our code will be more likely to meet its intended need and to continue meeting the needs of the application domain in the long term.

CHAPTER 2

Commonality Analysis

C ommonality and variability are two key characterizations of most software paradigms. This chapter introduces the first of these dimensions. Commonality defines *families* in an application. Families are the primary basis for abstraction in multi-paradigm development.

2.1 Commonality: The Essence of Abstraction

All major advances in software design have built on newfound insights into abstraction. Abstraction, in the common English language sense, means to focus on the general and put aside the specific. We abstract by emphasizing what is common and deemphasizing details. Abstraction is a fundamental analysis tool.

Let's say we're designing a package to process payroll data. We know we'll need to sort the data according to many different criteria. At some level of design, we may identify *sorting* as a key business abstraction. It's an abstraction not from the object paradigm, but from the procedural paradigm. Nonetheless, it's a key business abstraction. It's not a single piece of code. If we know the data are offered to the sorting algorithm in a largely random order, we're likely to use quicksort. We may sort large, partially sorted data sets with in-place insertion sort. If memory is available, we may copy the data into a list and then use list insertion sort, copying back when we're done. This typically is twice as fast as in-place sorting. And if we just want a function with a cute name for student exercises, we may use bubble sort. At high levels of design, we can treat all of these equally because of what they have in common: They all *sort*. This commonality is the basis of abstraction.

And if we're building a matrix algebra package, we'll talk about the abstraction "matrix," even though we know there are many different kinds of matrices. Sparse matrices, identity matrices, and upper and lower diagonal matrices all differ in their implementation. But we group them together by the behaviors they exhibit in common. The commonalities again support abstraction.

Commonality analysis goes hand-in-hand with the important design principles of coupling and cohesion. Software design strives to create largely independent design products that individually can be built, implemented, and maintained. A successful partitioning leads to design products that are largely decoupled (so that development teams can work more independently) and largely cohesive (so that each design product is a conceptual whole, thereby making the system easier to understand). For example, we strive to build inheritance hierarchies that group together classes that are independent of classes in other inheritance hierarchies. These hierarchies come about from a commonality analysis, though the commonality analysis is implicit in object-oriented techniques while we make it explicit in multi-paradigm design. We group classes together into an inheritance hierarchy because they share common properties: They have a common interface and may share a common implementation. Other language features capture other kinds of commonality. For example, templates let us group structures that have similar overall code and data structure but that vary in implementation.

Commonality analysis does three important things for us. First, it provides abstraction. By grouping together dozens of classes under a single design abstraction, it helps the designer "chunk" the design as an attack on complexity. A good example is an inheritance hierarchy, with the base class representing the abstraction of the classes in the hierarchy. Second, commonality analysis provides cohesion and coupling. Grouping by commonality naturally leads to chunks that are independent of each other because each chunk has low commonality with the elements in other chunks. Third, commonality analysis reduces maintenance cost. The broader a commonality, the more likely it will hold in the long term. Strong commonalities can be the invariant structures of design. For example, if we define the base class `Telephone` in terms of the methods `alert` (to ring the telephone), `DN` (which yields its telephone number, for which the term of the trade is "*directory number*"), and `talk` (which causes it to connect to a talking path), we will have captured an abstraction that characterizes most telephone terminals as they exist today, as well as most telephones over the past 100 years. We can put additional functionality in derived classes, but the base class captures the domain abstraction that is stable across space and over time.

2.1.1 Deductive and Inductive Commonality

We recognize commonality in two major ways: recognizing patterns we've seen before and recognizing recurring structures we haven't. The first of these relates to *experience*, and the second is a form of *learning*. Both are relevant to software design. Reuse is all about experience, and much of the rest of design—creating new abstractions—relates to the learning model. And it isn't much different for the way we view software than the way we think about the rest of the world around us.

Having seen cars all of our lives, we all recognize one when we see one. Even when seeing the first cars of a new model year, we recognize these hitherto unseen entities as cars. They differ in detail from the cars of our experience, but they share the same aspects in common as cars in general. The "archetypal car" in our mind helps us to recognize cars when we see them. Such archetypes shape the new systems we build. We don't have to invent "car" from first principles to build a new one.

The same is true in software: We can build on archetypes or "frames" as design foundations [Winograd1987]. When presented with a computing problem, most of us formulate abstractions drawn from our experience. For many of us, these abstractions are procedures with arguments. For others, they are database relations or tuples. And for many, they are classes or objects. All of these are *inductive* approaches to abstraction. Most methods draw on only a few rules from a single paradigm to abstract a complex system into a simpler model ("if you're a hammer, every problem looks like a nail").

Faced with a new situation in which no learned models apply well, we form abstractions by seeking repetition. In the absence of analogy and experience, we apply *deductive* reasoning to form models and abstractions. The first time we see the dwellings of a culture foreign to our own, it dawns on us that they are all related somehow. We form an abstraction that we tag "dwelling-for-that-culture." We can do the same in software.

Multi-paradigm design draws on available domain experience to partition the problem into commonly accepted domains. As the design progresses, multi-paradigm design draws more and more on the domain itself rather than on stock partitionings. Greenfield designs for new domains bypass the initial intuitive phase, borrowing from archetypes only as needed and looking to the domain itself for partitioning clues. We draw abstractions from the domain itself, instead of torturing abstractions from the problem by using preconceived partitioning criteria. If by happenstance a stock paradigm is the best choice for a given application, commonality and variability analysis will support such a conclusion.

This doesn't imply that every greenfield problem needs a custom paradigm to derive its solution structure. There are styles of partitioning called *commonality categories* (Section 2.3) that emerge again and again, and the designer should recognize these styles and capitalize on them. Most of these commonality categories map into C++ programming language constructs and the paradigms they support, such as objects and templates—this is presumably the reason such constructs exist in the language. We nonetheless can enumerate some "axiomatic" dimensions of commonality that are common to many world views. The perspectives we choose here don't comprise a complete set, and the choice is by no means unique. The dimensions we choose will shape our choice of C++ implementation techniques in Chapter 8.

2.1.2   Software Families

Software problems, and the solutions that address them, are rich with structure. We can group data structures and functions by criteria such as structure, name, or behavior. We call a group of related items a *family.* Parnas [Parnas1976] defines a family as follows.

> We consider a set of programs to constitute a *family,* whenever it is worthwhile to study programs from the set by *first* studying the common

properties of the set and *then* determining the special properties of the individual family members.

We can find many family abstractions in most applications.

The analysis of the domain of linear algebraic programming serves as an example. This domain produces a family of user abstractions called "*n*-dimensional matrix" that includes column vectors, 2-dimensional arrays, and higher-order matrices. Drawing on our experience with such programs, we know we also need a family of data structures for multiple internal representations of these data structures: sparse arrays (perhaps using a linked list), indexed sequential arrays, identity matrices, and diagonal matrices. Yet another family is the collection of algorithms for multiplying matrices: one to multiply sparse matrices, another to multiply an identity matrix by another matrix (a function that is easily made very efficient), another for the case in which one of the operands is a diagonal matrix, and so forth. There are analogous families for other operations. Further analysis may yield even more families.

Even this domain of matrices (which presumably comprises just one part of a larger problem) is rich with many families of its own. The larger domain of matrices can be broken down into subdomains: matrices, data structures, and operators. Each subdomain deserves its own commonality analysis.

Many design techniques focus on modules. There are many kinds of modules. Objects, classes, processes, and functions are examples of modules produced by popular design paradigms. Modules are the primary units of system abstraction, administration, and configuration. They need not delineate domains. There is a tension between the logical cohesion of some business concept and the ability of a programming language to capture that construct in a language construct.

Most traditional software design methods are top-down, and while the object paradigm may admit to being neither top-down nor bottom-up, it still relies strongly on hierarchy. We categorize by parts, and organize the parts hierarchically. What structured analysis, functional decomposition, modular information hiding, and object-oriented design have in common is that they produce *parts*. We use these parts to hide "secrets" of design. Whenever the domain allows us to hide design secrets in modules, we should do so—the design will be more resilient in light of change. But complex systems have many "tops," so top-down and hierarchical design paradigms are sometimes unable to expressively characterize some domains.

The matrix domain is one example. Instead of our capturing important domain dimensions in a traditional module—that is, a construct that corresponds to a consecutive block of source or object code—we look to capture them in language constructs. And we may apply those language constructs across modules. For example, we may capture matrix structure in a family of modules, with different modules for sparse matrices, identity matrices, upper and lower triangular matrices, and so on (though we'd probably use classes instead of modules, which we think of as being unlike modules in their support for instantiation). The operations on matrices are also a family, a domain, but they are a family of overloaded functions, and not classes or modules.

Finding Domains

At this point, an insightful reader will recognize that we might capture algorithmic commonality with overloading, behavioral commonality with public inheritance, and structural commonality with aggregation. But first we need to find the domains; this is the first step of commonality analysis. Most domains should be obvious to experienced practitioners in the field, who can formulate the abstractions from memory and experience. In new problem areas, we need to gather information about the problem to partition it into domains and subdomains and to characterize their properties. To get us started, we develop a dictionary of terms. Using this dictionary, we ascribe meaning to the "pieces" of the domain and to the domain as a whole.

Starting with the domain definition helps us separate a problem into aspects that can be separately managed, implemented, and perhaps reused. Consider the domain of matrices again. The designer must create structures to store and organize the data in a matrix. To swap or page large matrices to and from disk, one must know how to map back and forth between primary and secondary memory. One "top" is the domain of the representation; another addresses the semantics of matrices themselves. Dividing the matrix exercise into two subdomains—one for matrix semantics and one for memory management—leads to an architecture in which the modules are likely to be more cohesive and independently manageable than if these concerns were considered together.

The next section discusses how the domain vocabulary can help designers identify domains early in design.

2.2 Priming Analysis: The Domain Vocabulary

Vocabularies provide rudimentary building blocks for both the structure and interpretation of a domain model. A one-person programmer team can easily assemble an application vocabulary to be able to "communicate with one's self," and ambiguities can be deferred until the programmer chooses to deal with them. But most interesting software tasks—including most of those done as solo implementation efforts—require communication among several people: programmers, customers, testers, marketers, managers, software architects, the hardware folks, and so forth. These people must communicate among themselves to develop a solution for the problem presented, and a common vocabulary is essential to effective project communication. Even if solo programmers can avoid the social aspects of design, the problem of vocabulary resurfaces as they struggle with the translation from analysis concepts to solution constructs.

2.2.1 The Domain Dictionary

We start commonality analysis by building a *domain dictionary* that documents the vocabulary of the application area. The intent is to capture all relevant facets of the problem we are solving, and perhaps facets of the solution as well. Before we understand a problem in breadth or depth, we catch glimpses of it in words and word phrases that come from our customers, from requirement documents, and from our experiences. We call this a *domain vocabulary* or *domain dictionary*. It is a time-honored software design tool that is enjoying a renaissance of sorts in contemporary design methods (see [GoldbergRubin1995] for a particularly good treatment of this subject).

The domain dictionary is a catalogue of the technical terms of the problem area, or domain, in which we are working. It is not unlike the data dictionaries used to support structured design techniques. As we first approach a problem, we are faced with immediate needs. Most software development efforts are driven by an explicit problem, which is owned by a customer. By their natures, these applications are specific. This *specific* nature of most problem statements limits opportunities to find commonality. It is rare that a consortium of customers has considered their shared problems together, so it is unlikely that they would ever approach a software developer with *general* requirements hoping for a *broad* solution. It is often up to us, as analysts and implementors, to probe the business for other applications with similar abstractions. We want to broaden our scope to increase the chances that we will find commonality across the domain of consideration. We design for a *family* of applications, with the initial application at hand as one archetypal member of the family. The more broadly we examine a well-defined domain, the more commonality we find. We want to focus on *domain analysis*, not just analysis (either in the common English sense or in the sense it is used in classic software design methods).

Domain analysis has two major benefits over simple analysis, though these benefits are duals of each other. The first is generality, which may support reuse. If we are asked to build an FSM (finite-state machine) for a message protocol application, we can implement a general FSM that meets the specific need without excluding other opportunities. There is a cost to this generality in that it costs more to explore the properties of FSMs in general than it does to understand a single application. But if the same abstraction can be reused in the long term, we win.

The second benefit of domain analysis is resilience in the face of change. If we implement to the specification of the original, single customer, it will take rework to accommodate changes in that customer's world. But consider what happens if we broaden the design to accommodate similar customers, even if they are hypothetical ones. As requirements change for the original customer, they in effect characterize a new customer whose needs are similar to those captured by the original specification. If we design broadly, we can accommodate requirement changes more gracefully than if we optimize for the application at hand.

The designer must understand not only the commonalities that are stable across space and over time, but also the trends in change across space and over time. We can characterize change with a model based on parameters of variation. The range of values for parameters of variation generate software family members. Chapter 3 discusses *vari-*

ability analysis, a technique to build this conceptual framework of change. Domain analysis leads to more flexible software when its variability analysis complements the generality and resilience to change of the commonality analysis. If domain analysis is used to design an FSM so that the abstraction is sufficiently robust (general) and parameters of variation anticipate the range of changes well, the FSM can be customized across a wide variety of applications (reuse) without the price of generality being paid at run time. In fact, commonality and variability analyses cannot be separated in practice. Flexibility, resilience to change, and generality are closely related to each other as well.

Consider the vocabulary we would build to analyze an FSM. We could analyze the vocabulary for the first FSM that we were asked to build—perhaps one that can support a specific message protocol. But FSMs form a family. The same, basic FSM structure that serves a message protocol should also underlie the sequencing of dialogue boxes in a GUI. We want to capture what is *common* at that level of FSMs.

What do all FSMs have in common? They have a current *state.* The state is implemented as an instance of a *user-defined type* such as an enumeration or integer. They also have a conceptual *transition table,* which is a mapping from the *current state* and an *input event* (one of a family of such events, all of the same *event type*) to the new current state and a *transition function.*

Contemporary object-oriented analysis also starts with a domain vocabulary, the output of an activity often called "finding the objects." To a first approximation, the output of this activity is a list of classes (so "finding the objects" is an innocuous misnomer; however, see [GoldbergRubin1995] for a different strategy). The vocabulary that comes from an object-oriented analysis includes not only class names such as `Stack` and `Window`, but also other names that give `Stack` and `Window` meaning: `push`, `pop`, and `top`, or `displayText`, `refresh`, and `clear`. The domain vocabulary exercise of multi-paradigm design is a broadening of the "finding the objects" exercise of objects.

2.2.2   The Domain Dictionary Team

Developing the domain dictionary is an art. It defines the language of design for the domain. It should be a team activity. CRC cards [Beck1993] provide an example of how to draw on the perspectives of multiple designers to build a domain vocabulary. While the abstractions of CRC cards focus on the object paradigm—a more limited view than we must take in multi-paradigm analysis—they offer a good model for socializing a design.

Domain dictionary development is an iterative activity. As the dictionary grows, it is valuable for the team to pause and introspect on progress. There are important questions we can ask ourselves about the tentatively complete domain vocabulary.

- Are definitions clear? Do the architecture team, customer, and user have a shared understanding of what the terms mean?

- Are they all used? Do all of the terms pertain to the anticipated domain of application? Design teams have a tendency to get carried away and go beyond the demands of the business into areas best left alone. The vocabulary can help identify these.

- Is everything defined?

- Do the definitions fit the appearance of the terms in the requirements document? Without user contact (*not* just customer contact) and outside the context of the requirements document, domain terms can take on a life of their own. Revisit the vocabulary frequently with the user to make sure there is agreement about the meanings of the terms in the context of the requirements document.

These questions are meant to provoke thought, not to constrain the process. For example, the domain dictionary team may not strive for precise definitions. Instead it may characterize the domain by example or metaphor. Preliminary characterizations may omit even purpose and rationale. For example, the beginnings of an FSM domain dictionary might look as follows.

- *ABSTRACTFSM*: Consider an application that implements several message protocols across a link. An FSM will implement each protocol. Common application logic should be able to treat FSMs generically, so all FSMs can be used interchangeably. The *ABSTRACTFSM* domain captures the commonality at this level.

- *IMPLEMENTATIONFSM:* All FSMs will have an implementation to internally represent and manage tuples of the form {current state, stimulus, transition action, next state} using tables or some other data structure. This domain captures that commonality.

- *USERFSM*: Each FSM has definitions of specific transition actions and other code that are provided by the user. This domain provides a place to define and manage these tuples.

- *STATE*: States may be represented as enumerations, integers, or a class that abstractly represents some richer state of the application.

- *STIMULUS*: A stimulus is one element of the fundamental four-tuple of the FSM model. For each state, a stimulus causes the machine to sequence to the next state and to execute the transition function as a side effect. Potential synonyms or alternative names are *MESSAGE* and *EVENT*.

- *TRANSITIONACTION*: A family of functions that map a current state and stimulus onto a next state. Each function body implements the side effects of a state transition.

We'll use this domain dictionary as we elaborate the design in Chapter 8.

In FAST, Weiss [Weiss1999] annotates the requirements document by italicizing domain dictionary terms.

Commonality analysis is a generalization of object-oriented analysis. We are interested in finding not only the classes of interest (like event type or state type), but also common structure (transition table and current state), use cases (the external FSM interface and the scenarios and rules that govern their use), and common names or behaviors (state transition functions, which all share common behavior, argument, and return types). All of these abstractions are fair game for the domain vocabulary. In the following sections, we explore these facets of software commonality in more detail.

2.3 Dimensions of Commonality and Commonality Categories

Design is an innovative activity. Much of that innovation derives from how we apply the knife to carve abstractions into the system. We might do this first in the application domain and then in the solution domain, but in fact most people commonly do both together. If we look ahead to the solution domain during application analysis, using C++-shaped knives to partition the application domain, then we will more easily be able to express the structure of the problem as a C++ solution.

FIGURE 2.1 *Scalar number and matrix class categories.*

Number		Matrix

Design is more than cutting cookie-cutter modules from a two-dimensional piece of dough. The modular structure of a program is just one dimension we can capture in the design and implementation. When we do design partitioning, we may need to partition according to multiple criteria at the same time.

Think of how we divide classes in design. We may take a set of apparently unrelated classes (because their member functions are all different) and catalog them in some linear ordering. We may order them by importance or alphabetically by name or however we wish, first categorizing them at a level akin to what Booch calls *class categories*. The details of how we distinguish class categories isn't important except to the extent that we try to minimize commonality between the sets that result from the partitioning. For example, in a linear algebra package, we may have simple class categories such as scalar numbers and matrices, as shown in Figure 2.1.

Now consider adding derived classes to this categorization scheme. We want to arrange some classes together in an inheritance hierarchy because their member function signatures are a lot alike. We can no longer put them in the same line; that categorization exists in another "dimension." Notationally, it looks as shown in Figure 2.2.

FIGURE 2.2 *Capturing signature commonality.*

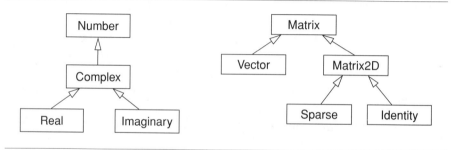

The dimension that differentiates base classes is orthogonal to the dimension that separates base and derived classes.

There may also be free functions that take several arguments, with different arguments declared in terms of different class categories. And each of these functions may exist in several different implementations, so some or all of the functions may be overloaded. That means the functions form families. Yet those functions operate on the classes. They have the same design stature as the member functions used to identify the class categories and to arrange the inheritance hierarchies. A good example is a family of `operator*` functions on some algebraic hierarchy (where `Vector`s are column vectors), as shown in Figure 2.3.

This function structure can't fully be separated from the class structure. However, neither does it align with the class structure. We can think of it as a third dimension of the design structure.

And we haven't yet talked about the internal structure of the classes, which may form a grouping different than the grouping by signature. If the original abstractions are templates instead of classes in closed form, then we have an additional dimension for each template argument, as shown in Figure 2.4.

And we can go on and on. The result is a rich, multidimensional space that models the design space available to the C++ programmer—much richer than the simple, two-dimensional plane of classes or objects. In fact, the design space (both in the problem and solution domains) is pretty complicated because these dimensions aren't totally orthogonal to each other. For example, overloaded member functions interact with inheritance in complex ways.

Design is the art of carving useful, expressive, maintainable constructs from this space. The "knives" we apply to this space must be

FIGURE 2.3   *A family of* `operator*` *functions.*

```
Vector operator*(const Matrix &, const Vector &);
Matrix operator*(const Vector &, const Matrix &);
Vector operator*(const Vector &, const Vector &);
Matrix operator*(const Number &, const Matrix &);
Vector operator*(const Number &, const Vector &);
Number operator*(const Number &, const Number &);
    .   .   .   .
```

FIGURE 2.4   *Another dimension: Template arguments.*

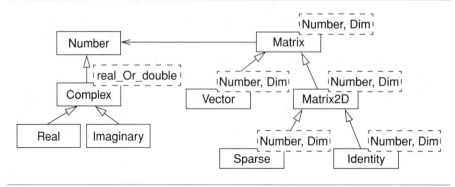

able to carve out a clean partitioning—and multi-paradigm design provides one set of techniques to manage the complexity of such design spaces. We will use the term *dimensions of commonality* for the aspects of this multidimensional design space. Example dimensions of commonality include the following:

- Structure
- Name and behavior
- Algorithm

These dimensions describe the kinds of *commonalities* we use to group family members into a subdomain. But commonality analysis alone isn't enough to select a solution structure suitable to the structure of the problem. We can also use those dimensions to characterize *differences* between individual family members. For example, all matrices behave the same, but they have different internal data structures. The study of differences in family members is called *variability analysis*, which is the topic of the next chapter.

These two dimensions—one for the primary commonality and one for the primary variability—together describe a *commonality category*. A commonality category, combined with requirements for binding time, instantiation, and default values, point to a unique C++ language feature. Each of these language features is designed to express abstractions in a particular paradigm. Commonality and variability analyses help the designer form software families. They also help the designer select the design paradigm for the family.

Assume that the matrix example is to use run-time binding; common behavior and variable data structure point to inheritance with virtual functions. That suggests a particular paradigm—in this case, the object paradigm. Each C++ language feature—templates, #ifdef, inheritance, or inheritance with virtual functions—corresponds to a combination of a commonality category, a binding time, and an optional parameter governing instantiation.

Commonality and variability analysis are rarely separated in practice; in fact, variabilities often can be derived from commonalities. So as we search the application domain for similarities along the dimensions of commonality, we look for variabilities along the same dimensions at the same time. The dimensions of variability are the same as those we use for commonality. For example, we note that different kinds of matrices *vary* in *structure*, while classes in an inheritance hierarchy *vary* in the *names* of some of their member functions and in the *algorithms* of some of the functions that retain the same names.

Commonality analysis is largely informal. The techniques presented in this book employ simple tables to organize abstractions and to document the analysis. The techniques use no mathematically formal factorings; we use no CASE tools. Rather, we rely on the intuition and insight of a good designer who is familiar with the domain to factor out the dimensions of commonality in a design. At this stage, we will just write them down informally, taking notes as we go along. Later, we will tabulate commonality and variability analysis results to support further analyses.

The following three sections describe the basic dimensions of commonality we use to define commonality categories: data, name and behavior, and algorithm.

2.3.1   (Data) Structure

In most good designs, data structures evolve more slowly than the algorithms that manipulate them. This may be because data more closely reflect the structure of the problem and are inherently more stable than procedures. Or it may be because the cost of data changes forces programmers to avoid changing data directly. In either case, good data design is key to maintainable systems. The tendency for well-formed data abstractions to remain stable over time is one advantage the object paradigm claims over procedure-based design methods. Data structure is an important dimension of commonality, though it is not the only dimension, and should not be confused with the dimensions of commonality that are central to object-oriented design.

Data design is a major concern of classical design methods such as structured analysis and its derivatives [Yourdon1979]. Before the advent of interactive user interfaces, and the rise in event-driven models of computation that came with them, data structures and control flows were the primary focus of design. The most important abstractions in a batch payroll system are the data structures and the sequence of processes that pass over those data. The legacy of classic data-focused design techniques lives on today in many popular design methods, such as Shlaer-Mellor, that consider data structure and data flows early on. In Rumbaugh, the notations and method suggest that we explore structural relationships early in design, though data are not the primary focus.

Recent trends toward interactive computing have moved software design focus from procedures and data *flow* to data *structure* and behavior. While batch applications are either holding their own or on the decline, most new software systems support interactive interfaces and "reactive" computation. Those systems must react to randomly sequenced data queries, whether from a real-time data link or the movement of a cursor across a GUI. In a sequential system, data flow cues the task sequencing, though the data just "go along for the ride." In an interactive system or real-time system, the system must route requests for service to the code that can handle them. The model of computation is no longer a smooth flow of data through sequential processes. Rather, it occurs in sporadic bursts of activity that happen in an unpredictable order. In the object paradigm, we create abstractions by grouping semantically related bursts of activity called *member functions*. These abstractions, called *classes,* usually have a data structure at their core. However, we are less interested in the data themselves or in how those data flow through the system than in how those data tie related operations together—it is the operations that form the abstraction. We call this abstraction an *abstract data type.*

The contemporary trend toward role-based design [Reenskaug1996] further emphasizes the distinction between an abstraction's "essence" and its functional behavior in a given circumstance (its *role*). In most responsibility-driven, object-oriented methods, behavior commonality drives the most important abstractions; we strive to defer structure until the end of design and the beginning of implementation. Examples include CRC cards [Beck1993] and Wirfs-Brock's responsibility-driven design [Wirfs-Brock1990]. In these methods, we focus on gross groupings of behavior that shape the *system*, instead of on the details of data and algorithm that shape the *code*. Even if data do sometimes drive the design structure, this analysis suggests that we should look beyond data structure as the primary source of partitioning criteria.

Yet most C++ programmers tie classes and inheritance hierarchy closely to their data designs; objects are too often thought of as "intelligent data" instead of loci of related behavior. Early proponents of the object paradigm jumped to the conclusion that the maintenance benefits of objects result from the time-honored principle that data are more stable over time than procedures and that classes were just a suitable mechanism to express that principle. Most methods that continue to underscore this perspective have their roots in an era that predates modern interactive user interfaces and the proliferation of real-time systems. They are "neo-classic" methods; they superficially use some object principles, yet they have their roots in data and process analyses. And old ways die hard. Few popular design methods in use today consciously defer data layout concerns. One common failure mode of modern methods is to cast member data as a collection of states and to treat all objects as FSMs. An FSM can be an object (more on that in Chapter 8), but many classes are not well-modeled as state machines. For example, a `Window` is a good class—a locus of related responsibilities—but it is hardly a state machine, and we aren't terribly interested in its data. Inexpert designers, apart from having a preoccupation with data in contemporary methods, often focus on data stores (such as the data for a report or form) to find the objects and fit the data into the object paradigm by annotating them with member functions that "give the data intelligence."

There is a grain of truth to the analogy between data stability and object stability, but it breaks down under scrutiny. Consider the case of class `Number` and its derived classes (see Figure 6.2). The behavioral hierarchy is clear, following the subtyping relationships that we derive directly from the application domain. The meanings of classes `Number`, `Complex`, and `Real`, and the relationships between them, are clear. Simple analysis produces a class hierarchy, in which `Real` is derived from `Complex`. The unwitting designer encapsulates a representation for complex numbers inside class `Complex`. This causes `Real` to inherit a lot of baggage it can't use.

We can learn several lessons here. A design derived primarily from data structure may be much different from a design based on distribution of responsibilities. Data structure is nonetheless an important design consideration. Even if data structures are implementation constructs, good design looks ahead to see how implementation shapes design decisions. Instead of our falling into the trap of the neo-classic methods that are overly eager to unify data analysis and object analysis, we need to separate those two dimensions of commonality and deal with each up front, during design.

Before we throw the baby out with the bath water, I will be quick to point out that data design often does line up with a good object partitioning. The point I am trying to make here is that we shouldn't *presume* such alignment. Rather, we should come by it honestly.

There is a whole paradigm suitable to the study of data structures and their access: databases. There is a place for relational modeling and other data-based modeling techniques in many data-intensive applications. (Object-oriented databases really don't fall into the same category because they are less a design regimen in their own right than a way of using object-oriented design structures in persistent storage media.) C++ does not express database relationships directly, so this book's treatment of multi-paradigm design treats them as an "outboard paradigm." I call them "outboard" because they don't come with the language; however, the language can accommodate them if we "connect them to the language on the outside." For example, we can link our C++ programs with database management libraries. Just because C++ doesn't support some paradigms does not diminish the value of such paradigms or of C++; both can be considered in the context of the multi-paradigm techniques of Chapter 7. Databases aside, we will focus on C++ mechanisms that support simple data commonality, particularly as it arises as a secondary concern in early design.

Let's consider some examples of data structure commonality.

- Disk file systems. An operating system may support many kinds of files: databases, unformatted character files, record-formatted files, indexed sequential files, blocked files, unblocked files, and others. All of these files must work in the context of a grander directory-and-file-structure design. Most files share basic data attributes: fields for creation and modification time, structures to map the logical file structure onto basic disk blocks, and so on. Note that the data structures may (or may not) cut across the major groupings of file system behavior.

- Protocol design. Message formats are regularized by size (as in fixed-size packet switching and transmission), fine structure (bit stream or 8-bit bytes), header format (a collection of fields, sizes, and offsets), and other parameters. Data commonality complements message semantics, though the two analyses can be separated.

- As we build software to audit the data structures of a fault-tolerant control system, we notice that most auditable data have links to parent, child, and sibling structures. Though not all data structures have all of these fields, early analysis brings them to our attention, so we include them in the domain dictionary. During commonality analysis, we can more precisely characterize the domain that forms around this commonality. We must deal with data structure differences as well, using the variability analysis approaches described in Chapter 3.

- Some memory management algorithms group data by size into equivalence classes: All blocks of like size are managed together.

- A data analysis application treats all scalars together; all ordered pairs (complex numbers, Cartesian points, polar coordinates) together; all ordered triples (Cartesian and polar 3-dimensional points) together; and so on.

While we are concerned primarily with the structure of data, we can also consider the structure of source code. Template functions have a single, common structure that can generate many variant implementations. For example, the following function captures the structure of a sorting algorithm, a structure that is common across most sortable types:

```
template <class T>
void sort(T s[], int nelements) {
    // a good sorting algorithm written in terms of T
    for (int top = 1; top <= nelements - 1; top++) {
        // vector is sorted in positions
        //        0 to top - 1
```

```
register int j = top - 1;
while (j >= 0 && s[j+1] < s[j]) {
    T temp = s[j];
    s[j] = s[j+1];
    s[j+1] = temp;
    j--;
}
    }
}
```

Template functions handle a small number of commonality/variability pairs well. For example, they can handle the case in which most of the algorithm is common with local variabilities that can be modulated through a template parameter. In this sense, they can be used like the TEMPLATE METHOD pattern in the design patterns book by Gamma [Gamma1995]. Template arguments manage the variability in algorithm template structure just as they manage data structure variability in class templates. Template arguments can be as specific as simple values or as complex as user-defined types.

We will see in Chapter 6 that inheritance is the most common tool to express common data structure and that templates capture both common data and code structure.

2.3.2   Name and Behavior

It is commonly heard that many interesting problems in computer science reduce to what's in a name and can be solved by one more level of indirection. Names convey meanings. We can use commonality of name to group items (such as functions) that have the same meaning. We must take care to avoid the analytical analogue of homophones. There are many kinds of programming language names: functions, types, parameters, data identifiers, and others. Modern computer science is sloppy with these terms, which often have noble and formal roots.

All this aside, for the moment we can take important design cues from names. As design and implementation move forward, we may discover a need for each of the following functions:

```
void set_date(const char *const);
void set_date(Year, Month, Day);
void set_date(time_t secondsSinceStartOfEpoch);
```

It's likely that these functions form a family, since they all have the same name and, at an intuitive level, the same meaning. This example shows how to take advantage of such commonality in C++ with function overloading. Overridden functions in an inheritance hierarchy are another kind of family of functions.

It is important first to identify the commonality during analysis and to defer language feature selection until the full commonality category is known. For example, consider the design of a general-purpose graphics system in which we may find a family of functions named displayOn. These functions display an object on some output medium. We could implement displayOn as a family of overloaded functions, as done in the previous example:

```
void displayOn(BitMap*, XWindow*, Point);
void displayOn(const char *const, XWindow*, Point);
void displayOn(BitMap*, MacWindow*, Point);
void displayOn(const char *const, MacWindow*, Point);
```

Or we could make displayOn a member function of each class whose objects are displayable:

```
class XWindow {
public:
    void displayOn(BitMap*, Point);
    void displayOn(const char *const, Point);
    . . . .
};

class MacWindow {
public:
    void displayOn(BitMap*, Point);
    void displayOn(const char *const, Point);
    . . . .
};
```

Or, we could make them part of a family of classes that we relate by inheritance:

```
class Window {
public:
    virtual void displayOn(BitMap*, Point);
    virtual void displayOn(const char *const, Point);
    . . . .
};
```

```
class XWindow: public Window {
public:
    void displayOn(BitMap*, Point);
    void displayOn(const char *const, Point);
      . . . .
};

class MacWindow: public Window {
public:
    void displayOn(BitMap*, Point);
    void displayOn(const char *const, Point);
      . . . .
};
```

There may be even more alternatives based on templates or on idioms or patterns (such as double dispatch). The selection depends largely on binding time; however, designer insight and experience should dominate.

We find names in requirements documents, in the user vocabulary, and in preexisting code. All of these sources are fair game for analysis. We start commonality analysis by scouring these sources for names, structures, sequences, and, more important, the trends and relationships among them. These trends and relationships form families, and we can capture the "genetic code" for these families in an abstraction.

There are several kinds of families that group by name. Functions, sets, and patterns may all have names; it should be clear that we want to group these separately from each other. We can define a few terms, as follows, to categorize common "name families," terms that are important dimensions of commonality in their own right.

- **Identifier:** An identifier is a name that is unique in some context, such as a scope. It is conventionally the name of a datum or group of data. In the more general sense, the name of a function or type is also an identifier, though we treat those separately later in this section.

- **Signature:** A signature is an interface to an operation, procedure, or function that is described in terms of the parameter and return types. We usually associate a name with a signature. Function declarations document named signatures. A signature connotes behavior and semantics. For example,

```
Complex &operator+=(const Complex&)
```

is a signature. A family of functions may share the same meaning at a high level but be implemented with different algorithms. Signatures convey high-level semantics, independent of any particular algorithm. In fact, a given program may have multiple functions that match this signature; for example, each in its own scope.

Every function has a signature. All functions of a given name need not have the same signature. An obvious case in point is overloaded functions, which are distinguished from each other by their signature. Functions of the same signature and name may form a family. An obvious example are the member functions in a class hierarchy.

Most programming languages technically define the return value type as part of the signature. The technical definition of C++ does not include the return type as part of the signature, but we can generalize the design notion of signature to include return types.

- **Type:** A type is a collection of signatures. It does not describe implementation, but behavior. We should think of "type" in the same sense as "abstract data type": the description of an interface apart from any implementation. We usually give types descriptive names such as `Stack`, `Window`, `TapeDrive`, or `ComplexNumber`.

  We sometimes find types directly during analysis, particularly "obvious" ones such as `Stack`, `List`, and `Window`. More formally, a type characterizes a set, or family, of abstractions that group by behavior. During analysis, we may find abstractions that group by behavior, recognize them as a family, and encode those properties in a collection of signatures, or a type. We should not focus on the data structure of the family members—that is a different dimension of commonality.

Note that *class* isn't among the abstractions considered here. A class is a programming language construct often used to implement a type. But each class brings together two dimensions of commonality in a single abstraction: behavior and structure. It is better to keep these two dimensions separate at the start of analysis. If the two analyses align, then a natural single class structure may result. We don't want to prejudice the implementation by prematurely imposing a class structure. Some contemporary design methods such as Fusion [Fusion1993] consciously recognize this.

Names are an important part of object-oriented analysis. We focus primarily on class names in most popular object-oriented methods. CRC cards help the designer focus on behavior and the names that convey the behavior, rather than on the data structures and algorithms that implement the behavior. The focus is on the signature.

A type is an abstraction that defines operations that take inputs (arguments to the functions in the type signature), produce outputs (through arguments and return values), and modify internal state. Classes are implementations of types. Instances of classes, called *objects*, connect in a network, passing inputs and outputs to each other to achieve the overall system function.

It is important to distinguish *behavior* from *meaning*. It is a fine distinction and, unfortunately, an informal one, but it serves us well to separate the two. Behavior is closely tied to implementation. We don't care *exactly* how an object behaves. For example, we don't care about the exact sequencing of instructions inside the member functions that implement type behaviors. The refresh responsibilities for an AsciiGraphicsWindow class and an XWindow class *behave* differently. However, refresh *means* the same thing to the client in both cases. Meaning is what the client cares about. A program can interchangeably use classes that have the same meaning but exhibit different behavior. (We take up this issue in more detail when we discuss paradigm and objects in Section 5.1.)

2.3.3   Algorithm

Procedures are one of the oldest and most widely used abstractions of programming. Historically, procedural design has been strongly hierarchical in nature, proceeding either top-down or bottom-up. Top-down design methods that focus on procedural decomposition rarely take the trouble to combine common algorithms or code fragments in the branches and leaves of the procedural hierarchy. Common code fragments are frequently duplicated—code for lists or sets or for walking project data structures—particularly in multi-person development projects. Bottom-up design addresses this problem at the expense of a weak or deferred notion of high-level system architecture.

If we do a commonality analysis of a top-down design, we find code fragments—use cases—that form families. Such commonality pops out when we have the entire system in view; this is a different perspective than that taken by a top-down designer who looks at one level at a time. During analysis, we want to consider threads of execution and the potential for commonality. Unlike procedural designers, who formally look only at one layer at a time, we want to find high-level use cases in which we analyze the system as a whole. And unlike object-oriented designers, who focus on individual member functions as the units of execution, we want to consider longer chains of execution.

2.4 Examples of Commonality

This section presents commonality examples for structure, for name and behavior, and for algorithm. These examples help demonstrate what we seek in commonality. They also show that C++ can express a given category of commonality in several different ways. The differences help motivate the discussion of variability in Chapter 3.

2.4.1 Structure

Structural commonality is intuitive to most software designers. To fall back on a tired example: All Shapes have a center of class Point. The C language tradition expressed such commonality like this:

```
typedef struct _Point { int xpos; int ypos; } Point;

typedef struct _Circle {
    Point center;
    . . . .
} Circle;

typedef struct _Rectangle {
    Point center;
    . . . .
} Rectangle;
```

In contrast, a C++ programmer is more likely to factor out the commonality using inheritance:

```
class Shape {
public:
    . . . .
protected:
    Point center;
};

class Circle: public Shape {
public:
    . . . .
};

class Rectangle: public Shape {
public:
    . . . .
};
```

That is, C++ can more directly express the commonality than can C.

C++ gives us other ways to express structural similarity. Consider the data structure for a List abstraction. All Lists are structurally *similar,* as shown in Figure 2.5.

Yet not all Lists are *identical;* the details vary according to the kind of element held by the list (for example, the exact size of each data block depends on exactly what X is). We can capture the similarity in a template:

```
template <class X> class ListRep {
friend class List;
    ListRep<X> *next;
```

FIGURE 2.5   *Data structure for* List.

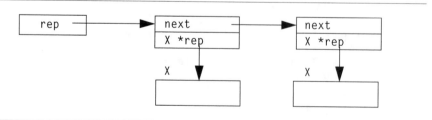

```
    X *rep;
    . . . .
};

template <class X> class List {
public:
    . . . .
private:
    ListRep<X> *theRep;
};
```

2.4.2   Name and Behavior

Consider the simple domain *Number*, in which we find several families of arithmetic operations such as operator+, operator-, and operator*. Each family of operators has several members that all "mean" the same thing. For example, addition always means the same thing, independent of its operands. This similarity in meaning is reflected in the *externally* observable behavior of the operators and is conveyed in the names we give them. We use the *name* operator+ to signify this commonality of meaning for addition.

C++ offers several language features to capture this commonality, and different contexts call for different C++ mechanisms. One such mechanism is the *overloaded* function. Here, we overload operator+ for assorted pairs of operands that are compile-time bound:

```
Complex operator+(const Complex &n1, const Complex &n2) {
    // would be declared a friend function in class Complex
    Complex retval = n1;
    retval.rpart += n2.rpart;
    retval.ipart += n2.ipart;
    return retval;
}

BigInteger operator+(const BigInteger &n1,
        const BigInteger &n2) {
    . . . .
}

Complex operator+(const Complex &n1,
    const BigInteger &n2) {
    . . . .
}
```

The name `operator+=` also conveys the meaning of addition, combined with an assignment operator. We can bind `operator+` at run time using *overridden* virtual functions in an inheritance hierarchy:

```
class Complex {
public:
    virtual Complex& operator+=(const Complex&);
    . . . .
};

class BigInteger: public Complex {
public:
    BigInteger& operator+=(const Complex&);
    . . . .
};
```

Note that the latter approach doesn't handle sequences of code such as the following:

```
int i;
Complex a, c;
a = i + c;
```

However, the overloading approach does handle it, provided `Complex` has a constructor that accepts a single `double` or `int`. It is common to use the overloading structure (to handle the latter problem) together with the overriding structure (to provide run-time genericity):

```
Complex operator+(const Complex &n1, const Complex &n2) {
    // would be declared a friend function in class Complex
    Complex retval = n1;
    retval += n2;    // a virtual function call
    return retval;
}

class Complex {
public:
    virtual Complex& operator+=(const Complex&) const;
    . . . .
};
```

Even this solution has limitations. If both the arguments are objects of classes derived from `Complex`, then the single-dispatching model of C++ virtual functions isn't enough—it doesn't accommodate the dynamic type of `n2` in the previous example—and the designer must resort to patterns such as VISITOR. We will discuss this class of solutions in Section 8.4.3.

In summary, for a family of functions bound together by a common meaning (such as addition), both function argument types and C++ language pragmatics drive the choice of language features. Binding time also governs the choice of specific implementation constructs. We cover this important aspect of multi-paradigm design in Chapter 3.

2.4.3   Algorithm

Procedures are one of the oldest programming abstractions, and procedural decomposition is a long-standing design method. We think of two kinds of procedural decomposition: top-down and bottom-up. Each approach has its advantages and disadvantages. Top-down design allows us to formulate higher-level abstractions, but it doesn't lead to much code reuse and can make it difficult to implement high-performance designs. Bottom-up design is more likely to create basic algorithms that can be broadly reused, but it requires more work to create higher-level abstractions and makes it difficult to foresee how well primitive functions will serve high-level needs.

Let's think about commonality in bottom-up design. We want to design one procedure that can be called from several different contexts. Of course, it would be even better to think about families of algorithms that share much logic in common. (Note that this is a different kind of commonality from behavioral commonality as described in Section 2.3.2.) One design trick of procedural programming is to package a family of algorithms in one procedure by using a formal parameter to discriminate between alternatives:

```
void FloorPlan::redraw(int showRoomDimensions = 0) {
    . . . .
    switch (showRoomDimensions) {
    case 2: // draw arrows annotated with room dimensions
        . . . .
        break;
    case 1: // just show square footage of room
        . . . .
        break;
    case 0: // no annotations at all
        break;
    }
    . . . .
}

    . . . .
```

```
FloorPlan *p;
. . . .
p->redraw(1);        // binding specified here in the source
```

Or we can factor the differences so that they are altogether outside
the function:

```
void FloorPlan::redraw(void FloorPlan::*f() = 0) {
    . . . .
    if (f) this->f();
    . . . .
}

void FloorPlan::drawArrows() {
    . . . .
}


. . . .

FloorPlan p;
. . . .
p.redraw(&FloorPlan::drawArrows);  // source-time binding
```

That approach encapsulates commonalities inside individual functions. Going a step further, we can meet the same design goals in a
more object-oriented way:

```
class FloorPlan {
public:
    // qualification is used just for emphasis
    void FloorPlan::redraw() {
        . . . .
        drawDimensions();
        . . . .
    }
    virtual void drawDimensions() = 0;
};

class FloorPlanWithArrows: public FloorPlan {
public:
    using FloorPlan::redraw;
    void drawDimensions() {
        // draw arrows for this floor plan
        . . . .
    }
};
```

. . . .

```
FloorPlanWithArrows p;
p.redraw();    // with arrows, compile-time bound
```

Or we can meet those goals in a slightly different use, given the same declarations of FloorPlan and FloorPlanWithArrows:

```
FloorPlan *q = new FloorPlanWithArrows;
q->redraw();    // with arrows, run-time bound
```

Each of these approaches captures commonality in algorithm. Each also expresses a different kind of variation, with a different binding time.

2.5 Reviewing the Commonality Analysis

It is useful to pause and reflect on the commonality analysis as the dictionary evolves and terms take shape. Dictionaries may evolve over weeks or months and sometimes longer, so the design team should revisit these terms and reflect on them frequently. Part of this introspection pertains to the vocabulary itself, as discussed in Section 2.2.2. We can broaden these questions to the analysis as a whole as follows.

- Are there unstated properties that are true for all members of the family?
- Can commonalities be stated more precisely?
- Are the commonalities accurate?
- Are the commonalities consistent?

We strive to answer these questions during commonality analysis and the (parallel) variability analysis (Chapter 3); when selecting implementation mechanisms (Chapter 6); and when design changes arise during maintenance.

2.6 Commonality and Evolution

The abstractions discovered during commonality analysis find expression in the most stable design constructs, those that carry the most inertia in the implementation structure. These include inheritance hierarchies, families of overloaded functions, and families of template instantiations. Once defined, these underlying structures are costly to change because of dependencies between the abstractions of a family or between the family and its clients. A designer who rearranges any portion of an inheritance graph is obliged to revisit the design decisions for all classes derived from any moved or removed class. If you add a new signature to a family of overloaded functions, it is a tedious job to evaluate the scope of coordinated changes that must be made. If a template parameter changes, the programmer must recompile the template itself and all of the code in the application that uses the template.

If our goal is to build systems that endure gracefully into the distant future, they must accommodate change gracefully. Ensuring this means making changes in ways that are unlikely to reshape or displace major system constructs. We want most changes to have local impact, to leave global interfaces unaffected, and, in short, to be invisible to as much of the system as possible. That, in turn, means that we want changes not to affect the constructs that implement the abstractions of commonality analysis.

So when we do commonality analysis, we should strive to carve out abstractions that will remain stable over time. That means that commonality analysis should draw on the analyst's knowledge of how the domain changes over time. Not only should we look for commonality between the constructs in the domain vocabulary, but we should ask whether the vocabulary will be the same tomorrow as it is today.

While we can encapsulate the stable parts of a domain as commonalities, we can't ignore the parts of the domain that change over time. In the next chapter, we'll see how variability analysis manages design assumptions that are not stable across applications or over time. Both commonality and variability analysis discover system structure: Commonality analysis seeks structure that is unlikely to change over time, while variability analysis captures structure that is likely to change. Variability analysis makes sense only in terms of the context defined by the associated commonality analysis. But it is the variability analysis that captures the way the system evolves. The maintainability of a system may depend more on what is *not* in the commonality analysis than on what it contains.

Fortunately, commonality often goes hand-in-hand with resiliency over time. The basic abstraction called "telephone" has remained unchanged in over a century, with a very few outliers, such as video phones. These telephone attributes are common to most telephones because they are essential to the commonly accepted model of telephone behavior, which is independent of the implementation. That these abstractions have remained in place for 100 years also owes to their fundamental relationship to what telephones do. Other parts of the telephone have changed as technology has changed. But most of the time, a good commonality analysis portends well for a resilient design.

2.7 Summary

This chapter explored the importance of commonality analysis. Commonality is the first thing we look for to formulate abstractions in both the application domain and in solution constructs such as programming language building blocks and user-defined types. We start looking for commonality by building a domain vocabulary. This vocabulary looks beyond a single application to a family of applications in anticipation of reuse and evolution. The vocabulary captures trends in structure, signature, types, and use cases. The common abstraction of contemporary object-oriented analysis—the class—is a second-order abstraction that unifies commonality in structure and signature. Because commonality analysis goes beyond classes, and even beyond types and responsibilities, it is a more general technique than object-oriented analysis alone.

The other side of analysis is variability. Life would be boring if we stopped at commonality; nothing would ever change! Variability is the interesting part of design, but it makes sense only in a well-defined context. With commonality and variability in hand, we will be able to survey the shape of both the application domain and the solution domain and gain insights into how to align the two structures for a given problem.

CHAPTER 3

Variability Analysis

I n the last chapter, we looked at commonalities, the first of two important dimensions that underlie most software paradigms. These commonalities can be expressed in a language such as C++. In this chapter, we discuss the second dimension of paradigm: Within a paradigm, how do similar items differ? There may be myriad differences between the members of a family, but we can gain tremendous abstracting power by parameterizing the variabilities of a domain. Here, we talk about variability analysis with an eye to the implementation of commonalities and variabilities in C++. The chapter also introduces variability dependency graphs, a simple notation for domain structure.

3.1 Variability: The Spice of Life

Commonality analysis is the search for common elements that helps us understand how family members are the same. As described in Chapter 2, we are good at finding commonality: We take note of it; it catches our eye. But commonality is monotonous without variability. If there is no variation in family members, there is no sense in creating abstractions to help understand a family as a whole. So while commonality forms the backbone and skeleton of design, variability gives it its flesh and blood. From an architectural perspective, commonality analysis gives the architecture its longevity; variability analysis drives its fitness for use.

As we also noted in Chapter 2, commonality analysis alone is insufficient to prescribe or even suggest a solution technique, particularly when C++ is our solution domain. For example, assume that we choose to make TEXT EDITING BUFFERS a domain because their behavior and much of their structure is common. (TEXT EDITING BUFFERS are a running example in this chapter. We'll discuss them in terms of their applicability to a text editor. We may as well have called them TEXT BUFFERS because they are broadly applicable to many text processing applications.) How do we represent abstractions that share common behavior and structure? Classes and inheritance come to mind, particularly to the object-oriented mind. But to choose an implementation strategy, you must understand not only how TEXT EDITING BUFFERS are similar, but also how they are *different*. If I tell you that text buffers differ only in their support for encryption, then a designer might break out each encryption algorithm using #ifdefs. If they differ in the character sets they support, a good C++ programmer would investigate templates as a solution. If they use different storage strategies and algorithms, then inheritance is one viable solution.

Application domain structures can vary along the same dimensions by which commonality is judged. TEXT EDITING BUFFERS share common behavior but may differ in algorithm, in detailed type characteristics, or in the argument types accepted by their member functions. Each of these variations leads to different C++ technology selections: inheritance for difference in algorithm, templates for type parameters, and perhaps overloading for different member function argument types.

Even if the dimension of variability is understood, we must also understand binding times and defaults. TEXT EDITING BUFFERS might contain source code for two different memory management strategies. Is all of the code present in a given running copy of the editor so that we can choose between memory management strategies at run time? Or do we compile one of the implementations into the program when we build it, using #ifdefs to bind the decision earlier? And, in either case, which buffer management strategy should be the default so that novice users encounter "reasonable" behavior if they don't choose either option?

We explore all of these questions during variability analysis. Because variability analysis and commonality analysis both use the same taxonomy of commonality categories, the two activities should be done together. Domain engineering supports commonality and variability analysis with notations that capture the details of commonalities, variabilities, binding times, defaults, and relationships between domains. The output of commonality and variability analysis is a collection of such notations. We can often use these notations as direct input to low-level design (writing classes and function prototypes) when variability analysis is done. This chapter introduces the dimensions of variability and a simple variability notation.

3.2 The Commonality Base

Variability makes sense only in a given commonality frame of reference. When we analyze variability, it is important to keep *something* fixed. Commonality analysis serves two purposes: to find the major dimensions of structure in a system and to provide a backdrop for variability analysis. The relationship between a variability and its commonality base is an important part of the published variability analysis.

We can't talk about variability in a context-free way, but we must always ask, "Variability in *what*?" Consider a `Message`. When we say that messages vary in length, the implied commonality comprises the characteristics that make a message a message. On closer inspection, we might find that these characteristics include a header of a given format and size, a trailer of a given format and size, and a message body of varying size and unspecified format. The commonality here is that every message contains a header, a trailer, and a body. For each message type, the format of the header and of the trailer is fixed. We ideally discover these properties during commonality analysis. There are many other commonalities for messages, too; for example, the algorithms used to dispatch them across a network medium or to compute their checksums.

Commonalities themselves often provide key hints to variabilities. Consider this commonality:

All Text Editing Buffers have some kind of working set algorithm.

Make no mistake; that's a commonality. However, it also points the way to a variability: TEXT EDITING BUFFERS vary in the kinds of working set algorithms they support. A large percentage of interesting variabilities fall into this category. Because of this tight link between commonality and variability analysis, the two are done together, not as separate, time-ordered activities.

3.3 Positive and Negative Variability

Let us reconsider the MESSAGE example of the previous section. All MESSAGEs have headers and trailers of a given format; we note that as an important commonality of the MESSAGE domain. Though the presence of a "message body" member is a substantial commonality of the MESSAGE domain, the body may vary substantially across members of the domain (but for the time being, we ignore messages that lack bodies). We can count on all messages having a header, a body, and a trailer. Note that the format of the header may be fixed for a particular system but may vary across systems or across time.

3.3.1 Positive Variability

Variabilities in message size and header field contents are independent of the commonalities that make a message a message. A message can leave certain header fields unfilled and still be a message; that is, it can have a 1-byte body or a 256-byte body and still quack, walk, and fly like a message. Yet the formatting of header fields and the size of the message body are important variabilities. Because these variabilities leave the underlying commonality model untouched, they "add" something to messages that refines their definition. I call these *positive variabilities* in that they add to the list of the base specifications that make a message a message without violating any of those original specifications.

If a parameter of variation is a positive variability, then a less abstract family results when we substitute a value for that parameter. As we bind more and more parameters of variation, we create an increasingly restrictive specification of the set of family members. For example, TEXT EDITING BUFFERS describe a large family at one level of abstraction. Particular editing buffers may support specific character sets, where CHARACTER SET is one of the parameters of variation. CHARACTER SET is a positive variability because a more restrictive specification results when we bind it to a specific selection. It is also a positive variability because its bindings do not violate the commonalities of the TEXT EDITING BUFFERS domain. The degrees of freedom become exhausted when all parameters of variation are bound. A single family member results.

3.3.2   Negative Variability

If all messages have bodies, then the variability is limited to the size of the message body (presuming that the body format is of no interest to message design). If most messages have bodies, while others (such as ACK messages) don't, the variability breaks our commonality assumptions. I call this *negative variability* in that it contradicts the assumptions that underlie what we mean by "message." It is a fundamentally different kind of variability than positive variability.

One might be tempted to claim that all messages have a body; it's just that messages like ACK have a body of size zero. If we take this perspective, we remove negative variability from the design. However, this is really lying about the semantics of ACK messages; in the very least, it violates common sense. Such a recasting of the design may have consequences for cost and complexity. It leads to embarrassing questions such as, "Can I take the checksum of the body of an ACK message?" If so, then ACK messages bear the "overhead" of checksum code. This might complicate the interface of the ACKmessage class. The appearance of checksum in the interface is semantic overhead. Depending on the types of commonalities and variabilities involved, it may also result in real memory or real-time overhead. These design decisions should be dealt with on a case-by-case basis because sometimes they *do* make sense. For example, all Shapes may report their angle of rotation, even though we could safely do away with this property for Circles. The consistency we gain by making the property ubiquitous (we do away with variability altogether) outweighs the slight economies of semantics and space we might gain by treating Circles differently.

There is a spectrum of negative variability. Multi-paradigm design offers creative but straightforward techniques to deal with *small* negative variabilities. For example, the absence of some message field can be controlled with an #ifdef that selects code according to message type:

```
// adapted from stropts.h in a UNIX header file

struct strrecvfd {
#ifdef KERNEL
    union {
        struct file *fp;
        int fd;
    };
#else
    int fd;
#endif
    unsigned short uid;
    unsigned short gid;
    char fill[8];
};
```

Assume that the KERNEL option is the predominate common base. The non-KERNEL version introduces a negative variability because it takes the fp member away from the presumed commonality of structure. If you assume that non-KERNEL code is the predominate common base, then the KERNEL version takes away the first-class standing of the fd member as a field whose value can be trusted as valid. In either case, the variation attacks the presumed commonality, so it's a negative variability.

This example may not scale or generalize well. If only half of the uses of strrecvfd messages are in the kernel and the other half are not, then it is difficult to claim fp as a substantial component of the STRRECVFD commonality domain. We may choose to break the structures into two separate domains instead: perhaps STRRECVFD for file descriptors and STRRECVFP for file pointers. Such a split makes the negative variability disappear.

We can apply these models of positive and negative variability across many domains and across many parameters of variation. These models of commonality and variability are well-developed for class inheritance under the object paradigm. Inheritance with cancellation, as dissected in the seminal analysis of Synder [Snyder1986], is a specific form of negative variability. Public inheritance with addition is a form of positive variability.

When using multi-paradigm design, try to express design using positive variability as often as possible. Multi-paradigm accommodates negative variability as well, often by appealing to existing techniques such as inheritance with cancellation. The most straightforward approach is to split such domains into disjoint subdomains along the lines of the negative variability. More advanced techniques range from judicious use of #ifdef to more generalized solutions that will be taken up in Section 6.11 and elsewhere in the book.

3.4 The Domain and Range of Variability

Variability distinguishes the members of a software family. The parameters that differentiate family members may be just a few, or they may be many. It is important to understand the parameters of variation that distinguish family members—how many of them there are and what values they can take on—and to understand how suitable parameter values meet design needs.

This section introduces vocabulary that describes the relationship between family members and the relationship between family members and the design trade-offs that shape them. Think of a family as a collection of members that can be produced by a machine to suit specific design needs. We use the term *range* to talk about the entire extent of family members that the machine can produce. The machine has inputs, knobs, switches, and levers that control the properties of the family member we want to make. We call these inputs *parameters of variation*. There may be few or many parameters of variation, and each may accept only a couple of values or a large set of values. We use the term *domain* to denote the valid combinations of values for all parameters of variation for a family or for a specific parameter of variation. Note that we use *domain* and *range* in much the same sense as in mathematics. The first job of domain engineering is to build this "machine" by finding the commonalities, variabilities, and parameters of variation that characterize the domain.

Commonality helps us abstract, and abstraction comes from deemphasizing detail. We think of variabilities as the complement of commonality; they express what is not common. Does that mean that parameters of variation express detail? Sometimes, variabilities are more pronounced than the commonalities against which differences stand out. We still want to capture substantial commonality during commonality analysis; that gives us a leg up on reuse. But we don't want to deemphasize variability. Instead, we want to *regularize* it. If we can abstract lots of variabilities into equivalence sets, there is hope that we can describe all of the variabilities in terms of a few simple parameters. This is a different kind of abstraction than we use to shape software families from the commonalities across family members. To make a far-fetched analogy, this is how nature manages variability across the individuals of a species that share a common genetic structure.

3.4.1   The Text Editing Buffers Example

All variability analysis takes place in the context of an established commonality domain. Consider the domain of TEXT EDITING BUFFERS for a text editor from Section 3.2. TEXT EDITING BUFFERS form a family around commonalities such as structure and algorithm. Different buffers vary over a range of output types, of character types, and of working-set management algorithms. Output types, character types, and working-set management algorithms are parameters of variation. It is these parameters that control the range of variability in the family.

Each parameter of variation has a corresponding *domain* of values, a set of independent design variables whose values we select to generate a particular member of the common family. A domain is a set of values that characterize the extent of variability in an associated range. For TEXT EDITING BUFFERS, the domain that controls output type variability includes databases, RCS files, screen output, and UNIX files. Character set properties are controlled by selecting from the set ASCII, UNICODE, EBCDIC, and FIELDATA.[1]

Variability domain sets are the "pressure points" of design. By assigning suitable domain set members to parameters of variation, we control the generation of family members for the software design. In a good design, the programming language captures the background commonality, but it emphasizes the way we express parameters of variation.

For example, we may know a great deal about the complexity of TEXT EDITING BUFFERS; we explore and capture this complexity during commonality analysis. The programming language should hide the complexity that is shared by all TEXT EDITING BUFFERS. We should use

---

[1.]   This is an archaic 6-bit character set used on UNIVAC machines of the author's experience in the 1970s.

the facilities of the language—inheritance, #ifdefs, overloading, templates, and others—to control the output type, character set, and working-set algorithm used in a particular text editing configuration. We will investigate the linguistic pieces to this puzzle more fully in Chapter 6 and will fully tie variability analysis together with the language facilities in Chapter 8.

3.4.2 Good Parameters of Variation

What makes good parameters of variation? Designers can ask themselves the following questions about parameters of variation as the design progresses.

- Do the domains of the parameters cover the range of application domain variabilities? It is crucial to select good parameters of variation if the design is to endure multiple releases and is to be used in multiple products of the enterprise. Parameters of variation encode the breadth of the domain.

- Are there parameters of variation that cannot be traced to variabilities, or vice versa?

- Are the defaults appropriate and within the domain? (Defaults will be discussed in more detail in Section 3.6.)

3.5 Binding Time

Analysis is largely a job of making associations; *commonality* analysis searches for associations common to families of application building blocks. Associations can be shaped by the application domain, by the use of a product, or by its implementation. A given product may need to serve several variability configurations. This means that we may need to accommodate many options in a given product.

3.5.1 Binding Time and Flexibility

When we need to foresee the need for multiple product options, how late can we defer *selecting* between members of a software family? Is it at compile time, or run time, or sometime in between? A software rule of thumb is that the later we can bind a decision, the better, since late binding and flexibility often go hand-in-hand (as discussed in Section 1.8.3). Of course, we need to balance this rule of thumb with nonstructural (and often nonfunctional) engineering considerations like performance and static type checking. But if flexibility is important to us, and if we incur no penalties for deferred binding times, we want to defer binding as late as possible.

One must often understand the binding time, in addition to the commonalities and variabilities, to select a suitable implementation technology for a given analysis. Multi-paradigm analysis makes binding times explicit. Binding time options are a function of the solution technologies available. These options are often richer than the simple compile-time-versus-run-time model so often portrayed in discussions of the object paradigm; we discuss them in Section 3.5.4.

3.5.2   Are Objects about Deferred Binding?

Deferred binding is one of the carefully taught lessons in many schools of the object paradigm. Under object-oriented design and programming, we usually defer the selection of a given class until run time and then select it from context. Object-oriented programming languages combine this flexibility with the ability to hide the decision beneath base class interfaces. Inheritance is the technique that hides the variability; virtual functions provide the run-time binding and complete the mechanisms necessary to support transparent variability. Inheritance and virtual functions provide powerful run-time variability against the backdrop of the commonality of a base class structure and interface.

3.5.3   Efficiency and Binding Time

We pay a penalty for run-time binding. In general, a program must contain code for all possible run-time options. If we used run-time binding for every function call, then every program we shipped would contain a complete copy of all code, whether or not we anticipated that it would be used. Furthermore, the programs would all need to contain logic to turn individual options on and off as context required. Such logic hampers program comprehension and carries a performance penalty. And there is the spectre of reduced confidence because of weakened static program checks, and we'd prefer to have complete compile-time type checking. Of course, we rarely go to these extremes. Instead, we usually bind some of the dimensions of variability at run time. (Dynamically linked libraries are a curious exception but are perhaps better thought of as a program engineering technique than as an important dimension of design.)

3.5.4 Binding Time Alternatives

Most designers think of two binding time alternatives: compile-time and run-time. We can be more precise, particularly with C++ as our implementation domain. Binding times include *source time, compile time, link time,* and *run time.*

Source Time

Source-time binding implies that the programmer consciously selects the appropriate family member in the program source. Template arguments are one example:

```
List<char>
```

where the programmer *explicitly* substitutes the parameter of variation.

Compile Time

Compile-time binding means that the compiler can select the proper binding from context at compile time. C++ function overloading is a typical example—the programmer doesn't consciously stipulate the parameter of variation, but the compiler does. An unusual example is #ifdef. Though the selection constructs are in the source code, the parameter of variation may be in a distant header file or may be supplied as a compiler flag. Compile-time binding informally implies source-time binding.

Link (and Load) Time

Link-time binding means that precompiled code can be selected to satisfy an interface before the program runs. It is usually environment-dependent and is not supported by C++, so we don't include it in our taxonomy here. For more on link-editing and load-time tricks for C++ programs, see Coplien [Coplien1992].

Run Time

Virtual functions are the canonical example of run-time binding. The compiler generates code at compile time to handle run-time alternatives, not knowing what the run-time context will be ahead of time.

FIGURE 3.1   *A fully general implementation of text buffers.*

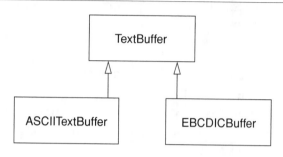

3.5.5   An Example

Consider the *Text Editing Buffers* example again. We could make the editor fully general so that it could deal with any character set at run time, probably by deriving several implementations from the same base, as shown in Figure 3.1. But then each editor would contain full copies of the code for `ASCIITextBuffer` and `EBCDICBuffer`. A given version of the editor must deal with only one character set at a time, depending on the platform for which it is compiled and linked. We might use templates so that we can continue to capture the variability in the source, while not remembering the full complement of alternatives in the implementation, as shown in Figure 3.2. Both designs cap-

FIGURE 3.2   *A general source structure that allows flexibility in implementation.*

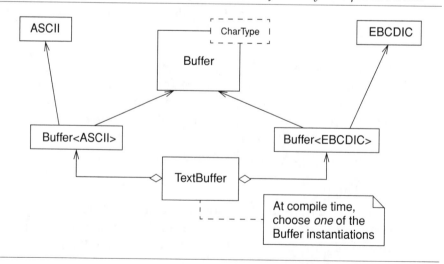

ture the same patterns of analysis commonality and variability, but they differ in their implementation binding time.

When we do variability analysis, we must capture the binding time for each parameter of variation, as it will guide us in the choice of a suitable programming language feature that captures the design intent.

3.6 *Defaults*

Defaults are useful conveniences when parameters of variation affect the application only rarely. C++ has useful facilities that express defaults, such as argument defaulting, base class member functions, and default template parameters. Defaults that we capture during commonality and variability analysis can often be directly expressed by the programming language.

Most of us are familiar with #ifdefs as a way to capture variability. We also are familiar with how to use them to vary the default behavior or structure of our code. We may wish to place debugging code in our text buffer implementation, but we may not want the code included in the production version of the object code. We may arrange debugging code to be the default:

```
#ifndef NDEBUG
    // include this code by default
    cerr << "got to " << __FILE__ << __LINE__ << endl;
#endif
```

If we turn on the #define, then we can generate a production version. If production versions are much less frequent than debugging versions, then it's appropriate to leave debugging on in the default case. That makes less work for the developer.

Designers should also remember that defaults are dangerous. A complex design may have many parameters of variation, each of which should be scrutinized to support a given deployment context. It is presumptuous of the designer to let a default value filter into an implementation unchallenged. Defaults should be chosen carefully (if they exist at all), should be explicitly documented as part of the project architecture document, and should be revisited for each application.

3.7 Variability Tables

We can produce a variability table to document the result of our variability analysis. There is one table for each commonality domain, and each application may comprise multiple commonality domains.

Table 3.1 shows the results of the variability analysis for TEXT EDITING BUFFERS. TEXT EDITING BUFFERS are a commonality domain in the grander context of a design for a complete text editing program. We recognize the TEXT EDITING BUFFERS domain during commonality analysis for its commonalities of *structure* and *algorithm*. That is what all TEXT EDITING BUFFERS have in common; the variability table describes how they differ.

We see that there is a *range* of TEXT EDITING BUFFERS defined over *domains* of output types, character sets, working set management techniques, and debugging code configurations. The columns of the table

TABLE 3.1 *Text Editor Variability Analysis for Commonality Domain:* TEXT EDITING BUFFERS

Parameters of Variation	Meaning (the decision being made)	Domain	Binding	Default
Output type	The formatting of text lines is sensitive to the output medium.	Database, RCS file, TTY, UNIX file	Run time	UNIX file
Character set	Different buffer types should support different character sets.	ASCII, EBCDIC, FIELDATA, UNICODE	Compile time	ASCII
Working set management	Different applications need to cache different amounts of file in memory.	Whole file, whole page, LRU fixed	Compile time	Whole file
Debugging code	Debugging traps should be present for in-house development and should remain permanently in the source.	Debug, production	Compile time	None

elaborate the domain for each of these ranges, the range's binding time, and the default value, if any. An additional column provides a simple description for the parameter of variation (the domain variable).

In Chapter 8, these tables will be used together with models of the C++ language structure to drive the solution structure.

3.8 Some Variability Traps

Consider the following variability table entry for a *TEXT EDITING BUFFER*:

Parameters of Variation	Meaning (the decision being made)	Domain	Binding	Default
Window type	Text buffers write to many different kinds of windows.	X, Curses, MS Windows	Run time	None

Here, we are not thinking of windows as output media analogous to the *OUTPUT TYPE* subdomain of Table 3.1, but as a separate, loosely coupled domain in the same system. The designer has designated the *WINDOW* type as a parameter of variation. Why? Because different *TEXT EDITING BUFFERS* coexist in systems with different kinds of windows. It's unlikely that these classes interact; it's more likely that a class such as `EditingLanguage` (analogous to an MVC controller) would dispatch contents from the buffer to the window. Even if the *WINDOW* and *TEXT EDITING BUFFERS* domains interact, the window type shouldn't change the implementation of *TEXT EDITING BUFFERS*; a given *TEXT EDITING BUFFER* can coexist with any kind of *WINDOW*. The two can be designed independently.

Just because there is a relationship between two domains doesn't mean that one of the domains is a *parameter* for the other. We need to be sure all domains are sensitive to the listed parameters of variation.

Here's another common pitfall, with an example suggested by Paul Chisholm. Consider the variability table for a `string` shown in Table 3.2. This analysis would lead to a design in which classes such as `PathName` and `RegularExpression` were derived from `string`. We would factor

TABLE 3.2   *Variability Table for* Sᴛʀɪɴɢ

Parameters of Variation	Meaning (the decision being made)	Domain	Binding	Default
Parsing algorithm	Different kinds of strings must be parsed differently; they obey different lexical grammars.	Character string, PathName, Regular Expression	Run time	None

the variability into derived class parsing functions that override a base class virtual function. The proper design is to separate classes such as PathName from string. This is because there are properties of PathName and RegularExpression that violate the commonalities of all strings (see [Coplien1992], Section 6.5). For example, you can't overwrite an arbitrary PathName character with an arbitrary character, such as '/' or '*' (as contrasted with pathname abstractions in Modula 3, for example).

Take care that you understand the commonalities and variabilities of the family and that all alleged family members exhibit the claimed commonalities and can be parameterized with the known variabilities.

3.9 Reviewing the Variability Analysis

It is important to review the results of variability analysis, just as it is important to introspect on the results of commonality analysis, as we did in Section 2.5. In practice, we review commonality and variability together because one makes sense only in the context of the other. Here are questions we can ask about the analysis from the perspective of its variabilities.

- Do the variabilities cover all members of the family?
- Can any variabilities be stated more precisely?
- Are there any variabilities that are inconsistent?
- Do the variabilities anticipate change well (domain analysis)?
- What family members are excluded (i.e., cannot be specified)?

3.10 Variability Dependency Graphs

Here, we present a trivial notation that uses simple graphs to show the relationship between domains and their parameters of variation. We call these graphs *variability dependency graphs*. We'll use this notation later in the book (in Chapter 7 and Chapter 8) to organize the software architecture.

Consider a domain ENCRYPTIONBUFFER that is used to gather and encrypt collections of text. We can envision a family of buffers that employ different encryption algorithms. A particular member of the ENCRYPTIONBUFFER family uses a particular encryption algorithm. In our simple notation, we depict ENCRYPTIONBUFFER as a node with an arrow pointing to the parameter of variation, as shown in Figure 3.3.

This isn't terribly interesting in its own right, but it becomes more interesting if we look deeper. First, ENCRYPTIONBUFFER may also take CHARACTERSET as a parameter of variation: Different encryption buffers need different internal storage structures for UNICODE than for ASCII. What's more interesting is that TRAPDOOR, which we view just as a parameter of variation, can actually be thought of as a domain in its own right. Its code also depends on CHARACTERSET, which means that as a domain, it also takes CHARACTERSET as a parameter of variation. So we can elaborate Figure 3.3 to capture these semantics, as shown in Figure 3.4.

These graphs can be used to map the relationship between domains in a design. There can be complex chains of relationships that propagate through parameters of variation. This simple notation helps the designer understand what the overall structure is, what the impact of change is for a given parameter of variation, and how domains depend on each other. We'll see in Chapter 7 and again in Chapter 8 that this simple notation has other much more powerful uses.

FIGURE 3.3 *Domain Dependency between* ENCRYPTIONBUFFER *and* TRAPDOOR.

FIGURE 3.4   *Adding the CHARACTERSET dependency to Figure 3.3.*

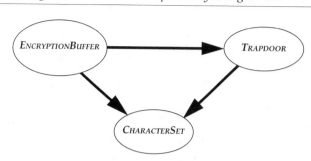

3.11 Summary

In this chapter, we presented a variability model to describe the differences between related software abstractions. Variabilities are the key to the genetic code of software families. Deep relationships exist between our commonality models and variability models, and we must be careful to discern between positive variability and negative variability. Wherever reasonable, negative variability should be addressed by dividing a single domain into subdomains. Where that can't be done, degenerate solutions such as #ifdefs might be considered.

We studied the domain and range of a variability, its binding time, and its defaults. These are the primary characteristics of a variability analysis. We can capture these properties in a variability analysis table and use that table to match analysis structures with C++ coding constructs that express them.

CHAPTER 4

Application Domain Analysis

This chapter introduces domain analysis. When doing traditional analysis, we study a particular problem or application. When doing domain analysis, we study a *family* of problems or applications. We will use the commonalities and variabilities in these domains to characterize family members.

4.1 Analysis, Domain Analysis, and Beyond

Analysis is a well-considered study of a problem. *Domain analysis* is a well-considered study of a *problem area of interest*. Most design methods emphasize application domain analysis, commonly called *problem domain analysis*. I use the term *application domain* to emphasize that not every software project should be viewed as a problem but as a focus of many kinds of change. Analysis provides opportunities not only to apply problem-solving and engineering techniques, but also to be creative and artistic. As you read about the techniques, notations, and procedures presented in this chapter, keep in mind that creativity is at the heart of design. It is important to understand that abstraction is at least in part an art. All designers draw on their experience, knowledge, and perspective to abstract the essential properties of a large or complex problem.

In this book, I treat domain analysis as part of the broader concern of domain engineering. Engineering disciplines focus not only on the problem at hand, but also on solution domain pragmatics and formalisms. Any formal analysis can be effective only if it looks ahead to implementation. Multi-paradigm design ties together the application analysis with the solution by using a common set of formalisms, called *commonality categories,* to characterize both aspects of design. Though this chapter focuses on application analysis, it will use notations and vocabulary that anticipate available solution strategies. In Chapter 6, we'll switch out of the application domain and examine *solution domain analysis.* These two analyses work together to provide domain-level solutions to domain-level problems in C++ domain engineering.

4.1.1 Traditional Analysis

Most formally trained software engineers are taught the art of analysis. The "thing" we usually are taught to analyze is a requirements document, and the result is something called an *architecture,* or a *high-level design document.* In any case, the term is only loosely defined. Others see it as the transformation from informal user needs into a requirements document. We learned analysis as an art, as it is, rather than as a component of computer "science."

The requirements documents we learned to decipher are complex, often ambiguous, and almost always incomplete, even though they usually represent the needs of a single client for a single application. As discussed in Chapter 2, abstraction is a key design and analysis tool that helps us manage or defer the complex details of large or intricate systems. Chapter 2 shows how commonality analysis helps us form the abstract stereotypes [Wirfs-Brock1990] and archetypes we use to think about systems. It also helps us find families of similar abstractions within an application; that is, it helps us abstract. It also helps us identify code that can be used by more than one part of the system; all members of a given software family may share code. Good analysis thus provides an important foundation for software reuse.

Occasionally, we discover abstractions during analysis that we think of as members of a family. We find the simplest kinds of software families within single systems. We can make an analogy to building architecture: Most of the windows for any given building share properties in common, while windows are likely to vary more widely across several buildings. In a piece of software, we may "discover" families of input/output (I/O) devices, or messages, or data structures, or behaviors, all within a single application described by a single requirements document. A diligent designer can gain insights into these families by building domain dictionaries (Section 2.2) and carrying out domain analysis with the client organization.

4.1.2   System Families: Domain Analysis

In most real software development projects, the developer must consider multiple deployment configurations from the very beginning. Even projects that start as singular systems usually branch into divergent, customized products as their markets grow and as customer expectations broaden. It is insufficient to analyze the application at hand. We broaden our scope to the entire domain of application, to the domain of our market, or to the domain of the corporate vision. Instead of application analysis, we do *domain analysis*.

What is a domain? The American Heritage Dictionary defines it as, "A sphere of activity, concern, or function; field . . . E.g. the domain of history." By domain analysis, most people mean the study of the fundamental business abstractions. Financial trading is a domain. Among its abstractions are transactions, stocks, bonds, securities, futures, derivatives, and exotics. Audio telecommunications is a domain. Calls, telephones, lines, trunks, subscribers, and features are its important abstractions. These are application domains. Each one defines a business, enterprise, or market in which we find families of complete systems.

The term *domain* also has a more formal meaning in mathematics, in the sense of the domain and range of a function. We alluded to this meaning of "domain" in Section 3.4. In multi-paradigm design, the term *domain* appeals to both of these meanings at once. It is in part this alignment of meanings that supports the way we express important abstractions of the application domain in the formal constructs of a solution domain language.

This book presents design and implementation techniques built around the domain concept. Domain analysis is a set of techniques for identifying software families, and application engineering is a set of techniques for implementing and managing software families. Domain analysis and application engineering together form a discipline called *domain engineering.* Multi-paradigm design is a form of domain engineering for which domain analysis applies both to the application and solution domains.

In Section 4.2, we will see that these broad domains are woven from smaller domains called *subdomains.* GUIs are a subdomain: windows, menus, dialogue boxes, text, fonts, and colors are among its abstractions. These abstractions often emerge as classes under object-oriented analysis, though many of them are too large to make good classes that are primitive and cohesive. Booch [Booch1994] uses the term *class categories* to describe the class hierarchies and associated classes for a given subdomain. Class categories group abstractions that emerge from object-oriented analysis and design. Under multi-paradigm design, we want to apply partitioning criteria that generalize beyond those offered by the object paradigm.

This is a wider scope of abstraction than we encounter in traditional analysis. We must seek commonality not only within an application but also across related applications. The application systems themselves form families. We talk about market product lines that are related by common properties and attributes and that vary according to their utility for specific markets. A good product line architecture separates the common parts from the variable parts. Good design encapsulates common properties and identifies architectural pressure points that express the variabilities for specific markets. The design must produce an implementation—in real code—that can conveniently be configured for each of the market segments by suitably binding the parameters of variation.

Family Members in the Application and Solution Domains

Some variabilities control low-level detail in algorithm and data structure. Many important *market* variabilities reach into the fine structure of the system *implementation,* while leaving the gross structure unchanged. Of course, many market dependencies can directly be expressed at a higher level by including and excluding specific modules. But, in general, the importance of an application variability may not correspond to the scope or abstraction level of its implementation.

For example, consider a text editor that has been designed to work with any one of several character sets. (The editor example serves to illustrate many points in this and later chapters.) There might be a domain named TEXT BUFFERS whose area of concern is the working set of text being edited at any given moment. This domain may support basic editing functions common to all text editors. It also may participate in output and input to and from disk files and in output to the screen. Most of the *object* code for this domain is different for chars than it is for wchar_t characters. These differences are small and are sparsely distributed throughout the object code. We might control the generation of object code for a given market by specifying a template parameter (for *TEXT BUFFERS* classes and functions) at the *source* code level. Templates provide a convenient, localized mechanism to express such market variabilities. The parameter easily can be propagated to all of the *TEXT BUFFERS* code, where it can fine-tune the generation of object code suitable to a specific market.

Because application domain analysis can affect the solution structure at many levels of granularity, it is important to conduct problem and solution domain analyses in tandem. For the same reason, it is important to consider all family members of a domain together. Domain analysis is an integrated view of commonality and variability across the abstractions of the entire domain. Though it may be done at a slightly higher level of abstraction than we would find in a traditional analysis, domain analysis should *not* be thought of as a layer that ties multiple analyses together. A single domain analysis cuts across all systems in a family at once.

Balancing Abstraction and Specification

Domain analysis is more abstract than traditional analysis. Abstraction is good because it facilitates the navigation of complex domains: The higher the abstraction, the lower the complexity. Weinberg [Weinberg1971] remarks that it's sometimes easier to solve a general problem than to solve the specific one. Furthermore, the general solution "generalizes" to the specific case, even though a direct solution for the specific case may have been more difficult to come by. The higher the level of abstraction, the more broadly an abstraction is likely to apply. It is this abstraction, supported by appropriate documentation and economics, that provides the foundation for reuse. The abstractions that come from domain analysis apply to all applications in the domain, whereas those that come from traditional analysis are guaranteed to apply only to the application at hand.

A good domain analysis balances abstraction with specification. Abstraction hides detail—it causes us to lose design information. The higher the level of abstraction, the less information is conveyed by the design. The level of abstraction should be commensurate with the scope of the business or enterprise. Broadening beyond the expected business application of a domain, or one of its abstractions, may result in discarding details that are important to the domain. On the other hand, if the abstractions do not cover the business domain, then evolution may take the system outside its architectural boundaries, thus leading to clumsy or costly architectural modifications. Domain designers must understand their business well.

For example, consider a software package that helps companies manage Federal corporate income tax deductions. Some of the interesting subdomains would be financial instruments, sales, purchases, and inventories. Good designers look for the parameters of variation in each subdomain, drawing on customer requirements and on their own domain expertise in Federal tax law. This may lead to an elegant, manageable product for the U. S. market. But if the company wants to broaden its product to address state tax issues, it will find domains that are absent at the Federal level. Things are even worse if the company wants to move into international tax. Looking at the initial problem as one of "taxability management" ignores the latent parameters of variation that capture the interests of the market. Designers can fall into these traps either because they don't understand the domain well enough (perhaps they are ignorant about differences between Federal and state tax liabilities) or because they don't understand their business vision well enough (they prematurely limit themselves to the Federal tax market, thinking that the state or international tax markets will never be of interest).

Returning to the editor example, consider a general-purpose editor we want to reuse across several domains. We might make the editor so general-purpose that it can accommodate graphical editing and text editing, as well as special-purpose editing such as editing the lighting sequences for computer film animation. An editor that general probably is striving for too much abstraction. There isn't enough commonality among the editing abstractions for graphics, text, and film animation lighting to benefit from considering the three together.

Levels of Domain Abstraction

During domain analysis, we abstract globally and reify locally. *Reification* means to talk about an abstraction in terms of how its instances are used in the real world. For each member of a family of systems, we use the general abstraction to meet a specific need. For example, if we are building a text editor to run under Motif, we can still talk about that application as though it needs X Windows. The same is true of another application that needs to run OpenLook. *XWINDOWS* is the abstraction that transcends this domain. We can talk about each domain as though it used something called *XWINDOWS*, though *XWINDOWS* may exist only as an analysis abstraction. Using an abstract concept from the domain, as if it were a concrete building block, is reification.

The abstractions of a domain analysis should be more abstract than those we consider during ordinary analysis only to the extent they are more *general*. The goal of domain analysis is not only to raise the level of abstraction (as an aid to problem cognition), but also to raise the level of generality and the breadth of applicability. "General" doesn't imply "vague," but it does mean that we suppress architecturally irrelevant detail and emphasize the commonalities that are important to the domain. One design is more general than another if it expresses fewer variabilities. We want to capture the essence of commonality and parameterize the variability. Rather than enumerate variabilities, we enumerate parameters of variation that characterize the application domain. For example, we wouldn't say that "we need `Stack<int>`, `Stack<Number>`, `Stack<Message>` . . . ," but that "we need `Stack<T>` where `T` is some type." This parameterized design is more general than an enumeration. But it is not vague—we can write every bit of source code for it.

To increase abstraction, we reduce specification. That is, a more general class has fewer member functions, or less restrictive interfaces, than a more specific counterpart. Sometimes, an abstraction can be made more general in this way, too. But we can also replace a family of related, specific classes with a single general template that captures the interfaces shared by the family members and whose parameters control individual instantiations. The template is perhaps less abstract, but certainly more general, than the original individual classes. As an example, consider parameterizing the text editor's *FILE* domain with different encryption algorithms (again, for different markets).

In short, we look for families of systems. By broadening to a family of related systems, we reduce the risks of requirements changes. If we derive a specific application architecture from a highly specified (very specific) architecture, then even small requirements changes will drive changes in major system structures or interfaces. If we keep the structure more general—by aligning it with the domain, instead of with a specific application or customer—it is more likely that the architecture will roll with the punches of system evolution. We can "reuse" the *design* across space and time—this was the central intent of the founders of domain analysis [Neighbors1980].

4.1.3   Application Domain Analysis and Solution Domain Analysis

In many of the traditional design methods, application analysis was something one did before starting on the design and implementation. In multi-paradigm design, we use foreknowledge of the implementation domain to our advantage. Consider this approach as an extension of one of the advantages claimed for the object paradigm, whose argument goes something like this: Presume that your programming language can express "objects." During analysis, look for "objects" as units of abstraction. When you go from analysis through design and implementation, you will find—surprise!—that you can express the abstractions of analysis in your implementation language.

The object paradigm was one of the first to popularize this technique. Classic software paradigms depended on intermediate forms, state charts, data flow diagrams, and many other artifacts that spoke of transformation after transformation between analysis and design. The object paradigm tried to linearize this with a "one-fits-all" approach for both the application and solution domains.

We do the same thing in multi-paradigm design, except that we broaden the design expressions available to the designer at implementation time. We open up *all* of the facilities of the language, not just the ones that are object-oriented.

4.1.4   The Activities of Domain Analysis

Domain analysis has three major activities: identifying the business domain, dividing the business domain into subdomains, and establishing the abstractions within each subdomain. Most software development efforts are shaped by the needs of a single customer. When we are doing domain analysis, it is important to broaden analysis into the needs of multiple customers. These multiple customer perspectives can help identify the critical business domains. In most business applications, the domains should be intuitive to experienced practitioners. Customers can help refine the domains of interest; a good domain is one to which a customer can relate.

Subdomains are the *specific* business or technical areas that are key to the success of the *general* business domain, or enterprise. Identifying the subdomains is the most crucial part of multi-paradigm design. Unfortunately, it is the part of design that is the most difficult to regularize. Splitting an application into good subdomains relies on intimate knowledge of the business or application being analyzed. Potential customers, or even hypothetical customers, can temper the list of domain commonalities and add to the list of domain variabilities. In the editing example, we may have a domain called PERSISTENT STORAGE with subdomains DATABASE and LINEAR FILE. Each subdomain can be used equivalently by the rest of the editing code. But the abstractions and algorithms that support database retrieval and update will be quite different from those that support ordinary files. They are different areas of interest that merit attention from development teams with the concomitant expertise, so we treat them as individual subdomains.

Historically successful subdomains of a business provide a good starting point to design new products for that business. To an experienced designer, subdomain partitioning follows the intuition that comes from experience in the domain, rather than from any formal or rigorous method. Once that is done, the design teams can proceed with domain analysis for each of the subdomains by using commonality and variability analysis. These activities point the way to system architecture and implementation.

Some domains lack an experience base, and intuition can't be trusted as the source of partitioning criteria. How does one discover the domains for a new business or for radically new problems in an existing business? For such problems, it pays to carry out an informal commonality and variability analysis at the system level before partitioning the domain into subdomains. The commonalities usually point the way to a domain partitioning.

The best subdomains are disjoint. "Disjoint" informally implies that domains have distinct parameters of variation and that each domain is sensitive to its own "localized" business drivers. A good domain or subdomain forms a family of related abstractions. It is useful to think of a subdomain as a unit of architecture and design reuse; the software of a subdomain can be independently reused only if it is adequately disentangled from other software. All interesting domains have some external coupling, usually through the parameters of variation. If they didn't, they couldn't be integrated with any other software. However, we want to minimize such dependencies in the interest of simple elegance and reuse. Chapter 7 focuses on multi-paradigm design for such independent subdomains. Sometimes, high coupling between domains is inevitable, even though we must keep the domains separate for business reasons or because the benefits of reuse still outweigh the costs of coupling. In these cases, we must factor related parameters of variation from multiple domains at once and must manage the dependencies *between* domains. In the editing example, the *Text Buffers* domain may overlap with the *Editing Language* domain, which deals with editing commands and the interaction between the commands and screen updates. Both are reasonable areas of interest and form good domains in their own right, but each must be considered in the context of the other. Consider a simple line editor: Its text buffer must manage only individual lines. Visual editors will probably manage buffers that are one or two screens large (or they may manage an entire file image at a time). Stream editors (such as **sed**) need a text buffer that is really a stream buffer.

Chapter 8 describes solutions to the problem of dependencies between domains. The success of the approaches of both Chapter 7 and Chapter 8 depend on subdomains that are as decoupled as possible, something we consider from the earliest stages of analysis.

4.2 Subdomains within a Domain Analysis

In the previous section, we noted that traditional development starts by exploring the needs of a single customer and looking ahead to the single integrated solution that will solve the problems brought to the surface in analysis. The next step usually is to partition the system into independently manageable parts. Paradigms are collections of rules that help us find the pieces in a system. These parts may be self-contained systems, which could be separately marketed, or separately manageable building blocks within a given discipline. Independently deliverable parts are called *subsystems*. To find these building blocks, a designer can use the object paradigm, database modeling, data modularization, procedural decomposition, or another paradigm of choice. Traditional design decomposes an individual application by using one primary paradigm. We broaden this in multi-paradigm design, following the principles of domain engineering. But we don't jump directly from a single paradigm to multiple paradigms; first, we revisit the question of design scope.

The scope of system domain analysis defines a context in which we look for abstractions. This scope is broader than a single system. Again, we could apply one primary paradigm to coax abstractions from the domain. But because domains are broad in scope, a single paradigm may be insufficient to express its abstractions. (In fact, the same is true for complex systems in which traditional analysis is used; it just becomes more apparent in domain analysis.) We could try to use multiple paradigms directly on the domain. But the question is, where do we start?

Most large problem domains are woven from multiple, smaller sub-domains. For example, the domain of financial trading includes the subdomains of financial instruments, human-machine interfaces, interprocess communications, databases, and others. In telecommunications, we find call processing, recovery, administration and maintenance, billing, and others. In a text editor, we find buffer management, human-machine interfaces, text files, and potentially others. Each of these subdomains is itself a domain—a "sphere of activity, form, or function"—that provides a focus for the designer.

Some domains may be modules or subsystems. But consider some of the domains listed previously. Financial instruments and databases may overlap each other, as do TEXT BUFFERS and EDITING LANGUAGE, as do most domains in telecommunications. We'll see later that even in the simple text editing example, domains can be intertwined in ways that make naive module boundaries unsatisfying.

While high-level domain analysis is concerned with families of systems that act like product lines, we can look across a domain of application for families of subsystems. A subsystem may not stand alone as a self-sufficient product, but it still may capture the design and implementation decisions for a business domain. Window systems are a good example: They rarely stand alone but capture design decisions[1] for a well-defined technical area. In our domain analysis of text editors, we discover "window" as a recurring abstraction. Window characteristics may vary from text editor to text editor, so the window packages form a family. These families themselves characterize a domain. We call these families subdomains to distinguish them from the broader business domains that are the popular topic of contemporary domain analysis. In most contexts, text editing would be a domain for which windows, files, and command processing would be subdomains, as shown in Figure 4.1. In the context of a broader domain like text processing, text editors may be a subdomain; we want a family of text editors to support a given text processing application. Subdomains will be our primary focus for commonality and variability analysis.

Subdomains transcend applications. In a particular implementation, we bind the parameters of variation for a subdomain to generate a subsystem. A subdomain is an abstraction that captures the commonality and variability of similar subsystems that recur across business applica-

FIGURE 4.1   *Subdomains in the domain of* TEXT EDITING.

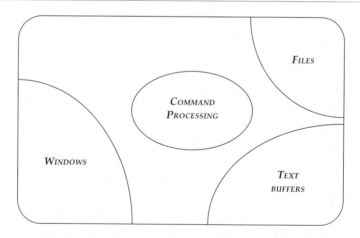

---

1.   Most paradigms are weak at capturing all design decisions and in particular at capturing the design rationale. We don't mean to address the issue of full design capture here. Sufficient to this context is that the code for class Window actually does capture the design intent for a specific application or domain, even though a user or reader of the code may not be able to reverse-engineer all that design intent.

tions. These subsystems form a family. The subdomain analysis characterizes that family, capturing its properties of commonality and variability. We should be able to generate any family member (any subsystem) with suitable choices for the parameters of variation. Frameworks are often a suitable way to capture commonality across family members, while providing parameters and interfaces that express the variability of an individual subsystem (Section 4.3.1). In the editor example, the domain *FILE* may depend on parameters of variation that control the buffering technique, the character set, and encryption. Suitable choice of values for these parameters of variation generates specific family members for specific applications and markets.

4.2.1 Domain Analysis and Reuse

As mentioned earlier in the chapter, good domain analysis is one key to reuse. Because traditional analysis focuses on the application at hand, its abstractions will have little better than an even chance of serving other applications as well. True reuse requires a broader perspective that encompasses multiple market threads. Domains should extend to the boundaries of the business, but not too far beyond. If they are too broad, they will be difficult to implement. If too narrow, their usefulness is limited.

Good system designers usually know the subdomains that are relevant to the business in which their expertise lies. That is, they know the patterns of commonality that recur in product after product. These intuitive subdomains form the bulk of the first level of analysis. Commonality analysis helps discover more subtle subdomains or subdomains relevant to new areas of application. A good domain exhibits common patterns of vocabulary, structure, name, behavior, and use cases (Section 2.3). A given domain may *not* exhibit commonality of customer (for example, both financial traders and interactive text-editing tool writers use human-machine interfaces), manufacturer (there are many window vendors), or target application.

Fortuitously chosen subdomains apply not only to many applications within a given business. They also may broaden to apply to multiple businesses in the enterprise. Databases, human-machine interfaces, interprocess communication, and file management are good examples of broadly applicable domains. That means that we can look beyond the current customer domain of interest to other domains in our business and in related businesses in order to shape a broader family of abstractions. Of course, many subdomains remain peculiar to individual business domains. For example, we wouldn't expect many of the abstractions of telecommunications administration and maintenance to apply broadly to other businesses. And we wouldn't expect the paradigms of highly parallel graphics rendering to contribute much to classic numerical analysis programs.

The outputs of business domain analysis include the following:

- A characterization of the families of products captured by the analysis
- A list of the subdomains of interest

These artifacts can directly drive the structure of the solution domain, which, of course, is taken into account from the beginning of application domain analysis.

A software artifact that encapsulates commonalities for a broad domain and that can be tuned with well-specified variabilities provides a solid foundation for reuse. The object paradigm supports this kind of reuse through inheritance; that is, new derived classes reuse the design and code of the base class. We use multi-paradigm design to express forms of reuse other than type specialization.

A good analyst has an eye to the implementation technologies available, even as the initial partitioning into subdomains takes place. One can more fully understand how to partition the domain into subdomains only when aligning the analysis with a solution structure. We take this up in more detail in Section 4.4.

Multi-paradigm design is only a technological enabler for software reuse. Good reuse and good domain analysis rely on good insights into business needs. Reuse itself is a business practice with business goals such as increased profitability and reduced time to market. These considerations are beyond the scope of this book, but I mention them so as to temper expectations a reader may create from the design perspective alone. The most important reuse issues involve sociological, organizational, and market issues that are beyond the scope of this book. It's important to recognize that a comprehensive reuse program owes as much to reward systems, organization issues, and economic models as it does to any technical concerns. For more on these issues, see the practical and accessible work by Tracz [Tracz1995].

4.2.2 Subdomain Modularity

Ideally chosen subdomains are modular; that is, the partitioning results in nonoverlapping pieces. We choose subdomains to break down the complexity of a larger system into smaller, manageable pieces. The pieces are manageable to the degree they are independent and cohesive. In some cases, modularization may be difficult and the success of a decomposition is sensitive to the domain. In fact, the more cohesive a domain is, the more difficult it is to partition it. There is little we can, or should, do about the properties of the application domain. We can only choose our knives carefully to extract the best possible partitioning from the problem definition. With these subdomain pieces in hand, we can start to apply commonality analysis to each one.

We could apply domain analysis to the entire spectrum of business domain systems, but it makes sense to start with the subdomains, for two reasons. First, many business domains are just too broad to analyze for commonality. Second, while the abstractions within a domain may be tightly coupled (such as keyboard to pointing device and window), coupling across domains limits the reusability of their abstractions and the ability to separately evolve domains (as discussed in Section 4.1.4).

Most contemporary analysis methods also suggest that design start with a high-level partitioning into separately maintainable chunks. Simple-minded procedural decomposition starts with procedural hierarchies. Simple-minded object-oriented analysis starts with objects. Most contemporary design approaches force the system into a single abstraction mold. Others, such as Booch's method, start with subsystems [Booch1994]. It is more important to find the patterns of commonality and variability that will lead to the best patterns of coupling and cohesion. These in turn promise good software evolution dynamics.

A domain often can be captured using conventional administrative constructs such as subsystems (as in [Booch1994]). However, domains are logical units of design and may not always map onto the contiguous bodies of code that usually define a subsystem. (An example follows in Section 4.3.) Domains may even overlap. A common example of this from object-oriented programming is the multiple dispatch problem. Consider the code that outputs the contents managed by the TEXT BUFFERS domain to a file managed by the PERSISTENT STORAGE domain. Which domain "owns" the code? The code structure and algorithms depend on both domains.

It is also important to note that not all subsystems are domains; subsystems are traditionally administrative units of code, not logical units of design. For example, enterprises may choose a domain to suit market interests or even market perceptions of system modularity and configuration even if the domain touches many parts of the code. Making the domain a first-class concern makes it easier to manage its evolution.

4.2.3   Iteration and Hierarchy

Software tradition and the even deeper traditions of Western culture usually lead us to attack problems in a top-down fashion. This hierarchical approach lends itself well to prevailing business structures—which are often hierarchical—and it serves the enterprise well to align the software structure with the business structure where reasonable and possible. In fact, much of the intuition that drives the initial partitioning of domains into subdomains derives from business experience (as opposed to being derived from, for example, software engineering principles).

In large systems, subdomain structures can be recursive. The initial partitioning from domains into subdomains may leave unmanageably large chunks that may be further subdivided. Subdivision should stop when the abstractions are more detailed than one finds in the vocabulary of the market. That's when to start choosing paradigms suitable to divide the subdomain into manageable design pieces.

A strictly hierarchical approach can leave serious blind spots, particularly in new domains. Work with the lower-level subdomains often yields insight into the higher-level domains, and the designer should take advantage of those insights by revisiting higher-level design partitionings. For example, ongoing work in the DATABASE and LINEAR FILE domains may yield insights on the parameters of variation and common code that can be factored into the PERSISTENT STORAGE domain. And the evolution of clients of the PERSISTENT STORAGE domain may suggest changes in their contracts with PERSISTENT STORAGE that in turn might affect the structure of its subdomains.

Domain analysis isn't an up-front activity we leave behind once we shape the application domain into subdomains. Increased understanding of the solution shapes the way we think about the problem. There is a danger in presuming that the results of domain analysis are conclusive. Any successful development process must embrace iteration.

4.3 The Structure of a Subdomain

We must structure the subdomains into parts that can be individually developed. This is the familiar territory of paradigms such as the procedural paradigm or the object paradigm. How do we judge a good partitioning, and what do we mean by the "best solution" to an analysis problem? Paradigms usually apply the tried and true principles of coupling and cohesion. Maximizing cohesion within a module is good, as is minimizing coupling between modules. Paradigms guide us to create modules that satisfy these guidelines, whether we use modules in the Parnas [Parnas1978] sense or whether our modules are procedures, objects, or abstractions from other paradigms.

If we dig deeper, we find that coupling and cohesion principles serve a deeper need—creating software that is easy to write in the first place and that is easy to understand and modify. A single, preconceived solution paradigm can hinder our understanding of the straightforward structure in the problem or application itself.

For simplicity's sake, we try to keep subdomains disjoint within a given application or application domain. As we partition subdomains, we pick up where most contemporary analysis techniques complete their first task: decomposing a problem into abstractions. Most paradigms seek to reduce a system to parts, each of which can be individually understood. Traditional techniques apply a single paradigm to one system at a time, perhaps choosing one that gives us the most intuitive partitioning. We use a paradigm to "chunk" a system into units that balance structure, behavior, and binding times. We think of the parts as *physical* entities that are distributed in space (either across our source code or through the memory spectrum of a running program or system).

An important tenet of C++ is that no single paradigm works best all of the time; this rule applies as well in the application domain as in the solution domain. We can use multiple paradigms within a single design as we find opportunities to apply them. These paradigms may overlap within a domain. Within a given domain, we are less interested in its "parts" than in the patterns of commonality that cut through the systems in many dimensions. Most paradigms focus on a physical view of the system, presuming we are going to decompose the system into "physically" separate modules. We desire a *logical* view, in addition to this physical view, that allows us to clearly see important abstractions that cut across any single physical partitioning. Instead of seeking a strict partitioning, we look for the logical groupings that make sense within a domain. That leaves room for the important abstractions that transcend objects (or procedures or modules).

We find simple conflicts between logical and physical partitioning in everyday C++ programming. For example, a system may have a family of functions that convert instances of user-defined types into strings. A common convention is to designate an `asString` function for each type. These functions are logically related—they all have the same name and the same meaning, but each applies to a different type. Architecturally, each such function is likely to be associated with the type to which it applies. We might write them as `friend` functions:

```
class MyType1 {
friend string asString(const MyType1 &s) { . . . . }
        . . . .
};

class MyType2 {
friend string asString(const MyType2 &s) { . . . . }
        . . . .
};


        . . . .
```

If each instance of `asString` is (or can be) implemented with a similar structure, then we might create a single template instance that can be written in terms of other member functions. This closed copy of the source "generates" the family of related functions:

```
template<class T>
string asString<T>(const T& c) {
        // really dumb implementation of asString
        string retval;
        char *buf = new char[BUFSIZ];
        strstream str(buf, BUFSIZ);
```

```
        str << c;
        str >> retval;
        return retval;
    }
```

If we look at all of the classes to which we wish to add `asString` behavior and note that those types all have similar signatures, then we broaden the commonality beyond the function to the classes themselves. We would express the commonality using inheritance hierarchies:

```
class Base {
public:
    virtual string asString() const;
    . . . .
};

class MyType1: public Base {
public:
    string asString() const { . . . . }
    . . . .
};

class MyType2: public Base {
public:
    string asString() const { . . . . }
};
```

And, of course, if the structures of all `asString` functions are common in this last case, we can factor their implementations into a single, closed copy in the base class. So, though `asString` is a legitimate logical abstraction, we may find that its implementation is not modular in the software structure.

Multi-paradigm design seeks to weave paradigms together, admitting that there are situations in which no single paradigm is a good fit. Most of the time, a single paradigm can give voice to the best abstractions for an application. The object paradigm provides the best fit for many applications. However, other paradigms still have their place, and some are better-suited to some applications than objects might be. If each domain can be managed with a single paradigm, we can use the simple multi-paradigm approach presented in Chapter 7. Once in a while, paradigms work well in combination, within a domain, to produce the best solution to an analysis problem. This more intricate form of multi-paradigm design is described in Chapter 8.

As an example of how multiple partitionings work together, consider the complementary type and class abstractions put forth in the design paradigm of Schwartzbach and Palsberg [Palsberg+1994]. Early object-oriented designs equated class and type. Schwartzbach and Palsberg laid many of the foundations that have helped us separate type—the behavior—from class—the implementation. Design then becomes a task of identifying not only the types, but also the classes to implement them and the mapping between them. Trygve Reenskaug's role-based design is similar in intent [Reenskaug1996]. In multi-paradigm design, we try to broaden our design scope even further.

4.3.1 Frameworks as Subdomain Implementations

A *framework* is an increasingly common software package that captures software architecture in source and object code. It is a partly filled-out implementation, with "holes" to be filled in on a per-application basis. Therefore frameworks are an abstraction and characterize a family of related implementations.

Frameworks describe the solution to a problem, so it is usually premature to focus on frameworks during analysis. I present them here in the analysis chapter to give the reader a firmer grasp on the usable end-products of design.

Frameworks usually capture the implementation that is common to an entire domain. The most common frameworks support user interfaces. Trygve Reenskaug's Model-View-Controller is a general model of human-machine interaction that is the foundation for a family of related frameworks. Proprietary frameworks in software corporations support families of software that are germane to a line of business.

A typical framework defines interfaces for which the user provides an implementation, abstract base classes from which a user derives implementation classes, or coupling relationships between classes in the framework. If a base class guides the implementor by stipulating the interface for a function that the user must define, then that function is a parameter of variation. If class derivation is used to capture the implementation of specific family members, then the structural or behavioral differences between the base and derived classes represent parameters of variation. Patterns of registration between classes (or their objects) bind abstract notions of the distribution of responsibility to real functions that are written for specific applications, as in the

Smalltalk Model-View-Controller framework. In each of these cases, we parameterize the generic framework with user-supplied constructs to generate a family member.

Sometimes, individual subdomains map closely onto frameworks. Good frameworks can be independently delivered, maintained, and evolved. The subdomains we discuss in Chapter 7 map closely onto frameworks. Tightly coupled subdomains are difficult to manage as independent frameworks. A rich framework usually combines multiple subdomains, sometimes by using multiple paradigms, to attack a business problem of broad scope. Frameworks usually emerge from the rich interaction of paradigms that we describe in Chapter 8.

4.3.2   The Activities of Subdomain Analysis

Section 4.1.4 established the principles for dividing a business domain into subdomains. Each of these subdomains must now be analyzed for pressure points of commonality and variability that can be expressed in a C++ implementation. This is the main focus of multi-paradigm design, and it is the activity that most distinguishes it from other techniques.

To do this, we apply the techniques that were introduced in Chapters 2 and 3. The first step is identifying the commonalities and variabilities of the subdomain. Though these were presented as separate activities in Chapters 2 and 3, we do them together in practice. Commonalities help reveal the variabilities, and vice versa.

Introspection and clear definition are key to a good domain analysis (Section 2.5), and there are many questions we must ask ourselves about the commonality analysis (Section 2.2.2). Are the definitions clear, complete, and consistent? Are the commonalities complete, precise, accurate, and consistent? The variability perspective is important as well (Section 3.9). Do the variabilities extend to the edge of the domain, both as it is defined today and as the team anticipates how it will change? Are the variabilities complete, concise, and consistent? Another audit on variability can be done through the parameters of variation (Section 3.2). Are they complete and consistent with the variabilities, and are their default values appropriate and within the domain?

And don't lose the big picture perspective: Could the subdomain product be marketed as a product in its own right? The answer won't always be yes, and the market may not always be broad. But a subdomain should be cohesive and should offer intuitive functionality that helps the business.

4.4 Analysis: The Big Picture

In this chapter, we started by motivating the need to broaden analysis to domain analysis. We do this by looking for software families either that transcend the products of our business or that we expect to transcend releases of a given product.

In theory, we can characterize domain analysis as a spectrum of techniques that lie between two extremes. In the first approach, we separate problem domain analysis from solution domain analysis. We can analyze the problem domain without regard for how to express the solution. This has the advantage that we can defer implementation details. However, it incurs the risk of delivering an analysis that cannot be implemented within the reasonable constraints of development technology and culture.

In the second approach, we take the implementation technology into account from the very start. For example, we would cast all domain abstractions in terms of C++ language constructs: classes, templates, functions, and so forth.

Neither of these extremes provides a satisfactory operating point, but it is nonetheless important to reconcile analysis techniques with the implementation strategies that follow. A good analyst starts with some notion of the implementation technology but doesn't let that knowledge dominate the abstractions that are created. When multiparadigm design techniques are used within subdomains to align analysis structure with programming language structure, the mappings will occasionally be awkward or even intractable. If it is difficult to express a subdomain using C++ constructs, consider rethinking the domain partitioning. In extreme cases, it might be useful to rethink the use of C++ as an implementation technology, particularly if other implementation technologies have proven themselves in the past. For example, rule-based systems should consider using tools that support expert systems (such as Prolog), while systems that deal with the management and concurrent access of large-scale data sets should use database tools.

Figure 4.2 summarizes the abstracting activities of multi-paradigm design. In this chapter, we have focused on the upper-left "bubble" of the figure. We start by identifying the application domain, or business, in which we wish to work. We split the problem into subdomains, relying more on our intuition than on any regularized or formal method to do so. Next, we do commonality and variability analysis on individual subdomains, as the figure demonstrates has been done for *Custom Protocols*. This is an iterative process, with commonality and variability analysis proceeding in parallel and converging on a first-cut selection of subdomains.

FIGURE 4.2   *The domains of analysis.*

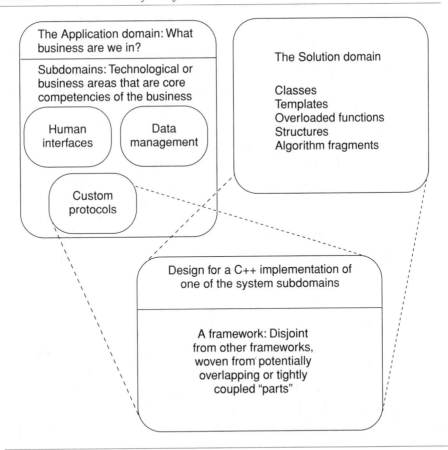

Once commonality and variability analysis are "complete," the designer must align each subdomain structure with the available structures in the solution space. To do that, the designer must understand the structure of the implementation space. The implementation language is a domain unto itself. Design and implementation are the arts of aligning the commonalities and variabilities of the application space with those of the solution space. The upper-right "bubble" of Figure 4.2 represents the analysis of the solution domain. We discuss that bubble further in Chapter 6. The structures of the application domain and the solution domain are combined to yield the framework of the bottom bubble. The techniques for combining these analyses will be covered in Chapters 7 and 8.

As we find that the implementation technology of choice doesn't fit the commonality and variability analyses for the application domain, we may revisit the analysis of the application, the choice of solution technology, or both. Multi-paradigm design—like all good design—is fundamentally iterative. It takes time to find the right knife that will cut the right solution in all of the right places. Good domain analysis is more time-consuming than simple analysis of a single application, with an eye to a single implementation paradigm. The benefits of this extra time spent come from products that may be more broadly applicable and that may better withstand the tests of time.

Even then, the picture isn't quite complete. The product is a framework whose parameters of variation can be bound for specific applications. This last step is done on a per-application basis, once for each occurrence of the subdomain in a given application domain. Over time, field experience feeds back into further iterations of the domain analysis process.

4.5 Summary

We strive to do domain analysis, not just analysis, to increase the likelihood that a system will evolve well. Once we establish the breadth of the domain, we try to decompose it into subdomains. Subdomains can be analyzed with commonality and variability analysis. Sometimes, commonality and variability analysis shed new light on the system as a whole, and the subdomain partitioning may be revisited. As commonality and variability analysis converge within a subdomain, implementation abstractions start to appear.

At this point, we can start aligning the results of commonality and domain analysis onto the structures supported by C++. But first, we'll take a look at object-oriented analysis as a specific case of commonality and variability analysis, exploring it as an extended example.

CHAPTER 5 — *Object-Oriented Analysis*

In this chapter, we look at the object paradigm as an example of a problem domain analysis technique. We develop object-oriented analysis from the principles of commonality and variability analyses presented in earlier chapters. We analyze an application, assuming that the object paradigm is the best-suited paradigm, by using principles of commonality and variability to derive design abstractions.

5.1 About Paradigms and Objects

The term *paradigm*, first popularized by Kuhn in his landmark book [Kuhn1970], became a household word in software with the popularization of the object paradigm. A paradigm is a set of conventions we use to understand the world around us. In software, paradigms shape the way we formulate abstractions. What is your world made of? Do you divide the world into procedures? Data records? Modules? Or classes and objects?

In practice, a paradigm encodes rules, tools, and conventions to partition the world into pieces that can be understood individually. The goals of a paradigm usually include a quality vaguely called *modularity*, which means that analysis should produce cohesive, decoupled abstractions. If abstractions are independent, then their owners can evolve them independently without tripping over each other. If we assume that we can evolve a system by evolving its parts, then a paradigm helps us by creating islands of change.

5.1.1   Classes and Objects

Classes and objects are the main abstractions of the object paradigm. Cohesion and coupling are the basic partitioning criteria; they are borrowed from the module paradigm and structured design [Stevens+1974]. We form *objects* around related groups of responsibilities or, sometimes, around a cohesive data structure. A *class* is a programming language construct that describes all objects that have the same responsibilities, that implement those responsibilities in the same way, and that share the same data structure. The same term is also used for design abstractions, as an informal synonym for Abstract Data Type, though this book will attempt to stick to the more precise definitions of these terms. Programs that use classes and objects are often said to use "object-*based* programming."

5.1.2   Liskov Substitutability Principle

The object paradigm, in the sense of object-*oriented* programming, goes one step further. Not only does it provide principles for dividing the world into parts; it also provides additional principles for grouping those parts into higher-order abstractions. These principles relate to *subtyping* and *inheritance*. Subtyping is the term usually used to describe the relationship between analysis and design abstractions, while inheritance is one mechanism used to reflect subtyping in most languages that support object-oriented programming. (Some languages such as *self* [Ungar+1987] use delegation instead.) We group classes into inheritance hierarchies by using strict rules of behavioral compliance. That is, Class B may be derived from class A if and only if there is an object of class B that can be substituted for each instance of class A in a program written in terms of class A, without changing the behavior of the program [Liskov1988]. This requires both that we design our classes appropriately and that the programming language cooperate by making substituted derived class objects "work." The programming language feature that allows a program to treat objects of different classes as though they were all of the same type is one form of *polymorphism*.

5.1.3 Virtual Functions

Inheritance and virtual functions implement this form of polymorphism in C++. Polymorphism literally means "many forms"; each C++ class represents one form, or implementation, of a general type. For example, the following declaration describes an abstract data type interface ("abstract" in the sense that operator+= has no implementation):

```
class Complex {
public:
friend Complex operator+(const Complex&, const Complex&);
    virtual Complex &operator+=(const Complex&) = 0;
        . . . .
};
```

This type may take one of several forms:

```
class PolarComplex: public Complex {
public:
    Complex &operator+=(const Complex &other) {
        // . . . . complex polar stuff
    }
    . . . .
private:
    double radius, theta;
};

class CartesianComplex: public Complex {
public:
    Complex &operator+=(const Complex &other) {
        rpart += other.rpart;
        ipart += other.ipart;
        return *this;
    }
    . . . .
private:
    double rpart, ipart;
};
```

The essence of object-oriented programming is that the implementation of a type operation is chosen according to the object's form at run time. Virtual functions dispatch member function calls (such as Complex::operator+=) according to the type of the object at run time.

This is a fairly formal definition of the object paradigm. More informally, we design loosely coupled, cohesive classes and arrange them into *specialization hierarchies*, with general classes at the root and more specific classes toward the leaves. From a programming language perspective, object-oriented programming is modular programming (encapsulation), plus instantiation (the ability to create multiple instances of any given module), plus inheritance and polymorphism. Peter Wegner gives the name *inclusion polymorphism* [Wegner1987] to the run-time type substitutability that supports the object paradigm so as to distinguish it from other forms of polymorphism, such as parameterized types and overloading (look ahead to Figure 6.8).

Object-oriented analysis derives object and class structures from the application domain structure, with most of the focus usually placed on class hierarchies.[1] Like any analysis activity, object-oriented analysis relies on the intuition of the analyst to know what makes good objects and classes, by knowing what good objects and classes have been in the past. In my experience, the most effective object-oriented analysis techniques are informal.

5.1.4   Object Orientation: Yet Another Definition

We can define the object paradigm in terms of commonality and variability. Presuming that we start with a domain dictionary, object-oriented analysis is based on a commonality analysis, in which we search for commonality of type. Recall that a type is a collection of signatures, where a signature captures name and behavior (Section 2.3.2). The first abstracting step of object-oriented analysis is to build families of abstractions grouped by behavior. So the idea of families should be intuitive even to students of contemporary object-oriented methods.

Positive versus Negative Variability

We look for variability in behavior against the background of type commonality. This variability includes positive variability in signature. If some family members exhibit a few behaviors not common to the family as a whole, that's OK; those family members will become derived classes. Negative variability isn't accommodated in the object models supported by most object-oriented design methods and programming languages. Negative variability in a family of types points to an implementation that would use inheritance with cancellation,

---

[1.]   Some object-oriented methods defer inheritance beyond the analysis phase, calling it an implementation activity. Some inheritance grouping inevitably takes place during analysis, even if analysis and the implementation considerations of design can be separated.

which good designers avoid. This, too, is apparent to designers who practice object-oriented techniques, but for reasons different than those developed in Section 3.3.

It is more common to find types whose signatures are the same but whose implementations are different. The signatures of XWindow and MSWindow might be the same, if they are suitably abstracted to the level of a domain abstraction named *WINDOW*. The behaviors of these two abstractions are clearly distinct, and their implementations will be different. This is variability in *behavior* against a common backdrop of *semantics*.

Binding Time

Binding time is a key attribute of domain analysis, as discussed in Section 3.5. The interesting variabilities of object-oriented programming are bound at run time. Deferred binding is the key to balancing commonality of semantics with variability in behavior and is what gives the object paradigm its abstracting power.

Defaults

Defaults are the final key attribute of domain analysis (Section 3.6). In any family of types, a more abstract family member provides defaults for more specific family members. These are the basic semantics of inherited properties. The inheritance mechanism propagates defaults through a graph that defines subtyping relationships between the family members. The subtyping graph, which is almost always the same as the inheritance graph in C++, captures relationships other than defaults as well. Its main purpose is to capture specialization of behavior, which can be explained in terms of the strengths of pre- and postconditions for individual signature elements of related types [Meyers1992]. Inheritance of (default) behaviors lines up nicely with the subtyping graph most of the time.

There is a large body of literature on the dichotomy of inheritance and subtyping. Much of the time, the two can be unified. It's important to recognize exceptions and to design accordingly. The exception arises as a collection of family members either that have common structure but not common behavior or that have common behavior but not common structure. This is a special kind of negative variability that is discussed in more detail in Section 6.11. The most common technique is to break implementation and interface into separate hierarchies. Pointers tie together instances across hierarchies. This is such a recurring problem that the solution can be regularized; such solutions have been captured as *design patterns*. This book covers design patterns in more detail in Chapter 9.

Neo-classic object-oriented methods (those that try to incorporate object-oriented semantics in traditional structured techniques) focus on commonality of structure instead of behavior. They treat structure as an analysis consideration instead of an implementation detail. An analysis based on structure isn't likely to capture the architecture as well as an approach based on types (see Section 2.3.1). Though structural commonality and variability often follow type commonality and variability, there are notable exceptions. A compelling counter-example can be found in the discussion of Section 6.7.

In short, the object paradigm is:

- A way to capture variations in structure and behavior in explicit programming constructs called classes
- A way to group these classes into abstractions by their commonality in behavior
- A way to share default behaviors between similar classes
- A way to unify behaviors that vary at run time into an interface that can be known at compile time and that relates to properties of the commonality analysis

Of course, we don't need to think of the object paradigm in terms of commonality and variability analyses. In fact, multi-paradigm design doesn't consider the object paradigm for its own sake, or on its own merits, at all. It's just that the techniques used in multi-paradigm design, based on commonality and variability analysis, result in abstractions similar to those that would be found through contemporary object-oriented analysis techniques when applied to problems for which object-oriented solutions are a good fit.

Using Proven Methods

A good designer will seek the benefits of one or more object-oriented design methods if multi-paradigm design suggests that objects are the dominant paradigm. An object-oriented method helps deal with important design considerations left untouched by multi-paradigm design, such as proper subtyping relationships between inherited interfaces and adequate attention to fat and thin interfaces.

5.1.5 The Suitability of Object-Oriented Design

How would we know to apply the object paradigm instead of another? Or, asked another way, how would we know, when doing analysis, to focus on object-oriented abstractions, instead of naively exploring the universe of paradigms supported by C++? The object paradigm produces a good architecture if the "pressure points" of the application line up with the dimensions of commonality and variability supported by the object paradigm. (Pree [Pree1995] calls these *hot spots*.) The object paradigm presumes commonality in type and structure; it expresses variability in implementation. If the members of a family can be cast into that framework, then the object paradigm is a good fit.

Language and Paradigm

Much has been said of C++ and Smalltalk and the degree to which they support the object paradigm relative to each other. One advantage claimed for pure object-oriented languages is that they force all design abstractions into an object-shaped mold. In a pure object-oriented world, other paradigms take second-class status and are difficult to express except in object-oriented terms.

Few designs are purely object-oriented because they express other important dimensions of commonality and variation. C++ captures some of these non-object-oriented design structures well. Most C++ programmers consciously use some degree of procedural decomposition. FSMs (finite-state machines) are part of many object-oriented designs and can conveniently be implemented in several ways in C++. Templates, overloading, and other language features aren't intrinsically object-oriented. There are other design structures that go beyond what C++ can express well, too. Industry experience suggests that objects do not express "units of work" well [Constantine1995]. Why? Because the commonalities and variabilities deal with steps and algorithms that are related to each other in time (succession of invocation), not with structures and collections of behaviors that are related in meaning. In telecommunications design, important business abstractions such as "call" or telecommunications features such as call forwarding and call waiting rarely make good objects because they are units of work. And of course there are database constructs, parallel programming constructs, and other important solution domain structures that C++ can accommodate only by convention, if at all.

Multi-paradigm design is important because it goes beyond objects to express other design structures that find rich expression in C++. To understand what this means is to understand the richness of expression of the solution technology that we will explore in Chapter 6. It also means understanding how to align the application space with the solution space, which we elaborate in Chapter 7. I mentioned previously that paradigms help us to the degree that we can evolve a system by evolving its parts. But that doesn't mean that to understand the parts is to understand the system. The object paradigm gives us the objects, the parts. Other paradigms help us understand other important relationships that make a system a system. And C++ can express some of those relationships directly.

Where *do* objects still work? The object paradigm excels at capturing stable domain resources and artifacts. Windows are a good example. Again, drawing from the telecommunications domain, lines, trunks, and ports make good objects. There are countless other examples in almost every other domain. Even so, one size does not fit all.

Objects also seem to work well in domains with direct-manipulation interfaces. If we think of a domain in terms of parts that we assemble or manipulate, objects are often a good fit. A library of graphical shapes is the time-worn canonical example. Computer-aided design (CAD) programs form another important software family well-suited to the object paradigm.

To illustrate the relationship between multi-paradigm design and object-oriented design, the following sections apply multi-paradigm design to an "object-oriented problem." Digital hardware design is the application domain, a domain full of resources and artifacts. The software written for digital design usually draws on a direct manipulation metaphor, another harbinger for objects.

5.2 *Object-Oriented Commonality Analysis*

We can illustrate how the object paradigm fits within multi-paradigm development by studying the objects of a system using commonality and variability analysis. Consider a digital circuit CAD program as a simple example. Instead of designing a circuit editor, simulator, or wire-wrap generator, we do analysis for the entire domain of circuit design. We do domain analysis, where digital logic design is the business domain (Section 4.1.4).

The first step of domain analysis is to build the domain dictionary, shown in Figure 5.1. This step not only establishes a vocabulary that helps design team members communicate. It also establishes the fundamental building blocks of multi-paradigm design.

The next step of domain analysis is to find the subdomains. This is an intuitive step that draws on our familiarity with the application domain. Drawing on the domain vocabulary, an experienced designer might derive the following domains:

LOGICAL COMPONENTS

NET

PORT

PHYSICAL COMPONENT

Each of these domains is a family with multiple members. Each family groups individuals by essential common characteristics (family members share the same commonalities and variabilities). For example, *LOGICAL COMPONENTS* is a domain of all of the logic elements that can be incorporated in a design. Designers use *LOGICAL COMPONENTS* as the logical building blocks of the design. They all have a graphical representation,

FIGURE 5.1   *The domain dictionary for digital circuit design.*

Design element: Any electrical or physical component of the circuit design

Network element: A design element with one or more associated signal values

Gate: A network element of primitive combinatoric logic design (NOT, AND, NAND, OR, NOR, etc.)

Flip-flop: A family of logic elements with single-bit memory

Net: An electrically passive connection between two or more network elements

Block: A logical grouping of related network elements, which itself behaves as a network element

Label: . . .

Input pin: . . .

Output pin: . . .

IC: . . .

Board: . . .

Counter: . . .

Register: . . .

Schmidt trigger: . . .

Line driver: . . .

Line buffer: . . .

all have input and output signals that can be connected to nets, and all can be asked about the physical components that implement them. They all *behave* the same. Gates, registers, counters, and flip-flops all fall into this domain. NETS are a domain whose elements can be connected to LOGICAL COMPONENTS or to PORTS; they can be reshaped, named, created, deleted, and so on. There are different kinds of nets: power nets, ground nets, signal nets, and others. But, again, they all *behave* the same at some level. Other domains such as PORTS (interfaces to a hardware building block) and PHYSICAL COMPONENTS (the real "chips" into which LOGICAL COMPONENTS are packaged) are also grouped because they behave similarly.

We could have formed these domains formally by using a process to optimize commonality within each domain and to minimize commonality across domains. An intuitive partitioning suffices and can incorporate insights that a formal approach might miss. Still, it is a good idea always to audit the commonality analysis results using the questions of Section 2.5.

5.2.1   Commonality Analysis

We grouped LOGICAL COMPONENTS together because they all *behave* the same. We did the same for NETS, PHYSICAL COMPONENTS, and other domains. It's likely that all of the family members in these domains also share some data structure and implementation. These commonalities are one set of traits that make a domain's members a family.

5.2.2   Variability Analysis

Each logical component implements some logic function, but each implements a *different* logic function. Each has pins, but the number of pins *varies* from component to component. Though components exhibit commonality in structure and algorithm, they also show variability in structure and algorithm. The fact that each member has these variabilities is itself a kind of commonality, but we use the variabilities to distinguish individual family members.

Each of these families exhibits commonality in behavior and structure and variability in algorithm and structure. These patterns of commonality and variability define our grouping criteria, the criteria we use to abstract. Such criteria form a paradigm. What paradigm did we use (whether subconsciously or not) to group family members into domains? The object paradigm captures commonality in behavior and structure and variability in algorithm and structure. In this example, commonality and variability analysis were a roundabout way of concluding that we should use the object paradigm, that each domain should be an inheritance hierarchy.

Booch's [Booch1994] *class categories* correspond closely to "domains" as used here. A class category comprises the classes in a class hierarchy, along with closely associated support classes and functions. We can use a class hierarchy to organize most of the domain abstractions. For example, the LOGICAL COMPONENT domain can be used to organize LOGIC GATES and *MSI* (medium-scale integration) Components (Figure 5.2). In general, this includes all components that the designer uses to implement the logical functionality of a hardware system. Logic Gates capture the commonalities of NAND gates, AND gates, OR gates, inverters, and many more. *MSI COMPONENTS* include flip-flops, shift registers, register caches, buffers, line drivers, and other "chunkier" design units.

Multi-paradigm design doesn't deal with the details of inheritance hierarchies: what is the base class and derived class, and what is public

FIGURE 5.2   *The LOGICAL COMPONENT domain.*

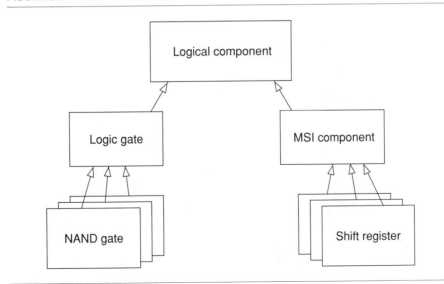

or protected. Those design decisions are well-supported by the popular object-oriented design methods listed in the References at the end of this book. Don't ignore them!

5.3 Summary

This chapter showed how simple commonality and variability analysis can help the designer choose the object paradigm for a suitable design. The purpose of the chapter was to illustrate the main principles of multi-paradigm design—commonality and variability—from the familiar perspective of object-oriented design.

The problem of designing a package for circuit design and simulation is much more complex than the treatment of it in this chapter. In particular, we ignored many important domains such as graphics, simulation, interfacing with analog circuit design and verification domains, and a host of others. Even the domains treated here depend on each other in contorted ways. For example, the logical and physical partitioning of gates can't really be separated.

In the next chapter, we lay some foundations that will help us move beyond the object paradigm into other architectural styles. We'll develop these foundations from the C++ language itself: What paradigms does it support?

CHAPTER 6

Solution Domain Analysis

I n this chapter, we revisit domain analysis, but this time in the solution domain instead of in the application domain. Many of the same principles of application domain analysis apply to the solution structure. The particular solution domain we investigate here is that of the C++ programming language.

6.1 The "Other" Domain

In Chapter 4, we studied how to capture the structure of the problem domain in commonalities and variabilities. Many design methods analyze only the problem domain—and then only with respect to a single paradigm. While we have already discussed why it is important to use multiple paradigms, we haven't carried the question into the solution domain.

Why study the solution domain? If we view design as the activity that derives a solution structure from a problem structure, it isn't enough just to understand the problem—we must understand the solution domain as well. The solution domain includes aspects of computer architecture, networking architectures, human interfaces, and other subdomains. But many of the abstractions of the solution domain live in the programming language. It is the structure of the programming language—or, more precisely, the way in which a programming language expresses commonality and variability—that determines the "shape" of the solution domain. In this chapter, we analyze the C++ programming language to discover its important dimensions of commonality and variability; that is, we analyze the solution domain from a C++ perspective.

Some readers may want to take offense to such a thorough treatment of language features that are obvious to them. I'd like to try to appease those readers by asking them to think of this chapter as a complete description of the design features supported by C++ that can help shape a vocabulary of design and implementation under multiparadigm design. We will investigate how to build on this design model starting in Chapter 7.

6.1.1 Analysis and Language

Different solution domains—such as different programming languages—call for radically different designs, even with the same problem domain analysis. Consider a simple Stack class, implemented in C++ and in Smalltalk (Figure 6.1). These languages employ

FIGURE 6.1 *Comparing a C++ design and Smalltalk design of class* Stack.

```
template <class T> class Stack:
    public ArrayedCollection<T>
{
public:
    Stack();
    ~Stack();
    T pop();
    void push(const T&);
private:
    int collectionSize, limit;
    T getElement(int);
    T *collection;
};


T Stack<T>::getElement(int index)
{
    return collection[index];
}


T Stack<T>::pop() {
    return getElement(limit--);
}
```

```
ArrayedCollection subclass:
#Stack
        instanceVariableNames:
            'collection
            limit
            collectionSize'
    classVariablenames: ''

Stack>>getElement: anIndex
    ^collection at: anIndex.

Stack>>pop
    |object|
    object :=
        self getElement: 1.
    collection replaceFrom: 1
        to: limit - 1
        with: collection
        startingAt: 2.
    collection at: limit
        put:
        self defaultElement.
    limit := limit - 1.
    ^object.
```

different kinds of commonality and variability that suggest, and even force, different designs. The code for the C++ design has a parametric argument, T, that is absent in the Smalltalk design. The object code is bound to the design much earlier in Smalltalk than in C++.

After we analyze the solution domain in this chapter, we will be ready to discuss how to mold and shape the architecture of the problem domain into the architecture of the solution domain. That done, the foundations of multi-paradigm design will be complete.

6.2 The C++ Solution Domain: An Overview

What does it mean to do domain analysis of the C++ programming language? We want to look for the families of abstractions that the language can represent. Now that we are armed with the tools of family analysis, it's straightforward to characterize these families as follows:

- Data, a mechanism to group families of related values
- Overloading, a mechanism to group families of related functions
- Templates, which group related algorithms or gross data structures
- Inheritance, which groups classes that behave the same (usually public inheritance; we treat private inheritance separately in Section 6.11)
- Inheritance with virtual functions, which also groups classes that behave the same but with later binding than inheritance alone provides
- Preprocessor constructs, such as #ifdef, typically used for fine-grain variations in code and data

Each of these language features characterizes a paradigm, a way of organizing the world. These language features shape the code in a C++ program. They also shape the way we think about and express the abstractions of banking systems, telecommunications systems, GUIs, and other application domains. The following sections focus on each of these features in turn, exploring the commonality and variability properties of each. Later, in Chapter 8, we will bring the application domain and solution domain together.

6.3 *Data*

C++ offers a rich variety of constructs to store and organize data, ranging from built-in types to `struct`s, all the way to full-fledged class objects. A data store represents a family of values. The commonality and variability analysis is simple, so trivial in fact that we would not present it here but for completeness.

> **Commonality: Structure and behavior.** A data item in C++ has a fixed structure that is established at source coding time and bound into object code at compile time. The type system associates valid operations with data values, also at coding and compile times.
>
> **Variability: State.** Data items vary only in their state.
>
> **Binding: Run time.** The value of a data item may be changed at run time through any non-`const` identifier for that data item.
>
> **Example:** Different color correction algorithms have formulae whose coefficients correspond to different display manufacturers. These coefficients can be treated as commonalities for families of similar displays and as parameters of variation that distinguish sets of displays.

6.4 *Overloading*

Classic C offers no language feature to group related functions. C++ offers several lexical and semantic groupings of different granularities: class scope, name spaces, and overloading. Overloading supports families of functions within a scope.

> **Commonality: Name, return type, and semantics.** Overloaded functions form a family whose members are related by name and by meaning. All overloaded functions have the same name and consistent return type. C++ does not enforce consistent semantics between overloaded functions, but common use follows that guideline.
>
> **Variability: Algorithm and interface.** Each overloaded function may have its own formal parameters, algorithm, and local data and

may call on other functions of its choice. Functions are distinguished (selected by the compiler for use) based on their interface.

Binding: Compile time. The appropriate function is chosen, from context, at compile time.

Example: There may be several functions for setting the color of a window. Some functions may take Xgcv values from the X system. Others may take red-green-blue intensity arguments. Others take other kinds of parameters suitable to other window technologies.

A classic example from Stroustrup's early book [Stroustrup1986] is the following collection of algebraic power functions:

```
int pow(int, int);
double pow(double, double);    // from math.h
complex pow(double, complex);  // from complex.h
complex pow(complex, int);
complex pow(complex, double);
complex pow(complex, complex);
```

6.5 Class Templates

C++ templates are an outgrowth of macro idioms used by early C++ programmers to capture common blocks of source code that could be parameterized with macro arguments. They retain similar design semantics today, though they are more integrated into the language. They also have matured to support highly idiomatic design expressions. Chapter 8 explores these more advanced constructs as a natural way to express dependencies between domains.

Commonality: Structure. Templates share the same structure. This includes the structure both of the code and of the data of a class template. Function templates are an analogous construct for individual algorithms in closed form. We treat function templates (later in the section) separately from class templates because applications treat them quite differently.

Variability: Detailed type or value. Templates take arguments that modulate and add to code generation. Template arguments usually aren't used for large structural changes.

A template may define a default for each of its parameters of variation. Defaults are an important component of multi-paradigm design, as described in Section 3.6.

6.5.1   Template Specialization

A template defines a family. Individual family members can be generated with suitable template arguments that capture parameters of variation. There is a way to generate other variant forms, too, using *template specialization*. Consider a template named Stack that takes a parameter T:

```
template <class T> class Stack { . . . . };
```

We can stipulate a peculiar form of this template for a given parameter of variation, say, for stacks of integers:

```
template<> class Stack<int> { . . . . };
```

This is an interesting form of negative variability that we will cover further in Section 6.11.

Binding: Source time. Template abstractions are bound to their clients at compile time or link-edit time according to parameters of variation (template parameters) that are explicit in the source. Template parameters may be defaulted:

```
template <class T, class SequenceClass = dequeue<T> >
class Stack {
    . . . .
};
```

Example: Collections, such as Stack previously, are common examples of templates.

6.6 Function Templates

Function templates and class templates build on the same C++ language mechanism. However, because one supports data abstractions and the other supports procedural abstractions, the two are used for different design purposes.

Commonality: Structure. Templates share the same source code structure. A function template is an abstraction of algorithm with details such as type dependencies, constants, defaults, and so on, factored out into parameters of variation.

Variability: Detailed type or value. This is much the same as for class templates.

Binding: Source time. Template abstractions are bound to their clients at compile time or link-edit time. The parameter of variation is explicit and direct in the code where the binding takes place.

Example: The sort function is the stereotypical example of a template function. The argument is a template type. The template expands into code suitable for the argument type with which sort is invoked:

```
template<class T> int sort(T[] elements, int size);
```

6.7 Inheritance

Programmers most often think of inheritance as a code reuse mechanism. More broadly, C++ inheritence can express both subtyping and code commonality. Multi-paradigm design tends to de-emphasize the code reuse perspective while focusing on—and carefully distinguishing between—code and behavior commonalities.

Commonality: Behavior and data structure. Inheritance figures prominently both in object-oriented design and in object-oriented programming. When C++ was still young, the industry's model of inheritance was much simpler than what we use today. Contemporary models separate inheritance of behavior from inheritance of structure. In other words, there are two separable components of commonality: commonality in behavior and commonality in representation.

When we do application domain analysis, we focus on behavioral inheritance. If we were to focus on commonality in the structure of the implementation, we might compromise the design's flexibility. A design based on implementation structure may not broaden to related domains, or even to new applications in the original application domain. Focusing on behavior tends to leave designs more flexible. This philosophy lies at the heart of design methods such as CRC cards [Beck1993] and responsibility-driven design [Wirfs-Brock1990].

Example: The Number hierarchy is a stock example often used to illustrate this point.[1] Consider the design of Figure 6.2. The first step of many contemporary object-oriented design methods is to establish class behaviors without undue consideration for implementation. The inheritance tree on the left (with the most abstract class at the top and the most refined class at the bottom) properly expresses a behavioral hierarchy. The operations on Number are a subset of those on Complex, which in turn are a subset of the operations on Integer. Each class inherits the operations of the class above it in the hierarchy. This is inheritance of types in the application domain, that is, inheritance of behavior. We might draw such a picture using a design notation such as UML [Fowler+1997], OMT

FIGURE 6.2   *A unified subtype/implementation inheritance hierarchy for Number.*

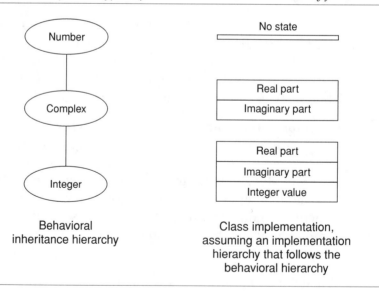

Behavioral
inheritance hierarchy

Class implementation,
assuming an implementation
hierarchy that follows the
behavioral hierarchy

---

1. Some designers object to this example because though Complex is closed under division, its derived class Integer is not. However, closure need not be inherited. There is nothing to prevent the inverse or division operations of Integer from returning Complex values.

[Rumbaugh1991], Booch [Booch1994], or ROOM [Selic+1994], apart from the C++ implementation that is to come later.

6.7.1   Aligning Domains

An important design step is to align the application domain structure with the solution domain structure. In C++, this often means translating the Rumbaugh, Booch, or ROOM classes directly into C++ classes. Assume that we derive the C++ classes from the behavior hierarchy at the left of Figure 6.2. We assign data fields to Complex for its real and imaginary parts and a simple integer field to class Integer. But because Integer is derived from Complex, it inherits all of its properties in a C++ inheritance hierarchy, including the real and imaginary data items. So sizeof(Integer) may be 12 bytes, if the machine represents both floating-point and integer quantities in 4 bytes of memory each. For efficiency (and because it goes against "the rule of least surprise" for an Integer to contain a real and imaginary part), we would like for Integer *not* to inherit these data fields.

The designer must take special care when structure and behavior have different hierarchies. C++ can capture implementation inheritance through private inheritance and behavioral inheritance with public inheritance. Private inheritance carries the semantics of encapsulation (called *implementation hierarchy* by some). The member functions of classes derived from private bases often invoke member functions of their base class, sometimes deferring all of their semantics to their base class counterparts. So Set might reuse the implementation of its private base class List, as shown in Figure 6.3. Set gets all of the machinery of List for free, including its algorithms and implementation. It contributes functions such as Set<T>::add, which maintains element uniqueness. The only behavior directly reused by the derived class is the size operation; the inheritance otherwise transfers only implementation and structure.

Though public inheritance expresses subtyping, it also makes a "logical copy" of the base class structure and implementation in the derived class. Programmers can often use this to their advantage. For example, the data common to all Window abstractions (size, location, and so on) are of interest to all derived classes as well. Inheriting the base class representation in derived classes relieves derived class authors of the burden of rebuilding common implementation structures. But

FIGURE 6.3 *Inheritance to reuse implementation and structure, not behavior.*

```
template <class T>                      template <class T>
class List: public Collection<T>        class Set: private List<T>
{                                       {
public:                                 public:
    void put(const T&);                     void add(const T&);
    T get();                                T get();
    bool hasElement(const T &t)             void remove(const T&);
        const;                              bool exists(const T&)
    int size() const;                           const;
    . . . .                                 using List<T>::size;
private:                                    . . . .
    T *vec;                             };
    int index;
};                                      void Set<T>::add(const T &e)
                                        {
void List<T>::put(const T &e)               if (!exists(e))
{                                               List<T>::put(e);
    vec[index++] = e;                   }
}
```

commonality in structure does not always follow commonality in behavior, as we saw in the Number example of Figure 6.2. Because there is a single mechanism called inheritance that represents two kinds of commonality and variability in C++—behavior and structure—we need exceptional mechanisms if behavior and structure commonalities and variabilities do not align with each other.

One solution to this problem is to turn to a language that supports behavior and structural abstractions separately, as one finds in Eiffel [Meyer1992] and Java [Flanagan1997]. Design patterns are another solution. Such patterns are described well by Gamma, Helm, Vlissides, and Johnson in their patterns book [Gamma1995]. Their *class structural patterns* in Chapter 4 of [Gamma1995] address just this problem. In particular, the pattern BRIDGE solves the Number problem directly, as shown in Figure 6.4. The programmer creates separate inheritance hierarchies for the interface and the implementation. Instances from these hierarchies are paired by "bridges" from the interface class objects (on the left) to the implementation class objects (on the right). This is similar to the envelope/letter idiom of [Coplien1992].

This pattern doesn't happen to find natural expression in C++, though there is no reason a programming language couldn't express

FIGURE 6.4   *A* BRIDGE *pattern for* Number, *adapted from [Gamma1995].*

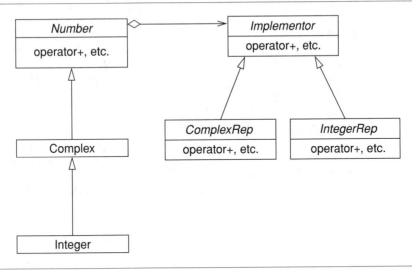

such rich commonality and variabilities. Even though the C++ language can't express patterns in closed form, we can still think of them as a language or implementation technology in their own right. Chapter 9 looks at multi-paradigm development and patterns in more depth. Without such patterns, we must stick to the C++ model of inheritance.

Because the semantics of private inheritance are **HAS-A** rather than **IS-A**, most programmers (especially the purists) prefer to explicitly use encapsulation rather than private inheritance, as shown in Figure 6.5.

If a class participates both in a subtyping hierarchy and in an implementation hierarchy, public inheritance can be used for subtyping, while private inheritance is used for implementation. This can be implemented using multiple inheritance, per the ADAPTER pattern, as Figure 6.6 shows. The more common alternative is to use an extra level of indirection, per the BRIDGE pattern, as illustrated in Figure 6.7.

Variability: Structure or algorithm. C++ inheritance inseparably expresses commonality and variability in both behavior and structure. We can use inheritance to express both either together when they align or separately when there is no variability in the other.

There is an interesting subtlety to the variability analysis. A class may exhibit positive variability (see Section 3.3) from other classes in

FIGURE 6.5 *Encapsulation to reuse implementation and structure, not behavior.*

```
template <class T>                template <class T>
class Set                         int Set<T>::size() const {
{                                     //   extra function call
public:                               //   beyond what is used
    void add(const T&);               //   with private
    T empty() const;                  //   inheritance
    void remove(const T&);            return theList.size();
    bool exists(const T&) const;  }
    int size() const;
    . . . .                       template <class T>
private:                          void Set<T>::add(const T &e)
    List<T> theList;              {
};                                    if (!exists(e))
                                          theList.push_front(e);
                                  }
```

the family established during commonality analysis. The stronger the positive variability, the further the class should be pushed from the apex of the class inheritance hierarchy. This is consistent with the definition of subtype and in good keeping with the Liskov substitution principle [Liskov1988]. For example, OrderedCollection might support a sort operation, while its base class, Collection, does not. And

FIGURE 6.6 *Multiple inheritance for implementation and interface.*

```
class RealRep {                   class Complex: public Number,
friend class Real;
friend class Complex;                     private RealRep,
    double rpart;                         private ImaginaryRep {
                                  public:
    . . . .                           . . . .

};                                };


class ImaginaryRep {              class Real: public Number,
friend class Complex;                     private RealRep {
    double ipart;                 public:

    . . . .                           . . . .

};                                };
```

FIGURE 6.7   *Separate implementation and subtyping hierarchies using* BRIDGE.

```
class NumberRep {
    . . . .
};

class RealRep: NumberRep {
friend class Real;
friend class Complex;
    double rpart;
    . . . .
};

class ComplexRep: NumberRep {
friend class Complex;
    double ipart;
    . . . .
};
```

```
class Complex: public Number {
protected:
    NumberRep *rep;
    Complex (NumberRep *r):
        rep(r) { }
public:
    Complex():
        rep(new ComplexRep) { }
    . . . .
};

class Real: public Complex {
public:
    Real(): Complex
        (new RealRep) {
        . . . .
    }
    . . . .
};
```

Set<int>, derived from OrderedCollection, may support an operation that adds all of its elements together into a single sum, as well as a sort operation, while these operations disappear nearer the top of the hierarchy.

If a class demonstrates strong enough negative variability against other classes in the family, it may not belong to that family. Negative variability in a family based on commonality in type points to inheritance with cancellation; this should generally be avoided ([Coplien1992], 237–239). The classic example of this problem can be found in the work of inexpert object-oriented programmers, who derive Set from List (or vice versa). Because a List can be sorted, it cannot be the base class for Set, which cannot be sorted (because there is no notion of ordering). And because Sets guarantee that their members are unique, and Lists don't, Set cannot be the base class for List. Both should be derived from a more general Collection class.

Binding: Compile time. C++ inheritance hierarchies are bound at compile time (but see the next section).

6.8 Virtual Functions

Virtual functions form families within a class hierarchy, and form much of the basis for commonality between inherited classes. They are the primary C++ mechanism that supports ADTs.

Commonality: Names and behavior. Virtual functions can be grouped in either of two ways. First, we group functions into classes that implement the abstract data types of the application domain. Second, we group functions from different classes into a single inheritance hierarchy. The grouping in class hierarchies captures the common relationship between the functions and the domain of the hierarchy, as well as their more obvious commonality of *signature*. A signature describes the name and argument types of a function. Related virtual functions all have the same name and apply to similar objects whose classes form an inheritance hierarchy.

The members of a family of virtual functions usually share the same signature. However, the return type in the derived class signature can be no less restrictive than the corresponding base class signature and the member function formal parameters in the derived class signature can be no more restrictive than those in the corresponding base class signature. The return types for derived class member functions must support at least the member functions supported by the base class return types. The formal parameters for base class member functions must support at least those member functions that the derived class formal parameters support.

In short, virtual functions share externally observable behavior, or *meaning*, in common. For example, classes that form a hierarchy under class Shape all share a draw member function, as well as many others. The ability to be drawn is a behavior shared by all shapes, they are like overloaded functions in this regard. The difference between overloading and virtual functions, from a design perspective, is that virtual functions are tied to a larger abstraction (a class) such that each family member (individual virtual function instance) is in a different class. Those classes are related by inheritance. Overloaded functions are less obviously tied to other abstractions or design relationships.

Variability: Algorithm implementation. Though virtual functions share the same behavior, each one implements its behavior in its own way that is suitable to the class to which it belongs. The draw member function for Circle is certainly different than that for

Rectangle. It is often useful to view this variability as an implementation detail. So virtual functions are a construct to express implementation variability for a behavior that is common to several related classes.

Inheritance lets the programmer bundle related algorithmic variabilities. If several algorithms vary together, they can be packaged into a single derived class. Such derived classes can be administrative units in their own right that become higher-level values for a conceptual parameter of variation. For example, we might define a class that implements behaviors for three levels of fault recovery; its derived classes might be implemented for a wide variety of recovery strategies. Classes (or subsystems) that need fault recovery support would take such an object (or class) as a parameter of variation. Inheritance, used to factor out algorithmic differences in this way, can be contrasted with techniques such as the STRATEGY pattern (Section 9.2.4), which are tuned to deal with functions one at a time.

Binding: Run time. How does a program select from a virtual function family, all of whose functions share the same name and same class hierarchy? The selection is done at run time based on the type of the object for which the function is called.

Example: Shapes in a graphics package are the stereotypical example of interchangeable family members related by inheritance.

6.9 Commonality Analysis and Polymorphism

Polymorphism means "many forms." Adapting our perspective of commonality and variability, we can just as well say that polymorphism means that there is something common to several related forms but that each form is distinct. C++ supports several forms of polymorphism; in fact, they have been the titles of the five preceding sections:

- Overloading
- Class templates
- Function templates
- Inheritance
- Inheritance with virtual functions

FIGURE 6.8   *The Wegner polymorphism taxonomy.*

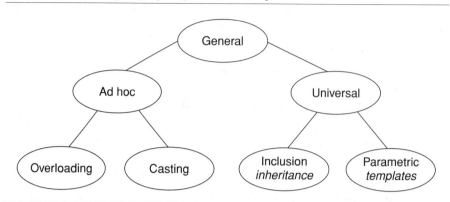

Wegner [Wegner1987] has characterized polymorphism itself as a family of four members structured into two groups, universal and ad hoc (Figure 6.8). In his model, objects are the artifacts of interest. *Overloading* describes a family of related functions having the same name and semantics but operating on objects of different types. *Casting* transforms one type of object into another; for example, one can cast between short and long integers. *Parametric polymorphism* means that the variability of an abstraction described in a single, closed form can be controlled through a parameter list. *Inclusion polymorphism* describes a hierarchy of sets of abstractions that include each other, all of which can be treated in terms of the properties of the most enclosing set. It is what we know as C++ inheritance hierarchies and virtual functions.

6.10 *Preprocessor Directives*

Preprocessor directives, such as #ifdef, #ifndef, #if, and the terminating #endif are commonly used for any fine-grain program changes. Because they are a preprocessor construct, they apply equally well to data structure and algorithms (code structure). Though they are defined as part of the C++ language, many programmers do not consider them full, first-class language features. This is because of relatively weak integration with the rest of the language and because of a common lack of symbolic tool support for them. They should be used selectively and with care.

Inheritance versus `#ifdef`

Notice that inheritance (Section 6.7) can also be used for fine changes in data and algorithm structure. What is the difference? Preprocessor directives can efficiently handle the finest level of granularity in a program. Inheritance can deal with fine data granularity, but that often comes at the expense of some overhead (for example, from C++ data type alignment constraints). The function is the unit of code granularity under inheritance; preprocessor directives can address arbitrarily fine code granularity.

Some design patterns manage arbitrarily fine code granularity by building on inheritance and virtual functions. That makes it possible to have arbitrarily fine code variability with run-time binding. The flexibility comes at some expense in efficiency; see Chapter 9.

Preprocessor directives are most useful to express negative variability: exceptions to the rule. When a line of code must be present most of the time, but absent in one or two cases that can be known at compile time, preprocessor directives are often a viable solution. Negative variability is discussed in more detail in Section 3.3.2 and in the following section.

6.11 Negative Variability

Positive and negative variability were introduced in Section 3.3. It is important to look for negative variability during application analysis. Having then found it, we must understand how to capture it in implementation. We can express negative variability in C++ by using techniques usually reserved for fine-tuning and implementation details. These techniques include template specialization, argument defaulting, indirection (for data member cancellation), private inheritance (for behavior cancellation), and `#ifdef`.

We can think of each of the paradigms of C++ as having a *rule of variation*. For the "object paradigm," the rule of variation says that family members can add new functions or data to the commonalities captured in a base class. The variabilities of most paradigms leave the commonalities untouched. Negative variability violate rules of variation by attacking the underlying commonality—they are the exceptions to the rules.

6.11.1   Deciding When to Use Negative Variability

For positive variability, we choose the appropriate C++ language feature according to the underlying commonality and the nature of the variability. We deal with negative variability in the same way. During variability analysis, how do we know whether to use positive variability or negative variability?

- If a parameter of variation can change only in ways that leave the underlying commonality untouched, then use positive variability. For example, a function may have the same logic for all of its applications, but it may need to use different type declarations for different applications. A template function would be one way to capture this positive variability.

- If some range of values of a parameter of variation leads to structures that violate the overall commonality, then use negative variability. For example, if a function needs to be slightly different for some set of target platforms, use #ifdef to demarcate the differences.

- Sometimes the variation becomes larger than the commonality. The design should be refactored to reverse the commonality and the variation. For example, a function has a body that must be substantially different on each of several platforms. Assuming negative variability, we initially use #ifdef to demarcate the differences. If we want run-time binding, we should use simple conditionals instead of #ifdefs. If we want source-time binding, we should capture the common name and semantics in a family of overloaded functions (possibly adding an additional function argument to serve as the parameter of variation) so that the implementations can vary freely.

A Template Example

Consider a Stack abstraction as a simple example. Most Stacks share a similar data structure, as shown in Figure 6.9. This implementation is fully general. It doesn't require that the stacked items have a default constructor, can handle polymorphic data types, and it can easily grow

FIGURE 6.9   *A common* Stack *data structure.*

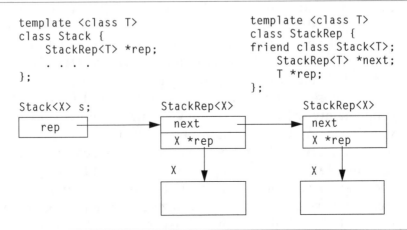

```
template <class T>                    template <class T>
class Stack {                         class StackRep {
    StackRep<T> *rep;                 friend class Stack<T>;
        . . . .                           StackRep<T> *next;
};                                        T *rep;
                                      };
```

as large as needed. But this implementation adds a lot of overhead to the memory consumed by the objects it manages, particularly if the managed objects are small. We can adopt a more efficient implementation for some Stacks, such as Stack<int>, by using a simple vector, as shown in Figure 6.10. If we know we need an integer stack, then we don't need the generality that supports polymorphism and we can remove the data structure overhead of all of those pointers. We pay a price for this efficiency when the stack grows, but that's acceptable for most applications.

Commonality analysis finds that most Stacks share the same structure, as well as the same code structure and the same external behavior.

FIGURE 6.10   *A simple stack.*

```
template<> class Stack<int> {
    int *rep;
        . . . .
};
```

Stack<int> s;   int[10]
```
+--------+
|  rep ——|——————————>  [ | | | | | | | | | | ]
+--------+
```

We look at one parameter of variation, *ELEMENT DATA TYPE*—the type of the element stored by the stack—to evaluate whether it violates any of the commonalities. `Stack<int>` violates the structure commonality, and some of the code structure as well. If we decide that this exception affects only a small set of choices for the *ELEMENT DATA TYPE* parameter of variation, then we treat it as a negative variability.

We choose an appropriate C++ language construct according to the commonality and variability. A given pair of commonality and *positive* variability uniquely selects a C++ construct. For the corresponding negative variability, we choose a C++ language construct that usually is related to the associated positive variability. For the commonality and positive variability that suggest templates as an implementation technique, we use template specialization for the associated negative variability. That is the technique we use for `Stack<int>`.

An Example of Argument Defaulting

Argument defaulting is another construct that can express a form of negative variation. Consider what to do if there is a predominate commonality in algorithm but minor variations in values used by that algorithm.

For example, assume we have an application that simulates chemical reactions. Some molecules have a member function called `hydrate`. Normally, we want to hydrate molecules with ordinary water, but we reserve the option to use heavy water in unusual circumstances. We would declare the function

```
void Molecule::hydrate(hydrationMolecule = Water)
    { . . . . }
```

and could call it using either of these forms:

```
Molecule *m;
 . . . .
m->hydrate();   // normal use
m->hydrate(HeavyWater);   // negative variability
```

An Example of Data Cancellation

Let's say that we're building a text editor and we decide to use a text buffer to hold text being edited. The class might look like this:

```
template <class CharSet>
class TextBuffer {
```

```
public:
    Line<CharSet> getLine(const LineNumber &);
    . . . .
private:
    LineNumber firstLineInMemory, lastLineInMemory;
    int currentLineCapacity;
    . . . .
};
```

`TextBuffer` may have several interesting derived classes:

- `PagedTextBuffer`, which maintains a working set of lines in primary memory
- `LazyTextBuffer`, which reads in lines as needed and retains them until they are written out.
- `SimpleTextBuffer`, which always keeps the entire file image in primary memory

Those classes can use straightforward inheritance. But let's say that we want to introduce a `SingleLineTextBuffer`, which we may use to edit the command line or for dialogue boxes instantiated by the editor. If we derive `SingleLineTextBuffer` from `TextBuffer`, it will inherit many data members that it will never use (or that it will use only in a degenerate way, such as the case where `firstLineInMemory`, `lastLineInMemory`, and `currentLineCapacity` are all set to 1). We can't "cancel" the base class members in the derived class. We can deal with this problem by factoring the data of both base and derived classes into separate structures that maintain a relationship to the original abstractions through a pointer. First, consider a hierarchy of classes used for the implementation of a family of *Text Buffers*, in an application such as a text editor (the following classes are body class objects in handle/body pairs):

```
template <class CharSet>
class TextBufferRep {
public:
    void appendChar(const CharSet&);
    . . . .
};

template <class CharSet>
class PagedTextBufferRep:
    public TextBufferRep<CharSet>
{
```

```
    friend class PagedTextBuffer<CharSet>;
    LineNumber firstLineInMemory, lastLineInMemory;
    int currentLineCapacity;
        . . . .
};

template <class CharSet>
class LineTextBufferRep:
    public TextBufferRep<CharSet>
{
        . . . .
};
```

The following classes are the corresponding handle classes,
which present the user interface through which the implementation
is managed. The common `rep` pointer in the base class `TextBuffer`
points to the body class, declared as a pointer to the (generic) type
`TextBufferRep<CharSet>`:

```
template <class CharSet>
class TextBuffer
{
public:
    Line<CharSet> getLine(const LineNumber &);
        . . . .
protected:
    TextBufferRep<CharSet> *rep;
    TextBuffer(TextBufferRep<CharSet>*);
    ~TextBuffer();
private:
    // encourage heap allocation - disallow instance copies
    TextBuffer(const TextBuffer<CharSet> &) { }
};
```

Each of the following classes inherit the `rep` pointer, but each may
choose to point at the appropriate variant of `TextBufferRep` suitable to
its own role:

```
template <class CharSet>
class PagedTextBuffer: public TextBuffer<CharSet>
{
public:
    PagedTextBuffer():
        TextBuffer<CharSet>
            (new PagedTextBufferRep<CharSet>) {
        . . . .
```

```
    }
    . . . .
};

template <class CharSet>
class LineTextBuffer: public TextBuffer<CharSet>
{
public:
    LineTextBuffer():
        TextBuffer<CharSet>(new
            LineTextBufferRep<CharSet>) {
        . . . .
    }
    . . . .
};
```

The pedagogical Complex example from Section 6.7 can be motivated from the perspective of negative variability. Consider this straightforward (but perhaps unrealistic) attempt at the design of a Complex hierarchy:

```
class Complex: public Number{
public:
    . . . .
private:
    double realPart, imaginaryPart;
};

class Imaginary: public Complex {
public:
    . . . .
private:
    ?
};

class Real: public Complex {
public:
    . . . .
private:
    ?
};
```

We want to cancel the imaginaryPart data member of Complex in the derived class Imaginary. The most flexible solution is to use the BRIDGE pattern [Gamma1995] to factor the data representation into two structures that are related by a common base structure, as in Figure 6.7. From the perspective of multi-paradigm design, we can view it as a special kind of negative variability that preserves commonalty in behavior but not structure or that preserves commonality of structure but not behavior. This book further addresses the ties between multi-paradigm design and patterns in Chapter 9.

An Example of Behavior Cancellation

Behavioral cancellation—usually called *inheritance with cancellation*—is the most infamous example of negative variability in object-oriented design. Novice designers sometimes presume that C++ allows them to cancel a public virtual function in a derived class. The C++ type system does not allow this, thereby enabling it to check for compile-time violations of subtype substitutability. It should be possible to use an instance of a derived class in contexts in which an instance of a base class is expected. This is called the *Liskov Substitutability Principle* [Liskov1988].

The C++ type system supports Liskov substitutability when public inheritance is used and disallows the cancellation of behavior in publicly derived classes. We can express inheritance with cancellation—cancellation of behavior—by using private inheritance. If we do this, we, of course, forfeit the right to use derived class instances in base class contexts (and the compiler ensures that no privately derived class object can ever appear in a base class context). However, we can create a new abstraction whose functionality is almost the same as the base class but with less specific operations. In Section 6.7, we viewed this as a way to reuse implementation without inheriting the behavior. Here we want to reuse selective parts of the behavior and implementation:

```
template <class T>
class List {
public:
    T front() const;
    T back() const;
    int size() const;
    bool exists(const T&) const;
    void insert(const T&);
    . . . .
};
```

```
template <class T>
class Set: private List<T> {
public:
    using List<T>::size;    // same--uses base class
                            // implementation
    using List<T>::exists;  // same--uses base class impl.
    void insert(const T&);  // different--check for
                            // uniqueness

    . . . .
private:
    // class qualification here is just for documentation
    using List<T>::front;
    using List<T>::back;
};
```

Good uses of behavior cancellation are rare. A design refactoring should almost always be used instead (see Section 6.11.2).

An Example of Contravariance

Contravariance is a relationship between the argument types for a base class member function and the derived class member function that overrides it. The arguments for a derived class member function are usually the same as those in the corresponding base class member function. Consider the case in which the derived class arguments are more restrictive than those in the base class:

```
class GIFImage{
// a class for general GIF images
    . . . .
};


class InterlacedGIFImage: public GIFImage {
// a class specialized for interlaced GIF images
public:
    . . . .
};


class GIF89aImage: public GIFImage {
// a specific format of GIF images
public:
    . . . .
};
```

```
class Window {
// a general window abstraction
public:
    . . . .
    virtual void draw(const GIFImage &, Point loc);
    . . . .
};

class HTTPindow: public Window {
// a proxy object for a Web window
public:
    . . . .
    void draw(const InterlacedGIFImage &, Point loc);
    . . . .
};
```

Now consider the following code:

```
Window *newWindow = new HTTPWindow;
GIF89aImage picture;
. . . .
newWindow->draw(picture, loc);      // woops
```

Imagine that the last line calls `HTTPWindow::draw`. That function expects an argument that can support at least the member functions of `InterlacedGIFImage`, and the actual parameter of type `GIF98aImage` presents a problem. C++ solves this problem by short-circuiting the virtual function mechanism when a member function argument is more restrictive in the derived class than in the base class. Thus `Window::draw` would be called in the last line of the previous code segment.

Contravariance can be treated as a special case of inheritance with cancellation, usually addressed with a pattern such as VISITOR [Gamma1995] or by refactoring:

```
class Window {
public:
    // handles GIF & GIF89a
    virtual void draw(const GIFImage &);

    // handles InterlacedGIFImages. In the base class
    // default behavior we do no interlacing, but derived
    // classes can override this behavior
    virtual void drawInterlace(const InterlacedGIFImage
        &image) {draw(image);}
};
```

```
class HTTPWindow: public Window {
public:
    // perhaps a special version for GIFs on a Web window
    void draw(const GIFImage &);

    // interlace interlaceable GIFs on a Web window
    void drawInterlace(const InterlacedGIFImage &image) {
        // code for interlacing
        . . . .
    }
    . . . .
};
```

An Example of #ifdef

One goal Stroustrup had in mind for C++ was to eliminate the C preprocessor. Language features such as the `const` type modifier and `inline` functions attest to this goal. The only preprocessor features not attacked directly by the language are those supporting conditional compilation: `#ifdef`, `#ifndef`, `#if`, `#else`, and `#endif`. We use these constructs to selectively introduce algorithmic or data structure fragments into the program. Many compilers attempt to optimize `if` statements so that they incur no more overhead than do preprocessor conditional compilation directives. However, `if` statements may be used only for algorithm structure, not for code structure, so programmers often resort to `#ifdefs` for small changes. Debugging code provides a typical example:

```
#ifdef TRACE_ON
#define TRACE_INIT_CALL_COUNT \
   static int trace_call_count = 0
#define TRACE(F) trace_show(#f); \
   ++trace_call_count
#else
#define TRACE_INIT_CALL_COUNT
#define TRACE(F)
#endif

void f(void) {
    TRACE_INIT_CALL_COUNT;
    TRACE(f);
    . . . .
}
```

Notice that you cannot use preprocessor directives for data variability within a program. Consider a program that uses #ifdef to implement two different family members that have different data structures (for example, different versions of the same class), selecting between alternatives according to a parameter of variation. No single program may contain both family members; C++ depends on a consistent representation of data layouts within a program.

6.11.2   Negative Variability versus Domain Splitting

The techniques of the preceding section apply to *small* negative variabilities. As a negative variability becomes larger, it ceases to characterize the variant: It becomes a commonality, and its complement becomes the variability! Large negative variabilities should often be treated as positive variabilities.

An Example of Behavior Cancellation

The most common example again relates to the problem of inheritance with cancellation in object-oriented design. Instead of cancelling the assumed base class commonality in the derived class, we can instead factor the commonality into a higher-level base class. Redoing the previous example, we introduce a (not very realistic) Collection base class:

```
template <class T>
class Collection {
public:
    int count() const;        // common to all derived
    bool has(const T&) const; //       classes, so not
    // virtual. insert is deferred to the derived class if
    // one likes, one can declare a placeholder here, to
    // capture the fact that the behavior is common to all
    // family members
    virtual void insert(const T&) = 0;
        . . . .
};

template <class T>
class List: public Collection<T> {
public:
    T head() const;           // peculiar to List;
    T tail() const;           // this, too
```

```
        using Collection<T>::count;    // just use the
        using Collection<T>::has;      // base class
                                       // version
        void insert(const T&);         // simple list
                                       // insertion

        . . . .
    };

    template <class T>
    class Set: public Collection<T> {
    public:
        // no head, tail -- not meaningful for Sets
        using Collection<T>::count;    // just making the
                                       // default
        using Collection<T>::has;      // explicit (good
                                       // documentation)
        void insert(const T&);         // different--must
                                       // check
        . . . .                        // for uniqueness
    };
```

That is, instead of using a relatively narrow List abstraction as the commonality base for Set and expressing Set as a variant of List with negative variability, we create a broader base abstraction Collection, which is common across both List and Set. Both List and Set can be described in terms of Collection by using only positive variability.

A Template Example

Template specialization admits a broad variety of changes in implementation code and data structure. This degree of flexibility makes it unnecessary to make a special case of templates that have little in common with the (nonspecialized) original instance. For example, a typical vector might look like this:

```
    template<class T, int size = 50>
    class vector {
    public:
        . . . .
        T operator[](unsigned int index)
            { return rep[index]; }
        . . . .
    private:
        T *rep;
    };
```

However, the implementation of the specialized bit vector might look completely different. We capture the difference with a straightforward application of template specialization:

```
unsigned short vectorMasks[16] = {
    0000001,
    . . . .
    0100000
};

template<int size = 50>
class vector<bool, size> {
public:
    . . . .
    bool operator[](unsigned int index) {
        return rep[index / (8 * sizeof(unsigned short))] &
        vectorMasks[i % (8 * sizeof(unsigned short))];
    }
    . . . .
private:
    unsigned short *rep;
};
```

An Example of Data Cancellation

The technique described previously in the section, "An Example of Data Cancellation" (in Section 6.11.1) is intentionally broad enough to handle both isolated cancellation of data members and completely unrelated data layouts across family members. Even if the data are completely different for every layer of an inheritance hierarchy, the extra level of indirection accommodates the variability.

An Example of #ifdef

Sometimes variability leaves a single procedure with little common code—all of the code goes into the variant part:

```
void f() {
#if C1
    . . . .
    // lots of code
#else
    . . . .
    // lots of code
#endif
}
```

Conditional compilation constructs can be used to express almost any variability. They should be used sparingly, if at all. Other techniques, such as the factorings available through inheritance, function overloading, and sometimes templates, are often more suitable than conditional preprocessor constructs. There are many idiomatic preprocessor techniques that are only on the fringe of language concerns. For example, in the previous case, we might create two complete and separate functions that would be put in header files as static functions. To select the appropriate function, just #include the appropriate header (perhaps using a #ifdef).

6.11.3 A Summary of Negative Variability

Table 6.1 summarizes negative variability and how it interacts with C++ features used to express commonality and variability. The first two columns reflect the commonality and nominal variability from the domain analysis. The third column recalls the C++ feature used for the commonality/variability pair, and the last column prescribes a remedy for exceptions to the variability. The first three columns are expanded in more detail in Table 6.2.

The table does not cover the situations in which variability "takes over" and becomes the commonality. Those should be handled on a case-by-case basis according to the analyses of Section 6.11.2.

TABLE 6.1 *Choosing C++ Features for Negative Variability*

Kind of Commonality	Kind of Variability	C++ Feature for Positive Variability	C++ Feature for Corresponding Negative Variability
Name and behavior	Gross structure or algorithm controlled by a parametric type or value	Templates	Template specialization
Structure, algorithm, name, and behavior	Fine structure, value, or type	Templates	Template argument defaulting

Table continued on next page.

TABLE 6.1   *Choosing C++ Features for Negative Variability, continued*

Kind of Commonality	Kind of Variability	C++ Feature for Positive Variability	C++ Feature for Corresponding Negative Variability
Semantics and name (of function)	Default value in a formula or algorithm	Function argument defaulting	Supply explicit parameter
	Signature	Overloading	Overloading
Commonality in some data structure; perhaps in algorithm	Membership in data structure	Inheritance, adding data members	Refactor using pointers to alternative implementations
Some commonality in structure and algorithm	Behavior	Inheritance, overriding, or adding virtual functions	Private inheritance or **HAS-A** containment
Most source code	Fine algorithm	`#ifdef`	`#ifdef`
All others	All others	Usually none	See Chapter 9

TABLE 6.2   *Commonality and Positive Variability in the Domain of the C++ Programming Language*

Commonality	Variability	Binding	Instantiation	C++ Mechanism
Function name and semantics	Anything other than algorithm structure	Source time	n/a	`template`
	Fine algorithm	Compile time	n/a	`#ifdef`
	Fine or gross algorithm	Compile time	n/a	Overloading

Table continued on next page.

TABLE 6.2   *Commonality and Positive Variability in the Domain of the C++ Programming Language, continued*

Commonality	Variability	Binding	Instantiation	C++ Mechanism
All data structure	Value of state	Run time	Yes	`struct`, simple types
	A small set of values	Run time	Yes	`enum`
(Optionally, related operations, too, for this row)	Types and values, as well as state	Source time	Yes	`template`
Related operations and some structure (positive variability)	Value of state	Source time	No	Module (class with static members)
	Value of state	Source time	Yes	`struct`, `class`
	Data structure, as well as state	Compile time	Optional	Inheritance
	Algorithm (especially multiple), as well as (optional) data structure and state	Compile time	Optional	Inheritance (compare with Strategy, Section 9.2.4)
	Algorithm, as well as (optional) data structure and state	Run time	Optional	Virtual functions

6.12 A Summary of the C++ Solution Domain: A Family Table

We can summarize the C++ solution domain in Table 6.2 that provides a uniform view of how the language features relate to each other. At one level, this table summarizes the value of specific C++ language features. It is a useful tool for programmers to learn the language from a design perspective once they're beyond the novice stage. But at a higher level, we'll use this table as the "virtual machine" that will guide design decisions that start at higher levels of analysis and design. Some language features seem to apply better at high levels than others do. For example, we think of templates and derived classes as powerful architectural constructs, while we rarely think of conditional compilation constructs or argument defaulting in the same way.

The design model now in hand, we can move to the next chapter and use it to design systems using multiple paradigms.

CHAPTER 7

Simple Mixing of Paradigms

I n this chapter, we break a problem into parts so that each part can be designed with a single paradigm. This "divide-and-conquer" approach is the simplest form of multi-paradigm development.

7.1 Putting It All Together: An Overview of Multi-Paradigm Design

Most software projects require multiple paradigms. Even on the most "pure" object-oriented projects, we fall back on procedural thinking inside individual methods or member functions, both for the logic of the code and for common engineering practices such as loop optimizations. Multiple paradigms often surface to the highest levels of design in complex applications; templates, overloading, and other C++ language features may appear as first-class architectural abstractions. Multi-paradigm design can help us choose which C++ paradigms to use. In previous chapters, we established a foundation of commonality and variability analysis as building blocks for multi-paradigm design. Now, it's finally time to move into design and create some abstractions!

In this section, we'll briefly preview ways to use multi-paradigm design and define the steps that take us from commonality analysis to implementation.

7.1.1   One Size Does Not Fit All

Chapter 1 motivated the need for multiple paradigms. Even if we have an extensive palette of paradigms at our disposal—as we do in C++—we still need techniques to combine these paradigms in implementation. There are different ways to mix paradigms. The most intricate techniques are those that weave together the paradigms of multiple subdomains as described in Chapter 8. If we are building a framework as a reusable module that won't be further subdivided, then the internal coupling incurred by multi-paradigm design is justified by the increased expressiveness and ease of evolution in the framework's external sites of parameterization and extension.

It is often possible to cleanly partition a system so that paradigms don't cut across the design partitioning. This can be true at many levels of design, even at the highest levels of architecture. Sometimes, major system chunks are GUI or database libraries—implementation paradigms foreign to C++. We'll explore such "outboard paradigms" in Section 7.6. In the more detailed levels of implementation, we may find large sections of regularly structured designs that can easily be treated with a single paradigm. That paradigm is often the object paradigm; sometimes it is procedures; and sometimes it is modules. Though a single overall design may need to be attacked with several paradigms, we often can divide and conquer so that individual pieces can use a single paradigm and its methods. It is this common case of homogeneous subdomains that we take up in this chapter.

One goal of design is to minimize coupling between parts and to maximize cohesion within them. Close attention to commonalities can help us achieve these ends when we partition a domain into subdomains. We find subdomains by grouping the domain's family members *along the lines of commonality that naturally can be expressed in the implementation technology.* We start with simple commonality analysis. When that is complete, we make sure that we can express those commonalities in the programming language. For example, if we find that family members share common data structure, we look for a way to express that in C++ and find that inheritance fits the bill. If we find that family members share the same interface, with each one implementing it differently, we might use inheritance with virtual functions. If we find common code structure and behavior but variability in the interface, we might use templates.[1] This process may repeat recursively.

For example, consider the domain of matrices and vectors. We may first group all matrices together because they share common behaviors, and may likewise group all vectors. Vectors and matrices are each a subdomain in their own right. We may also note families of functions: multiplication (for vectors and vectors, matrices and vectors, matrices and matrices, sparse matrices and vectors, vectors and diagonal matrices, and so on), division (likewise), addition (likewise), and subtraction (likewise). Each basic operation becomes a subdomain whose members can be expressed using overloading.

Though coupling and cohesion are applied as design or architecture principles, they directly benefit the quality of the code less than the quality of life of people that maintain the code. Good decoupling makes it possible for teams or individuals to work independently. Tighter coupling makes it difficult for small teams to maintain their code independently; this means that decisions can't be made locally, and so productivity suffers. Software decoupling is the means; team decoupling is the end. If politics, culture, policy, or history dictate a team structure independent of software considerations, then the software structure should follow the organization, not vice versa.[2] This means that the best (pragmatic) domains often come from an intuitive market or business perspective rather than from the domain analysis principles of commonality and variability. So not only is it true that any single paradigm should yield to multi-paradigm design driven by a good domain analysis, but also that multi-paradigm design should yield to common sense and the prevailing structures of the business. There just isn't a single recipe that works all of the time.

One example is the domain of auditing in fault-tolerant systems. Audits exist to glean data structures to detect problems and escalate recovery actions to restore the system to a consistent state. A simple commonality analysis might note that critical data structures have both ordinary traversal methods and auditing methods and that each

---

[1.]   See an analogous example (number 42) in Scott Meyers's *Effective C++* [Meyers1992]

[2.]   For more on the relationship between organization and architecture, see the patterns "Organization Follows Location" and "Conway's Law" in [Coplien1995a].

of these methods references internal data structures in detail. There is likely to be commonality there. The variability is in the style of traversal, and we can well imagine using an iterator to visit each element in turn to apply a function that is selected according to a parameter ("audit" or "traverse"). This approach is sometimes called *delegated audits*, in which audits are not a domain in their own right but a responsibility of critical data structures. Auditing has historically been a domain in its own right in many of these systems. There are some plausible technological arguments for factoring audits into a separate domain. First, it is sometimes necessary to audit data structures against each other. This means that there needs to be an independent agent that audits multiple data structures against other aspects of system state. Second, audits use their own clever strategies and tricks for auditing, tricks that build on domain knowledge specific to auditing itself, tricks that go beyond the expertise of the designers of the data structures. Such tricks might depend on the underlying hardware or software platform, and it is best to factor them into a domain of their own instead of distributing the knowledge about the system. Third, audits need to be scheduled like any other system activity and audit scheduling needs its own locus of control. Even if these reasons are lost to history, one might take a cue from the presence of a well-formed audits organization in historical developments for a given product line and follow such strong traditions instead of submitting to overly technical analyses. As a rule of thumb, it's easier to deal with imperfect software structures than to change an organization. That rule of thumb sometimes guides domain formulation.

When we talk about variability, the backdrop of commonality is often implicit. That means that the vocabulary of the *variabilities* in the *application* sometimes provides hints about *commonalities* in the *implementation*. Variability in implementation, assuming common behavior, points to inheritance. For example, all matrix abstractions (sparse, identity, upper- and lower-diagonal, and so on) *behave* alike (all can be added, multiplied, and divided with other matrices) but implement their operations and data structures differently. Therefore there should be an inheritance relationship between matrix abstractions. If we talk about variations in the signature of a function, we imply some commonality. We might capture that commonality as a family of overloaded functions, all sharing a common name (as with the algebraic operations for matrices).

7.1.2 Degrees of Complexity

Designers face problems that cover a wide range of complexity. Simple design problems can be coded up directly; difficult ones require more planning, introspection, and analysis. We can develop a simple model of complexity ("all models are lies, many models are useful") to illustrate how multi-paradigm design contributes to design robustness.

We often think of complexity in terms of scale, either in lines of code or numbers of people. But some voluminous projects are conceptually simple (large databases of satellite data still use proven database techniques), and populous projects vary in what we intuitively call complexity. What makes a project complex?

We use abstraction to address complexity. The more complex a problem is, the more we must use abstraction to understand it. Some projects seem easy to decompose into abstractions. Most design methods use hierarchical refinement, building either on top-down or bottom-up strategies. Hierarchical organization seems to be hardwired into the Western mind; it dominates the way we formulate abstractions and organize the world. If a project lends itself well to hierarchical refinement, it really doesn't look that complex—we can choose to view it from an arbitrary level of detail.

There are many kinds of design hierarchy. First and foremost came procedural decomposition—algorithms building on other algorithms. A related but richer hierarchy can be found in block-structured design, whose primary structure follows procedural decomposition, but whose design rules accommodate the scoping of data along with the procedures. Object-*based* programming uses "implementation hierarchy" [Booch1994] to build hierarchies of objects. Object-*oriented* programming augments object-*based* programming with hierarchies of classes that comply to a common interface.

We also find paradigms that are less hierarchical in nature. Among these is the seldom-practiced functional paradigm, which serves languages such as FP, ML, and Tim Budd's **leda** language [Budd1995]. But it's important to remember that many popular paradigms, such as relational databases [Date1986], also depart from the hierarchical model.

Some projects are so complex that they defy common abstraction techniques. What makes many of these projects complex is their lack of a *single* hierarchy. Complex systems exhibit many interacting hierarchies. If we were to use top-down techniques to formulate abstractions for these systems, we would have to analyze them from many "tops."

A telecommunications system has a call processing top, a billing top, a maintenance top, an operations top, an evolution and administration top, a fault-tolerance top, and many others. The abstraction trees beneath these tops interfere with each other in pernicious ways. This is what makes systems complex. *Complexity is proportional to the number of distinct, meaningful views of a system.*

Where does multi-paradigm design fit into this application taxonomy? We can use multi-paradigm design in several different ways to tackle different classes of problems. These problems lie on a spectrum that ranges from uniform application of a single paradigm in a single domain to the application of multiple paradigms across multiple, tangled subdomains. Consider the number of meaningful views for the examples in each of the following cases.

Single Domain, Single Paradigm

This is the simplest case: building a single family of products, all of which obey one set of commonality and variability categories (commonality and variability categories were introduced in Section 2.3).

> *Example:* There aren't too many real-world examples because the world is rarely this simple. However, a family of sorting algorithms may fall into this category if the algorithms are truly independent.

Multiple Decoupled Subdomains, Single Paradigm

Designing a system with multiple domains, all using the same paradigm, isn't qualitatively different from the case for a single domain and paradigm. The project can still use a single tool set and single training program. Each domain has its own vocabulary that is relevant to the domain's business interests, but all abstractions are the same "shape."

> *Example:* Think of software that monitors an industrial control process. Object-oriented design may be used for the architecture of the software that interacts with industrial implementation, since the object paradigm is often a good fit for physical devices. Object-oriented design may also be used for the system graphical interface, which is a different domain in the same system.

Multiple Decoupled Subdomains, Single Paradigm for Each Subdomain

Such a project can be run as multiple, independent projects that contract with each other through well-defined interfaces and mechanisms.

Each project has its own tools and design methods. The software of one domain can communicate with the software of another domain either in terms of the other domain's paradigm or through a globally agreed-upon interaction paradigm (procedures, objects, messages, database, and so on).

> *Example:* An example is an inventory tracking system, with product lines for data management (database paradigm) and human interfaces (object paradigm).

This is the class of problems we focus on in this chapter.

Multiple Decoupled Subdomains, Multiple Paradigms for Each Subdomain

Many projects fall into this category. Multi-paradigm design helps identify the parameters of variation for each domain and the paradigms that translate those parameters into design structures. Multi-paradigm design does not stipulate how to weave these paradigms together. However, the design dimensions are often orthogonal, and an experienced C++ designer can usually foresee the "obvious" design that mixes the paradigms together.

> *Example*: A *FILE* domain may have both *CHARACTER SET* and *RECORD FORMATTING* as parameters of variation. *CHARACTER SET* becomes a template parameter. *RECORD FORMATTING* can be handled with inheritance (both for the supporting data structures and the algorithms that format those structures to and from disk). The design looks generally like this:

```
template <class CharSet>
class File {
public:
    virtual int read(const CharSet*);
        . . . .
};

template <class CharSet>
class WindowsFile: public File<CharSet> {
public:
    int read(const CharSet*);
        . . . .
};
```

We address this level of complexity in Chapter 8.

Multiple Subdomains in a Directed Acyclic Graph (DAG), Multiple Paradigms

One domain may depend on another. If the dependency graph contains cycles, then the graph behaves as though it has infinitely deep dependencies. There is no problem as long as subdomain dependencies form a directed acyclic graph (DAG): Each subdomain can treat other domains as modular, self-contained units.

> *Example:* Consider a compiler example. Both the *Parser* and *Code Generation* domains depend on the *Machine Architecture* domain. The architecture may in turn have *Instruction Mappings* and *Word Characteristics* as parameters of variation. *Word Characteristics* may be a domain in its own right that can be parameterized as little-endian or big-endian, with a length in bytes and with specific fill and alignment characteristics for primitive hardware types.

Circular Subdomains

It is possible—and common—for domains to take each other as parameters of variation. Consider the classic trio of domains *Model*, *View*, and *Controller* *(MVC)*. The *Model* domain represents application information such as application state that might be of interest to other clients (usually a person interacting with the software). The *View* domain presents an abstracted view of the *Model* information, usually on a human/machine interface. The *Controller* domain dispatches user input to the *Model* and the *View* domains. These classes obey a set of simple update protocols to keep the *View* in synchronization with the *Model*. For example, all interested *Views* register themselves with the *Models* whose data they care about; all *Models* notify interested views when an interesting application state change occurs. These protocols are independent of the application semantics, which implies that no *Model*, *View*, or *Controller* can depend on any specific version of the other two. But these three domains often fall short of this idealized decoupling because each domain often depends on details in one or both of the other two domains.

Consider an entry form application,[3] perhaps for a spreadsheet, for which the form itself is a special kind of view. The *EntryForm* domain takes data fields of the *Model* as parameters of variation; it builds a

---

[3] The example is inspired by an EntryForm pluggable view once posted on the World Wide Web by Alan Wills, alan@cs.man.ac.uk.

form so that users can view and change those data fields through the *ENTRYFORM* view. The model shouldn't depend on a particular *ENTRYFORM* or controller, though it must support behaviors common to all models (such as alerting the *VIEW* when its contents change). The *CONTROLLER* depends on the structure of the particular *ENTRYFORM*, since it must know where text fields, buttons, and slide bars appear on the screen so that it can dispatch mouse clicks and keyboard events in a sensible way. The *ENTRYFORM* depends on the *CONTROLLER*. This is because it may take mouse input and keyboard input that elicit interactive highlighting or take input from a separate process, such as a monitor or a debugger process, for which highlighting should be disabled. In the standard *MVC* framework, this causes coupling at the derived class level; normally, derived classes are coupled only through their base class level interfaces as shown in Figure 7.1.

These dependencies conflict with the classic *MVC* architecture, whose domain dependencies are captured in abstract base class interfaces. Though *CONTROLLER* depends on the interface of the abstract base class `View`, the class `EntryForm`—which is in the *VIEW* domain—depends on `SomeController` in the *CONTROLLER* domain. This design violates the classic *MVC* architecture because *CONTROLLER* depends on the structure of *VIEW* (that is, of *ENTRYFORM*). It goes beyond simple multi-paradigm design because of the circular dependency between

FIGURE 7.1   *Relationships in classic **MVC** and in the more coupled* `EntryForm` *example.*

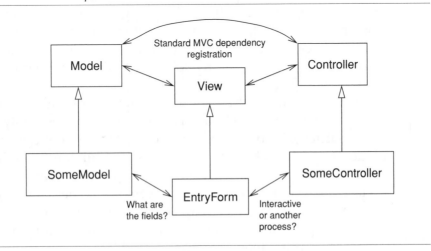

VIEW (*ENTRYFORM*) and *CONTROLLER*. Designers frequently solve this problem by combining *VIEW* and *CONTROLLER* into a single domain. Here, we try to keep them separate and to better understand the design relationships between them.

The trick in such designs is to break the dependency cycle. We can use one coupling technique for one direction of the dependency and another technique—usually based on pointers—for the other direction. Here, we might treat *CONTROLLER* as a "pluggable" class that provides an interface that *ENTRYFORM* can use to teach it about the screen structure at start-up. *ENTRYFORM* can interact with different kinds of *CONTROLLERS* through a single abstract base class interface that generalizes to all family members.

Such designs commonly arise from the coupling between application classes and their I/O interfaces. We defer a more thorough treatment of such designs to Section 8.4.

7.2 Activities of Multi-Paradigm Design

Earlier chapters in the book introduced the building blocks of multi-paradigm design: commonality and variability analysis, and application and solution domain analysis. Now that all of the pieces are in hand, we can consider how to integrate them into a design strategy.

We have studied both application domain analysis and solution domain analysis in depth. Both are specific applications of domain analysis. Design is the activity of aligning the structure of the application analysis with the available structures of the solution domain. Here, we'll call that activity *transformational analysis*. It is an analysis activity—a study of mapping structures—that deals with a transformation across domains.

We can assemble the techniques as steps in an overall design method. This is at least a little misleading, since design rarely proceeds as a predictable sequence of steps. Many of these steps can and should be done in parallel. Staffing profiles and business needs dictate whether some steps, such as application domain analysis and solution domain analysis, might be done concurrently. Some steps may already be complete when a project starts (such as a solution domain analysis of the C++ programming language), thus making it possible to eliminate or abbreviate steps.

As with any method, it's dangerous to treat the steps too literally. The team should engage only in those design activities that carry them to a shared vision of progress. The techniques in this book stand as principles that shape and support design. The team should use them to support broader schedules and business objectives that are peculiar to the project or the business. Roughly, these are the steps of the multi-paradigm design process:

1. *Divide the problem into intuitive subdomains* (Section 4.1.4).
   An experienced designer lets domain experience shape new system architectures. Most high-level system structuring is intuitive. The first-cut "pieces" are independent business areas, each of which has its own history and expertise. (See the discussion about this in Section 7.1.1.)

   Once in a while, we build something entirely new and cannot draw on domain experience for the first-cut architecture. In that case, we analyze the entire problem using the techniques of Chapter 4 (see the following step 3). The design team can seek commonalities in the problem domain and use those commonalities to partition the problem into subdomains. This activity can help develop intuition about the domain.

   This chapter focuses on domains whose subdomains are largely decoupled. One major consideration for good subdomains might be whether they can separately be marketed (Section 4.3.2). If domains are tightly coupled to each other, then they might be combined into a single, larger domain. If there are market forces or other design considerations that suggest that tightly coupled subdomains retain their identity, then the techniques of Chapter 8 apply. Patterns (Chapter 9) may also address this class of problems, if suitable solutions can be found in the patterns of the domain of interest.

2. *Has this been done before?*
   Maybe you want to reuse existing designs before starting from scratch. Multi-paradigm design is a good choice for domains that are immature and not well understood.

3. *Analyze each application subdomain* (Chapter 4).
   Multi-paradigm design, and in particular the activities of commonality and variability analysis, support effective dialogue between designers and customers and within the design team. Application domain analysis is in part a marketing activity

whose job is to assess the breadth of the market for the application and to anticipate how the market will evolve.

Not all domains succumb to multi-paradigm analyses. Some can be implemented with little or no variation across platforms or members of a product line and with little variation over the life of the product. These "monolithic domains" often adhere to traditional design practices. We find examples of such domains in embedded systems, such as overload control, processor maintenance, and other domains. Commonality analysis can help designers partition these domains, but they won't have the same kinds of "hot spots"—parameters of variation—as we find in domains that represent software families. Some domains aren't easily separated from others, and the designer must manage the coupling between them using techniques such as those described in Chapter 8.

Most application domain analysis foresees available solution techniques. This means that application domain analysis should either proceed concurrently with solution domain analysis or proceed with an eye to previous solution domain analyses.

A project may renew its application domain analysis on successive releases.

4. *Analyze the solution domains* (Chapter 6).

A project typically has many solution domains at its disposal. This book focuses on C++ as a solution domain, and (in Chapter 9) it accommodates common *solution* domain patterns as well. Both for C++ and for patterns, the solution domain analysis activities are complete; for C++, just use Chapter 6. Looking ahead to how you will align the application analysis with the solution space, familiarize yourself both with relevant solution domain patterns and with patterns relevant to the application domain. Think of patterns as a separate kind of solution domain, one that should be considered early: It's better to build on past successes than to reinvent the experience yourself. Patterns may not make commonalities and variabilities explicit, even though commonality analysis is one of the underlying themes of pattern-based design (see Section 9.1). You should not feel compelled to recast patterns into commonality and variability analysis terms; use them as they stand. However, some patterns *can* be captured in the multi-paradigm design framework. We will discuss this topic further in Chapter 9.

Some solution domains are a better fit than others for a given problem domain. A design team can often build on past experience to select suitable solution techniques. For example, a trouble tracking system might build on databases as one solution domain and a GUI-builder as another. This step of multi-paradigm design might take the solution outside the realm of objects or C++. One could arrive at the database-and-GUI solution using the techniques developed in this book. However, this book can only touch the surface of all available solution techniques; for example, it doesn't have anything specific to say about databases or GUI-builders. Even if it did, wholesale use of the formal techniques is overkill. Multi-paradigm design works best for solution domains that are specific to a programming language, supporting those design decisions that trade off one language feature against another.

The design problem is more challenging in new domains. The application domain analysis often strikes the designer's intuition about a suitable solution domain technique. That technique joins other stock techniques (such as those analyzed in Chapter 6) as candidates for solution domain analysis.

The designer might be tempted to do a comprehensive analysis of all available solution techniques, testing each for a good fit to one of the application domain analyses. Such a blind search is rarely cost-effective. We should build on experience when possible and on the intuition of respected designers otherwise. Multi-paradigm design becomes an audit for that intuition and provides techniques and vocabulary to regularize the design.

5. *Map from application domain analysis onto available solution domain analyses* (Chapter 7).
   This is the core of multi-paradigm design because it tackles one of the main problems of design: selecting an implementation structure that fits the problem. We analyze each application domain for its commonality categories, binding time, instantiation, and defaults. These parameters together direct the designer to a solution paradigm: objects, templates, template specialization, overloading, or whatever.

Transformational analysis frequently points to classes and inheritance—the object paradigm—as the appropriate solution domain technique. There are many tools, techniques, and methods beyond multi-paradigm design that leverage the object paradigm more fully than described here. It is wise to build on these mainstream techniques—*if* multi-paradigm design or experience show that they are applicable to the domain of interest.

Mature solution domains such as client/server architectures, human interface design, distributed processing, and fault-tolerant computing now enjoy a growing body of pattern literature describing stock patterns for general problems [PLoP1995], [PLoP1996], [PLoP1998]. Patterns can short-circuit much of the effort of design by raising the level of design reuse.

Any single project may use several solution domain techniques. It even may be feasible to use multiple programming languages within a single project. Project management must carefully balance the technical suitability of multiple solution domain tools with pragmatic concerns such as education and tool support.

For more on this approach, see the book by Lai and Weiss [Weiss1999].

6. *Evaluate opportunities for Application-Oriented Languages (AOLs).* Sometimes it's difficult to find *any* implementation domain technology that fits the application domain well. The commonalities and variabilities of the domain may not fit any existing solution domain structures. It's often best to build a custom solution domain structure for such problems, that is, build a new language specifically for the domain. Such languages are called application-oriented languages (AOLs) (also "application-specific languages" and "little languages" [Bentley1988]). This is one of the central strategies of the FAST method [Weiss1999] and was discussed briefly in Chapter 1.

Even if existing solution techniques are a good structural fit for the problem, they may prove economically infeasible or fall prey to other pragmatic considerations. For example, we may want to design a language for a pigment-mixing control language in a fabric dye application. We could represent pigments as classes and use overloading (for example of `operator+`) to express the mixing of pigments. Some semantics of this problem could be captured by an AOL, but they can be dealt with gracefully in C++ only at run time. For example, we might want to include pigment properties such as acidity and alkalinity in the type system—certain alkaline pigments should not be mixed with certain acetic pigments! An elaborate class system might address that. But consider this example: Though pigments of classes A and B may be mixed, and pigments of classes B and C may be mixed, pigments of classes A and C may never be mixed. A C++ rendition couldn't easily catch this error at compile time:

```
A a;
B b;
C c;
Dye d;
d = a; // mix in initial pigment
d = d + b + c; // whoops, mixing pigments we shouldn't
               mix
```

If we parsed this same statement in an AOL, the language processor's semantic analysis could pick up the error—it understands domain rules that C++ compile-time semantic analysis can't.

AOLs can be more expressive than C++; this is particularly important for languages targeted to inexpert users. This expressiveness goes hand-in-hand with convenience. That's why languages such as **yacc** and **lex** exist. They don't do anything that can't be done in C++, but they succinctly (more or less) express the domain semantics in their syntax.

AOLs are frequently motivated by automatic code generation—an unusual motivation if you think about it. The goal isn't to generate lots of code—code takes memory to store and time to run, so more code means more cost. The insightful benefits are convenience of programming and, in the long term, ease of maintenance.

These benefits come with some costs and downsides. A good AOL is difficult to design and expensive to maintain. Time will uncover opportunities to improve on the initial language design, but it's costly for legacy programs to track changes in the programming language in which they're written. Unless language design foresees evolution perfectly, there will be pressure to change the language, and such change is expensive.

A good AOL enjoys a rich support environment with analyzers, debuggers, and translators that can easily be retargeted across platforms (operating systems, processors, and so on). Each environment must be kept current with all platforms used by the project; this can increase the technical head count. The support cost increases with the number of distinct AOLs that have been deployed. The benefits of an AOL—convenience of programming, static analysis, formal verification, debugging, automatic documentation generation, and optimization—must outweigh the cost of developing and maintaining it.

7.3 Example: A Simple Language Translator

This example will use procedural design to build a recursive-descent parser, with object-oriented design for symbol table information. Compilers typically contain code for multiple well-defined subdomains: lexical analysis, parsing, semantic analysis, code generation, and others. The domains are largely disjointed. And each of these domains can best be managed using a single mainstream paradigm.

7.3.1   Partitioning the Domain into Subdomains

As we discussed in Section 4.2, it is important to divide the application domain into disjoint subdomains. An ideal subdomain contains code that can be reused in other applications. For example, the symbol table management code written for the compiler should meet the needs of the link editor, the debugger, and other software generation tools.

Choosing a Partitioning

We don't use a formal process to factor the problem into subdomains; rather, we rely on the intuition of experienced designers. A designer who has seen and built many compilers knows the gross recurring patterns of architecture that all compilers share. These domains typically include the following:

- Lexical analysis
- Parsing
- Semantic analysis

- Symbol management
- Code generation
- Optimization

How do we know that these are good domains and that this is a good partitioning? Ideally, the partitioning is modular with domains that are cohesive and decoupled. Some domains may be independently marketable in their own right; that is often a sufficient (though not necessary) condition for a good domain. Domains should overlap as little as possible and interfere with each other as little as possible. We don't want to find the same commonalities in multiple domains. In a simple compiler, lexical analysis, parsing, and semantic analysis are independent "phases." Lexical analysis is a cohesive activity; its code does one thing and does it well. In the ideal case, a lexical analyzer shouldn't have to worry about parsing issues. We can claim that lexical analysis and parsing are decoupled enough to be separate domains.

In a practical compiler for a rich language such as C++, or even for a portable assembler such as C, the domains can't be perfectly separated. One important design consideration is the interaction between domains such as lexical analysis and syntax analysis or between syntax analysis and semantic analysis.

Even at this level, the partitioning may reflect the programming language used to implement the compiler. A programming language may have primitives for lexical analysis; for example, it is unlikely that a compiler written in SNOBOL would have a separate lexical analysis module. Even more language sensitivity arises at the next level, inside the individual domains. For example, a design based on a parser generator such as **yacc** has a much different structure than one based on a hand-coded recursive-descent parser. But both parsers would have the same relationship with the symbol table management and code generation domains—unless the parser generator, or other implementation technology, provides parameters of variations that we would ordinarily ascribe to symbol management or code generation.

Domain Analysis

We have established a starting point for analysis by dividing the application into domains based on our experience writing compilers. Now, we need to broaden the analysis. Broadening the analysis improves prospects for reuse, as described in [[Coplien1992], Chapter 8]. We can broaden the analysis in two phases. First, we want to look at the (obvious) application of these subsystems to the family of tools that work with and support the compiler: the assembler, the link editor, the browser, and so on. Second, we want to broaden to the families of tools that support language translation in general, including compilers for other languages.

Assume that the domain analysis was originally done to create a family of C language support tools. Does it follow that the analysis extends to tools for other languages? It is difficult to regularize the interplay between lexical analysis and parsing that arises from constructs such as `typedef`. When we do commonality analysis across languages, we find variability in the parsing complexity of the language. Some are LL grammars, some are LR(0) grammars, some are LR(1) grammars, and so on. The parsing complexity of the language affects context sensitivity and therefore the independence of lexical analysis, parsing, and semantic analysis. For example, the designer of a C compiler may choose to push the recognition of `typedef` names into the lexical analyzer so that the grammar can deal with `typedef`s just as it can deal with any other type. For example, given the statement

```
typedef int Int;
```

it follows that the language production

```
type_name decl_list
```

should accommodate both of the following source statements

```
int a, b;
Int c, d;
```

The lexical analyzer can identify `typedef` names by consulting with the parser. The designer has another alternative, though, by using a grammar that accepts productions of the form

```
name decl_list
```

where the first name is presumed to be a type identifier, a presumption that must be validated in semantic analysis. Such a grammar relieves the lexical analyzer of the burden of recognizing `typedef`'d names as valid type names (perhaps at the expense of tighter coupling with semantic analysis). Architectural trade-offs such as this affect the details of the commonality analyses for each subdomain. They also affect the independence of the subdomains and the modules used to implement them.

The "Glue" Domain

Some abstractions transcend individual domains. In a compiler, we will find string in all subdomains of analysis. Where does it belong? We follow common sense and put string in a separate domain of basic building blocks. Support for these abstractions can often be found in standard libraries, in commercially available support packages, and in common or standard operating system APIs. These are sometimes called "toolkits," as in the GOF book [Gamma1995]. They are usually familiar enough to merit little formal analysis.

Domain Analysis and Iteration

Once domain analysis is complete, the designer should revisit the subdomains to ensure that good partitioning criteria are still met. Domain analysis may broaden or skew abstractions in ways that change the coupling between domains. Such a shift in coupling may suggest changes in subdomain boundaries. If so, the problem should be repartitioned into subdomains based on the newfound understanding (usually by doing some fine-tuning). The process iterates until it converges.

For example, imagine that the initial compiler design comprised the domains of *Parser*, *Code Generation*, *Symbol Management*, and others. The hardware architecture would be one parameter of variability for the *Code Generation* domain, but we would presume that other domains are insulated from the hardware. Design experience might show that the compiler front-end (the parser) can take advantage of hardware characteristics to generate more compact parse trees, which in turn result in more efficient code. For example, the hardware may provide instructions that dispatch case statements directly—this would be of value to the parser. The designer can take advantage of these architectural features by capturing them in a separate *Machine Architecture* domain. Both the *Parser* domain and *Code Generation* domain can use the *Machine Architecture* domain as a parameter of variation.

7.3.2 Finding the Right Paradigms within a Subdomain

Once we identify subdomains, we must design and implement each one. If we have chosen our domains well (and if we have the good fortune to work on an easily partitionable system), most design at this level can proceed without interference between domains. Each domain must be partitioned into manageable parts, such as algorithmic steps and object structures. We may be able to group these parts into abstractions, such as functions and classes. Both the parts and the associated abstractions should support product evolution by hiding design secrets (modularity) and by aligning their interfaces with the stable characteristics of the subdomain that contains them.

The choice of paradigm within a domain is often obvious for an experienced practitioner in the domain. But new domains challenge the designer to choose the right paradigm to meet software maintainability goals. To find the right paradigm, we analyze the subdomain for commonality and variability using the techniques of Chapter 2. Let's investigate the SYMBOL MANAGEMENT subdomain of the compiler, choose a paradigm, and find the important abstractions of that subdomain.

Some paradigms are supported by C++, as we found in Chapter 6. We try to use those paradigms to express the commonality and variability in the SYMBOL MANAGEMENT subdomain.

The Domain Vocabulary

The SYMBOL MANAGEMENT domain is an important part of any compiler. We can think of SYMBOL MANAGEMENT as a module in the sense that it can be separately designed, developed, and configured. If we use domain analysis to drive analysis and design, then a well-designed symbol management model suits not only the compiler, but also the assembler, link editor, debugger, and other tools.

The first step of domain analysis is to capture the domain vocabulary. Figure 7.2 presents a first-cut at the vocabulary for the SYMBOL MANAGEMENT domain. These are terms familiar to practitioners in the domain. Many of the terms are familiar also to external clients of symbol tables: the people who use compilers, debuggers, and link editors.

Commonality Analysis of the Domain

Now that we have established a vocabulary, we start looking for structure in the domain. Some vocabulary items group naturally with others. Each of these groupings forms a family of abstractions. The family members share properties in common and distinguish themselves by their variabilities. If we codify these commonalities and variabilities, we can align them with programming language features that

FIGURE 7.2 *Symbol management vocabulary.*

Typedef: A `typedef` clause, alias for another type

Identifier: Any identifier for a user-defined type, function, "variable," or label

Function name: The fully qualified name for a freestanding or member function

Line number: Source line number within a compilation unit

Label: For `goto`

Size: Size, in bytes, of a data element

Structure tag name: . . .

Address: . . .

Offset: . . .

Storage class: . . .

Scope: . . .

Alignment: . . .

express these design dimensions directly. We capture that analysis in a variability table. The result will be a paradigm, or lists of paradigms, suitable to each domain.

Note that we don't go directly from the domain vocabulary to the variability table. We use our intuition to shape the abstractions of the domain wherever possible. We can use rules of thumb to guide this intuition by suggesting likely places to look for abstractions with a broad commonality base. Weiss [Weiss1999] suggests looking at the design from three perspectives, in the following order:

1. Abstractions in the external interfaces of the domain
2. Units of work in the domain (for example, internal states and state transitions)
3. Everything else

The symbol domain is simple, and its groupings are intuitive. The vocabulary entries TYPEDEF, IDENTIFIER, FUNCTION NAME, STRUCTURE TAG NAME, and LABEL are all kinds of *names*. They establish a range of values for some parameter of variation, so each of them probably appears as a single row in a commonality analysis table. The subdomains SCOPE, ALIGNMENT, SIZE, OFFSET, LINE NUMBER, STORAGE CLASS, and ADDRESS are all attributes of symbol table entries. We may think of a LINE NUMBER as a special (implicit) kind of label that delineates a place in the code; for the time being, we can think of it as a degenerate kind of NAME.

We follow our intuition and establish NAME as a commonality domain. NAMES are an abstraction over the entries TYPEDEF, IDENTIFIER, FUNCTION NAME, STRUCTURE TAG NAME, and LABEL that we find in the domain dictionary. All *Names* are the same in many respects. We want to capture and characterize that commonality to drive the commonality analysis. What characteristics do all *Names* share? They all behave similarly, and we can store them in the symbol table, organize them into search tables, ask for their name string, and so on. We find commonality of *behavior*. Following business intuition, we derive the primary commonalities from abstractions in the published (external) interface of the domain.

Our experience and intuition may tell us that *Line Numbers* and *Labels* are not part of the *Names* subdomain. A *Line Number* just isn't a *Name*! We can think of a broader domain—perhaps *Symbol*—that accommodates both *Line Numbers* and the other symbol table attributes we ascribed to the *Names* subdomain. At this point in analysis, we could yield to this intuition and abstract one level higher. If we treated all these vocabulary entries as *Symbols*, we miss an important axis of commonality that ties *Names* together. So we still treat *Names* as a subdomain and will come back and either fit *Names* into the more abstract *Symbol* domain along with *Line Numbers* and *Labels* or deal with *Line Numbers* and *Labels* as negative variabilities.

We also know that most (though perhaps not all) *Names* have some form of address or offset and some designation of the scope in which they are found. These are structural elements or data fields common to all *Names*. We find commonality of *structure*. This follows Weiss's suggestion about the second place to look for commonality: internal state. Another facet of internal structure—the algorithms used to build disk representations of *Name* structures—can be thought of either as common internal structure or as common external behavior. Both suggest the same grouping around the *Name* abstraction.

Does the solution domain offer mechanisms to express these commonalities? If we look at the Commonality column of Table 6.2, we find an entry for "Related Operations and Some Structure." C++ can capture and express that commonality, so we go with it.

We now understand how *Names* are alike. How are they different? Even though all *Names* use the same rudimentary routines that format symbol table entries for the disk image, we find a family of algorithms whose members vary with the type of symbol table entry.

We capture the differences, or variabilities, in a commonality table as in Table 7.1. The major variability is the kind, or type, of symbol: typedef, identifier, function name, label, line number, or structure tag name. We bind the type to a given family member at run time; this allows us to reason more abstractly about the type in the application code that uses symbol abstractions. Looking again at the "Related Operations and Some Structure" row in the language commonality table (Table 6.2), we see that for a variability in algorithm, data structure, and state and for run-time binding, we should use C++ virtual functions. The main paradigm we will use for this design will be the object paradigm. We record that mapping as an italicized annotation in the final column of the SYMBOL TYPE row of Table 7.1. (Italicized items in the table are annotations we add to the table during transformational analysis.)

We go through the remaining rows of Table 7.1 in the same way. We deal with SCOPE using enums, with LAYOUT using inheritance, with ALIGNMENT using simple data value variation, and with STORAGE CLASS again using enums. Because we choose virtual functions to support the previous type variability, inheritance is already implied. The inheritance that supports variability in layout falls along exactly the same lines as the inheritance that supports the virtual function variability that expresses different symbol types, so there is nothing new we need to do for LAYOUT. Dealing with data value variation is always trivial; note that the design accommodates data structure and state in the row we had chosen from Figure 6.2. Enumerations behave much like data values: They just "go along for the ride" in the classes that we organize into the inheritance hierarchies.

Note that two rows of the table are almost the same. The second row captures the variability by symbol type: typedef, identifier, function, and so on. The last row captures the variability in formatting algorithms. Each row defines a separate range of variability. However, these two parameters of variation cause the same kinds of changes in the design: run-time structure and formatting. We say the two parameters of variation are *covariant*—the formatting algorithm is germane to the symbol type. Both rows suggest the same paradigm (virtual functions) as a solution, so we can think of one of the rows as being superfluous (either the first or the last, but not both). Project documentation should capture the description of both parameters if the rows are folded together. Or the table can be left as shown.

We depict this condensation graphically using a *variability dependency graph* as in Figure 7.3. The nodes of the graph are subdomains. The central node represents the focus of the current analysis, the NAME

TABLE 7.1 *Compiler Transformational Analysis for Commonality Domain: NAMES (Commonalities: Structure and Behavior)*

Parameters of Variation	Meaning	Domain	Binding	Default
Symbol value *Object value*	The actual name of the function, identifier, and so on.	[a-zA-Z_] [a-zA-Z0-9_]*	Run time	None *Value of state*
Symbol type *Structure,* *Algorithm*	A major category of the symbol's use and meaning	`typedef`, identifier, function name, label, line number, `struct` tag name	Run time	None *Virtual* *functions*
Scope *Data*	The scope in which a symbol appears	Global, file, function, class	Run time	None `enum`
Layout *Algorithm* *(because an* *algorithm* *generates the* *layout)*	Different symbols carry differing amounts of state and have unique layouts in the symbol table file	`typedef`, identifier, function name, label, line number, `struct` tag name	Compile time	None *Inheritance*
Alignment, size, offset, address *Data*	Data value attributes of symbol entries	Variously constrained integers	Run time	0 *Data values*
Storage class *Data*	A description of how a data item is stored in the application program	`register`, `static`, `auto`, `extern`	Run time	0 `enum`
Symbol table formatting *Algorithm*	Each symbol has its own appearance in the object file	Irregular	Run time	None *Virtual* *functions*

domain. The surrounding nodes represent the parameters of variation, labeled with the parameter names. Later (in Section 8.4), we treat parameters of variation as subdomains in their own right, and the arcs in the graph capture domain dependencies. Parameters of variation *do* correspond to domains, even here, but for the time being we'll call on the notation only to capture the relationships between a domain and its parameters of variation. I have omitted the variabilities we can express as differences in data value, since they don't affect the structure of the abstraction.

In addition to the explicit dependencies in the variability table, there are additional dependencies *between* rows in the table. Figure 7.3 includes arcs between *Layout* and *Symbol Type* and between *Symbol Table Formatting* and *Symbol Type* to show the dependency between those domains. In fact, *Symbol Table Formatting* depends *only* on *Symbol Type*. The parameters of variation *Symbol Table Formatting* and *Layout* are covariant. When two parameters are covariant, we can remove the nonleaf node in the subgraph comprising the two parameters. *Layout* only passes the effects of *Symbol Type* on to the *Names* domain; *Layout* itself contributes nothing else to *Names*. If we do that for all of the parameters of variation in Figure 7.3, we end up with just two nodes in the dependency graph: *Name* and *Symbol Type*, as shown

FIGURE 7.3 *Variability dependency graph for commonality domain:* NAME.

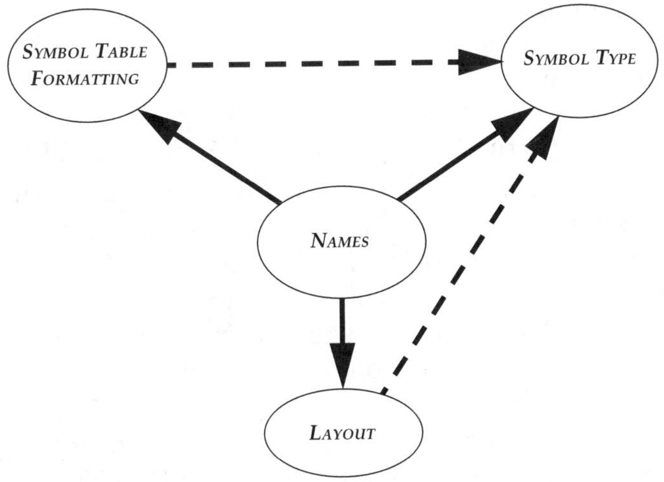

FIGURE 7.4   *Reduced variability dependency graph for commonality domain:* NAME.

in Figure 7.4). If we think of each node in the graph as a domain, then we can treat LAYOUT as part of the SYMBOL TYPE domain. What's important for LAYOUT is (already) important for SYMBOL TYPE.

By using inheritance and virtual functions, we have chosen to use the object paradigm. We arrived at this decision in a roundabout way and reached a conclusion that was probably obvious to many readers before going through the analyses. The reason for the analyses is that they don't always proceed so simply, and it is better to arrive at the object paradigm honestly than to use it where it doesn't belong.

The commonality analysis alone isn't enough. The object paradigm has many other design rules that tell how inheritance should be effectively employed. We should organize the symbol table entries by types into specialization hierarchies and cast those hierarchies directly into inheritance trees. Analyzing the specialization relationships between symbol abstractions isn't part of commonality analysis per se, but it is special to the object paradigm. Commonality and variability analysis get us to the right paradigm with the right parameters of variation. The rest is "SMOP" (a simple matter of programming) to the informed C++ designer.

Returning to the Question of Line Numbers and Labels

We noted previously that LINE NUMBER and LABEL didn't fit well into the commonality analysis. It is time to return to that question. We will discuss two choices here. The first is to treat LINE NUMBER as a kind of negative variability. The second is to solve the problem with a hierarchy of subdomains. The subdomain hierarchy solution is more general and usually leads to more extensible designs than the negative variability approach.

Negative variability (Section 3.3.2) is a way of saying, "The commonalities of a commonality analysis hold, *except* . . . ." We can say that a LABEL or a LINE NUMBER is a NAME, *except* that it doesn't have the type attributes common to other names. We can ignore the type attribute ascribed to *LABELS* in multi-paradigm design and just hope no one ever tries to interpret it sensibly. We can also "turn off" the type attributes at the language level so that the designer doesn't accidentally come to depend on them. How might we do that?

We express commonality within the symbol domain using public inheritance. To express negative variability, we must cancel some base class properties on their way into the derived class. This is called *inheritance with cancellation*. Public inheritance with cancellation is illegal in C++ because it violates the parallelism between class derivation and subtyping that is enforced by the language. The temptation to apply inheritance with cancellation is one of the most recognized forms of negative variability in object-oriented programming languages; see Chapter 6 in [Coplien1992] for a discussion of this problem. We can use one of the other techniques described in Section 6.11, but we should try to avoid a negative variability if we can.

Many negative variabilities can be viewed as positive variabilities from a different perspective. We hinted at this kind of solution earlier. Instead of viewing *LINE NUMBER* and *LABEL* as degenerate kinds of *NAMES* (degenerate in the sense that they have no type information), we could look for more abstract common ground. Is there a higher domain of which both *NAME* and *LINE NUMBER* are subdomains? Yes: Intuitively, we would call that domain *SYMBOL*. Now we have a hierarchy of domains, with *SYMBOL* at the top, followed by *NAME*, *LINE NUMBER*, and *LABEL* beneath it, with *NAME* heading its own subordinate domains.

Because we are using the object paradigm, these hierarchies *are* inheritance hierarchies. It's instructive to note that the top-level domain name we ended up with was *SYMBOL*, which was the domain we chose to start with back at the beginning of Section 7.3.2. We will see this hierarchy in the implementation.

7.3.3   Implementing the Design

At this point, the designer can often capture the structure directly in code. Designers may use an interim graphical representation if they feel it would help clarify the design or if pictures would make the design more accessible to the rest of the development organization. The skeleton code in Figure 7.5 is a direct distillation of the design. The

FIGURE 7.5   *Some C++ class interfaces capturing the analysis of Table 7.1.*

```
class Symbol { . . . . };

    class Name: public Symbol {
    };

        class Identifier: public Name {
        };

            class FunctionName: public Identifier {
            };

        class Typedef: public Name {
        // not an identifier!
        };

            class StructTagName: public Typedef {
            // in C++, a structure tag is a typedef
            };

    class LineNumber: public Symbol {
    };

    class Label: public Symbol {
    };
```

inheritance hierarchy reflects another kind of commonality that we know from the object paradigm: Base classes capture the structure and behavior common to all of their derived classes. Building the inheritance hierarchy becomes a simple matter of sorting the classes by their commonalities.

The commonality analysis has "discovered" that the object paradigm is the best fit for the symbol domain. In one sense, the multi-paradigm techniques have done their job, and at this point, the object paradigm can "take over." Now is the time to get out your Booch and Rumbaugh and to use the subtyping and inheritance rules that work well for inheritance hierarchies.

What if the solution commonality table had no entries that matched the commonality we found in our analysis of symbol management? The designer might be tempted to force the problem into a dimension of commonality that C++ can express. Inexpert designers use inheritance for every commonality on the face of the planet. We want to avoid doing that because it strains the architecture of the resulting system and makes the system difficult to evolve. We need paradigms beyond inheritance, and in general we need paradigms that go beyond what C++ can express. We take up that topic in some measure in Section 7.6 and in broader measure in Chapter 8.

7.4 Design, Not Analysis

Let's step back and look at what we have accomplished. We used our domain knowledge to our advantage. The coarsest architectural divisions came from our intuition, supported by experience in compiler writing. (If you haven't written a compiler, take my word for it.) Other architectures may have worked as well; most problems have multiple satisfactory solutions.

7.4.1   Analysis, Architecture, or Design?

Do multi-paradigm design activities best fit the traditional concept of analysis, architecture, or design? It isn't analysis in the classical sense, since we are organizing domain knowledge, not acquiring it. We have considered structure and partitioning criteria, and we have focused on "how" (in the structural sense), which goes beyond "what" (in the behavioral sense). The same techniques we used here to organize our domain knowledge can be used to help us organize new domain knowledge as we acquire it. We can cluster the vocabulary items into related subsets; this gives us strong hints about the domain structure. But the final partitioning still draws on our insight and intuition. In the best of all possible worlds, the partitioning also draws on our foresight about how the system will evolve: A good architecture encapsulates change. Here, again, experience and intuition are the best guides—history is often the best predictor of the future.

If the first level of architecture is a gross partitioning following application domain criteria, the second level of architecture creates abstractions supported by solution domain structures such as those supported by the programming language. This may seem like an abrupt transition, but I believe both that it is necessary and that it is a more direct transformation than it might first appear to be. C++ allows us to build our own abstractions. By building abstraction on abstraction, we often can raise the level of expressiveness to the same plane as the domain vocabulary. In that sense, C++ is a suitable vehicle to capture and structure the domain vocabulary (though it may be the lowest reasonable level of expression).

Consider the quote from Whorf that we hear so much these days, "Language shapes the way we think and determines what we can express." [Whorf1986] We would have chosen different abstractions even at this second level of architecture (the intuitive domain partitioning is the first level) if the implementation language had been Smalltalk. We would have chosen yet a different architecture if the language had been CLOS, and yet something else if it had been APL. That is why it is important to shape the architecture around the forms and foundations of the programming language. That we shaped the architecture around C++ constructs does not mean that C++ is the "best" or "right" language. We might have derived a different architecture from commonality and variability tables for Smalltalk.

Though multi-paradigm design shapes the architecture according to what the language supports, that does not imply that it is a low-level or back-end technique. Language considerations and concerns touch the earliest design considerations. Programming language is less a consideration of early design than of back-end design and implementation, but that doesn't mean that it is absent at the high levels of abstraction.

7.5 Another Example: Automatic Differentiation

Max Jerrell presents a simple but powerful design that provides automatic differentiation of mathematical functions [Jerrell1989]. In this section, we look at the domains of automatic differentiation and derive a design for such an application. This application demonstrates effective use of design constructs that fall outside object-oriented programming. It also illustrates the difficulty in separating the application and solution domains.

Computers have long been used to calculate and print the values of the derivative for mathematical functions across some range of independent variables. These derivatives can in turn be used for other interesting applications, such as finding local minima or maxima of the original function (because the derivative is zero there). So let's assume that we are trying to solve this problem:

Compute the derivative of a complex function with as much design and programming convenience as possible.

There are three classic techniques for calculating the derivative:

1. Calculate the derivative directly as the slope of the function at a given point, dividing the rate of change in *y* by the rate of change in *x*:

$$f'(x) = \lim_{h \to 0} \frac{f(x+h) - f(x)}{h}$$

The programmer need not derive the formula for the derivative ahead of time. The computer does all of the necessary work, and the derivative for any function f could be captured in an algorithm encapsulated in a function named fprime, perhaps using Newton's method or a straightforward quotient:

```
const double h = 0.001;

double differentiate(double f(double), double x) {
      return (f(x + h) - f(x)) / h;
}
```

But the accuracy is closely related to the value of *h*. This technique may not be suitable for functions with steep derivatives even when an iterative technique is used.

2. Let the programmer differentiate the function (for example, f) manually and encode the derivative as a new function fprime. For example, for the code

```
double f(double x) {
      double a = sin(x);
      return a * a;
}
```

the programmer would write the following difference function:

```
double fprime(double x) {
      return 2 * cos(x) * sin(x);    // derivative of
                                     // sin squared
}
```

However, this makes the programmer do most of the work (working out the derivatives), and it can be slow and error-prone, particularly for long equations.

3. The third alternative is to use *automatic differentiation*. Automatic differentiation asks the programmer to specify simple derivatives; for example, the programmer must tell the computer that the derivative of *sin* is *cos*. But the computer can be "taught" the rules of calculus for the basic operations of addition, subtraction, multiplication, and division. For example, the derivative of a sum is the sum of the derivatives. And we can use the data abstraction of the object paradigm to handle composition. For example, for the expression

```
g(f(x))
```

we can let the computer calculate the derivative information for f(x) and pass the result as an object—with derivative information included—as a parameter to the function g. The derivative information can be passed as a gradient vector (first derivative) and Hessian matrix (second derivative); the formulae for calculating their contents are specified by rules of calculus. The values from all functions—including constant functions and simple parameters—can be treated as a uniform type Value. (This superficial description leaves out many important details, but this is a proven technique, substantiated in the literature, as described in [Jerrell1989].)

We can note—almost in passing—that each of these approaches leads to a different design, each of which is a solution to the same problem. This example illustrates that the structure of the design may not be obvious in the structure of the problem alone. The solution structure emerges when we understand something of the implementation strategy, such as the exact solution technique.

It is often convenient to capture these implementation considerations as part of the problem statement. The original problem definition was cast in the general terms of calculating derivatives. But we might use the following alternative formulation of the problem:

Compute the derivative of a complex function using automatic differentiation.

That seemingly pollutes the problem statement with solution concerns. We'd like to defer solution concerns because binding them prematurely can constrain design options. But if the design options radically change the structure of the problem, they should be made part of the problem. There are many such solution choices that are better treated as requirements: the choice between centralized and distributed processing, the choice between implementation languages, the choice between operating systems or scheduling regimens, and many others. Don't take these too lightly.

We wish to do a software design for an automatic differentiation program: Find the domains, establish their parameters of variation, choose the appropriate paradigms, and write the code.

To find the problem subdomains, we can think of the family groupings that appear in the problem definition shown in Figure 7.6. Basic operations also form a family; a major commonality of this family is that their derivatives can be mechanically derived without too much effort. Do other functions (such as, $f(x) = \sin(x) + \cos(x)$) form a family? In automatic differentiation, we treat them as part of a larger family called *VALUE*. All members of the *VALUE* family share the same structure—matrices and values that capture their state—and they share the same external behavior common to any algebraic expression. Last, there is a parameter of variation, *DEGREE*, that drives the structure of the other two families. We treat this parameter of variation as a subdomain in its own right, consistent with the reasoning of Section 8.4.

7.5.1 Basic Operations Domain

Table 7.2 shows the analysis for the subdomain *BASIC OPERATIONS*. These are the "functions" (addition, subtraction, multiplication, and division) that operate on two arguments—which may be functions, scalars, constants, or other *VALUES*—for which calculus provides formal differentiation rules. Since these functions are so commonly used and their derivatives can be regularized and because they are built-in C++

FIGURE 7.6 *Automatic differentiation domain vocabulary.*

Value: An abstraction that represents an expression, its value, and its partial derivatives, at a specific ordinate value

Basic operations: One of the operations
  *, -, +, /

Degree: The solution has a different structure for problems of different degree (in particular, the shape of the matrices changes)

TABLE 7.2   *Transformational analysis for domain BASIC OPERATIONS (commonalities include arity, argument types, and return types)*

Parameters of Variation	Meaning	Domain	Binding	Default
Operation type *Algorithm*	The algorithm that generates the derivative (and value) varies with the operation type	$*, /, +, -$	Compile time	None *Overloading*
Degree of equation *Structure, Algorithm*	The number of independent variables	Positive integers	Compile time	1 *Global constant*

operations, we can factor them out as a family of common, expressive operations.

7.5.2   Degree Domain

An algebraic expression contains one or more independent variables. The *degree* of the expression is the number of independent variables. We may differentiate an expression with respect to any or all of the variables. Each such derivative is a partial derivative with respect to the corresponding variable. Each member of the BASIC OPERATIONS domain must know the degree of the system it is working on, since it must differentiate its arguments with respect to each independent variable. Thus DEGREE becomes a parameter of variation for the BASIC OPERATIONS domain.

7.5.3   Value Domain

Automatic differentiation evaluation takes place in the same way as any other algebraic evaluation. That is, the innermost subexpressions are evaluated first, and evaluation works outward as results are combined by operations higher in the expression tree. In ordinary algebraic evaluation, the result of each subexpression is a scalar value. In automatic differentiation, that result includes not only the scalar value, but also the coefficients for the first derivative of the expression (the gradient matrix) and the second derivative (the Hessian matrix). This holds whether the expression is constant, a scalar, one of the *BASIC OPERATIONS*, or an arbitrary user-defined function. These abstractions form a family, or domain, as well, which we'll call *VALUE*.

Table 7.3 shows the transformational analysis for subdomain *VALUE*. Notice that the use of the Hessian and gradient matrices is an explicit commonality of this subdomain. This is a bit of a surprise. If one steps back to consider other solution alternatives, such as Newton's method or manual differentiation, these matrices are a variability against the broader background of the universe of differentiation techniques. It's an issue of scope. Here, we are concerned with families of abstractions within the domain of automatic differentiation, *not* the domain of differentiation in general. Automatic differentiation depends on such matrices, and that's what makes *VALUES* an interesting domain.

If we had not chosen automatic differentiation in particular, the top-level domain analysis itself would have been different. The subdomains would have been different for Newton's method than they are for automatic differentiation; symbolic differentiation would be supported by yet another domain structure; and so forth. The choice of solution technologies can alter the domain analysis; this is a solid argument for iterative development. And this is particularly important in new domains.

The Hessian and gradient matrices are a form of structural commonality, thereby suggesting inheritance as an implementation technique. However, this use of inheritance relates not at all to the interface of the base or derived class—it is done solely for the implementation commonalty. In this case, the astute C++ programmer might lean toward private inheritance or even a **HAS-A** relationship. However, we define the family members of the *VALUE* domain using public inheritance, anyhow, in order to capture the variations in algorithm (Table 7.3).

Figure 7.7 shows the variability dependency graph for the previous domains. Note the "domain" *DEGREE*. We don't think of *DEGREE* as a real domain; it simply defines the degree of the equation under study. But it is a parameter of variation for the domains *VALUE* and *BASIC OPERATIONS* and an important aspect of the design.

The *DEGREE* domain is a simple numeric parameter. We might represent it as a global C++ const int, which works fine for a single system

TABLE 7.3   *Transformational analysis for domain VALUES (Commonalities: Includes the use of Hessian and gradient matrices, a representation of the current value, and most behaviors)*

Parameters of Variation	Meaning	Domain	Binding	Default
Calculation of the value and its derivatives *Algorithm*	Each kind of value has its own algorithm for calculating its value, its matrix values, coefficients, and so on.	Constants, scalars, all kinds of functions	Compile time	None *Inheritance*
Degree of equation *Structure, Algorithm*	The number of independent variables	Positive integers	Compile time	1 *Global constant*

of equations. If we are solving multiple systems of equations, we might scope the implementation of each in its own class, each of which has its own value for the degree of the equation. Let's call the symbol NDegree:

```
const int NDegree = 3;      // suitably scoped
```

The *VALUE* domain carries around the value and derivative matrices. We make it a class, since it groups commonly related data items. The declaration looks like this:

```
class Value {
friend Value operator+(const Value&, const Value&);
friend Value operator-(const Value&, const Value&);
friend Value operator*(const Value&, const Value&);
friend Value operator/(const Value&, const Value&);
```

FIGURE 7.7   *Variability dependency graph for automatic differentiation.*

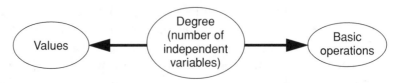

```
public:
    Value():
        gradient(NDegree),
        hessian(NDegree, NDegree) { }
    operator double() const { return value; }
protected:
    double value;
    vector<double> gradient;
    matrix<double> hessian;
};
```

The friend relationships appear only to grant access permission to the common operations.

BASIC OPERATIONS uses straightforward overloading, with the operator itself (+, -, /, or *) being the parameter of variation. We hand-code the algorithms that vary according to the operators, and the compiler selects the appropriate algorithm from context at compile time. The code for the basic operations looks like this:

```
Value operator+(const Value &x, const Value &y) {
    Value f;
    f.value = x.value + y;     // operator double()
                               // eliminates
                               //    the need to say y.value
    for (int i = 0; i < NDegree; i++) {
        f.gradient[i] = x.gradient[i] + y.gradient[i];
        for (int j = 0; j < NDegree; j++) {
            f.hessian[i][j] = x.hessian[i][j] +
                                    y.hessian[i][j];
        }
    }
    return f;
}
```

Each family member must compute not only the (scalar) return value but also its associated gradient and Hessian matrices. It computes these results from the (scalar) values and first and second derivative matrices of its operands. Here are more examples:

```
Value operator*(const Value &x, const Value &y) {
    Value f;
    f.value = x.value * y;
    for (int i = 0; i < NDegree; i++) {
        f.gradient[i] = x.gradient[i] * y + x *
            y.gradient[i];
```

```
            for (int j = 0; j < NDegree; j++) {
                f.hessian[i][j] = x.hessian[i][j] * y
                    + x.gradient[i] * y.gradient[j]
                    + x.gradient[j] * y.gradient[i]
                    + x * y.hessian[i][j];
            }
        }
        return f;
    }


Value operator/(const Value &x, const Value &y) { . . . . }

Value operator-(const Value &x, const Value &y) { . . . . }
```

Specific primitive functions can be added as the application requires them . They, too, take the function (cos, sin, and so on) as the parameter of variation and are selected by the compiler from context at compile time. Here is an example:

```
Value cos(Value &x) {
    Value f;
    f.value = cos((double)x);
    double fu = -sin((double)x);
    double fuu = -f;
    for (int i = 0; i < NDegree; i++) {
        f.gradient[i] = fu * x.gradient[i];
        for (int j = 0; j < NDegree; j++) {
            f.hessian[i][j] =
                (fu * x.gradient[i] * x.gradient[j]) +
                (fuu * x.hessian[i][j]);
        }
    }
}
```

More complicated functions can be written in their natural algebraic form, for example:

```
Value w = exp(t) * cos(omega * t);
```

which uses a suitably defined exp and cos (as previously) function and (twice) uses the overloaded operator*. A framework developer might write code for basic operations, including the four arithmetic functions and other basic functions. Those done, the framework user can write expressions such as the previous one—ordinary C expressions, which now have the intelligence to differentiate themselves.

The reference ([Jerrell1989]) shows how to use such a design for function minimization and explains how the design supports other applications.

This design isn't object-oriented. Multi-paradigm design helped identify appropriate solution techniques such as overloading that capture important abstractions of the problem. Many of these "problem" abstractions foresee the solution structure. That is, it would be difficult to find a single solution structure well-suited to automatic differentiation, Newton's method, and manual techniques.

7.5.4   Evolving the Design

The most important goal of domain analysis is to support reuse and minimize evolution cost. Good design anticipates evolution; good structure accommodates change gracefully. In a good structure, the parameters of variation express what is likely to change.

In this design, there are two levels of reuse. Many users reuse this framework to evaluate the values and derivatives of arbitrary algebraic expressions. New expressions can be written and evaluated without changing any of the framework code on the previous page. We may also want to change the framework itself, "teaching" it new facts of calculus. It should be convenient to make those changes, too.

There are parameters of variation for several subdomains in this design. The design anticipates change in operation type (for the primitive operators), algorithm (for non-built-in operations and functions), and degree. We should be able to change the degree of the system of equations easily. We can, through one global parameter. And we should be able to change algorithms (and, in this case, add algorithms) to calculate the values and derivatives of new functions (for example, if we wanted to add `tan` for trigonometric tangent). We also should be able even to add a new primitive function and the definitions for its computation and derivative.

Let's assume we want to define the semantics of the built-in `operator^` to mean exponentiation. (Of course, we can't add operators that the C++ grammar doesn't understand, and for any built-in operations, we must live with the precedence and association rules those operators obey for C++.) It's a relatively straightforward change—we just need to add the function to the framework:

```
Value operator^(const Value &x, const Value &y) {
    Value f;
    f.value = pow(x.value, y);
    for (int i = 0; i < NDegree; i++) {
        f.gradient[i] = y * x.gradient[i];
        for (int j = 0; j < NDegree; j++) {
            f.hessian[i][j] = x.hessian[i][j] * y
                + x.gradient[i] * y.gradient[j];
        }
    }
    return f;
}
```

7.6 Outboard Paradigms

It is unreasonable to expect a single programming language to capture all conceivable analysis abstractions. General-purpose languages such as C++ are broad, but not deep. Some problems are served well by specific, well-understood paradigms that go beyond those supported by C++. Databases and parser generators are examples of tools that capture important design constructs in an implementation technology. The wise designer avoids forcing such architectural constructs into C++ features by using the right tool for the right job.

We could construct a commonality and variability analysis for all such tools in the designer's toolkit. Multi-paradigm analysis could easily be extended to find the best fit between an application domain analysis and the available solution domains. Here, we leave such an approach as an exercise to the reader—or to the Ph.D. student looking for a thesis topic. Such an exhaustive analysis would be, well, exhausting in practicality. Just as we relied on experience and intuition to divide problems into sensible domains, so we rely on experience and intuition to select the right paradigm for those domains.

Let's return to the compiler example from Section 7.3. One of its domains is parsing. We could do a commonality analysis of the vocabulary of parsing (productions, actions, reductions, targets, and so on) and then look for matching patterns of commonality and variability in the C++ solution domain analysis. With luck, we would fail to find a match. If we were unlucky enough to coerce the analysis to match, we would have "found" a way to design parsers using the design paradigms that C++ supports. We also will have missed the opportunity to use tools such as **yacc** and **bison**, which are perfectly suited to the problems, commonalities, and variabilities of this domain.

The general design strategy, then, is to divide the domain into subdomains according to the tools and techniques that are suited to the problem. C++ alone often will not be enough. We use "obvious" techniques like parser generators, databases, existing GUI frameworks, and state machines as they apply and use multi-paradigm analysis for the remaining subdomains.

7.7 Management Issues

The impact of paradigms and technologies on project success is small relative to that of management policies. This book certainly can't do justice to management practices; one might look to books like the recent work of Goldberg and Rubin [GoldbergRubin1995] for more holistic guidance. Other outstanding sources include [McConnell1997] and [Cockburn1998]. Some of the activities and decision points of multi-paradigm design have clear project management overtones, and we touch on just a few of those closely related issues in this section. Related topics are covered elsewhere in the book: Section 2.2.2, "The Domain Dictionary Team"; Section 2.5, "Reviewing the Commonality Analysis"; Section 4.1.4, "The Activities of Domain Analysis."; and Section 4.3.2, "The Activities of Subdomain Analysis."

7.7.1   Occam's Razor: Keeping Things Simple

There are no prizes for using the most paradigms. A paradigm helps define a culture through its vocabulary and world-view; a shared culture is an invaluable component of a successful development team. A development culture can support only a small number of paradigms and tools. On the other hand, it is important to use the right tool for the right job and to avoid being blind-sided by the stereotypes of a single paradigm. Successful projects balance these two concerns.

Try as they might, organizations rarely avoid becoming dependent on the idiosyncrasies of individual tool versions. That sometimes makes it hard to upgrade the version of one tool without reworking code in the domain of other tools. If the tool inventory is small, the chances increase that a project can move forward to accommodate change in the tool set. If the number of tools is large and if the tools introduce coupling between domains (and hence to other tools), then it becomes difficult for the project to track advances in technology.

My experience working with organizations has borne out a rule of thumb that suggests that organizations can rarely manage more than three "major changes" at once. A "major change" may be a new design paradigm, a new management paradigm, a new hardware platform or operating system, a new language, or a new way of working with customers. Once a project is established, it can accommodate gradual change. The technology choices that shape the long-term system architecture usually come early in the project and usually must be considered and introduced together. The obvious conclusion is that the number of paradigms should be kept small. As time progresses and the system market expands, projects can explore new tools, technologies, and paradigms, particularly if the projects can localize their impact (to a single subdomain, or organization, or processor, or other domain of some local context). New paradigms should be introduced gradually and only against a relatively stable base. Another good rule of thumb is not to introduce new paradigms to a system until it's passed its third release. And we should remember the rule of thumb that limits the number of concurrent changes to three—and the lower, the better.

One strength of multi-paradigm design as presented here is that it strives to use a single, general-purpose implementation platform—the C++ programming language—as the delivery vehicle for a host of paradigms. This greatly minimizes the shock of introducing those paradigms that C++ can express: objects, abstract data types, procedures and generic procedures, parametric functions and templates, and so on. It is tempting, and perhaps possible, to count all of these paradigms as a single paradigm when considering the three-changes rule of thumb. But it cannot help with the paradigms outside the reach of C++: the kinds of multi-threaded execution one finds in Java, the rule-based abstractions of Prolog, or the functional abstractions of ML. Techniques exist to emulate these styles in C++ (see, in particular, the latter chapters of [Coplien1992]). If the programming staff is unusually expert in C++, such paradigms can be accommodated using C++ constructs and can be thought of as not assaulting the three-change limit. But such organizations are rare, perhaps one out of one hundred. (It is probably best for you not to think of yourself as belonging to such an organization, in spite of the human tendency that tugs each of us to that misplaced conclusion.)

Keeping a small tool inventory reduces cost (of tool procurement or licensing). It also reduces training time (and cost) and the cost of other support infrastructure.

Once a project has been divided into subdomains (see the next section), Occam's Razor may yield insights that lead to compromises either in the selection of paradigms or tools. For example, a system might have five domains, four of which are well-suited for implementation in Java (perhaps for concurrency) and one of which is better-suited for implementation in C++ (perhaps for its efficiency). Unless there is a compelling case for the outlier, the project would be better off reducing its tool inventory and adapting the design of the last subdomain so that it can fit a Java implementation.

7.7.2   Divide and Conquer

Most of us are culturally conditioned to attack complexity with a separation of concerns. One measure of a maintainable architecture is the degree to which it can be treated as a collection of independent parts. Such architectures can be maintained by teams that are smaller and more independent than if the same code were organized under a monolithic structure.

Experience, market familiarity, and intuition are often the best foundations for a good domain partitioning. We should try to partition a problem into subproblems that have independently deliverable solutions.

Once the system is subdivided, the designer can evaluate each subdomain for the paradigms best-suited to its structure. It is possible, and even common, for all subdomains to use the same paradigm. That would be a fortuitous result that serves Occam's Razor well. But a project should first formulate its subdomain partitioning, *then* choose the paradigms for each subdomain, and *then* choose the tools to support those paradigms. At that point, enter Occam's Razor to audit whether the project plan is tractable, reasonable, and cost-effective. The whole process is iterative, not only at the outset of a project, but conceivably over its lifetime.

Capturing the Big Picture

Perhaps the hardest question in a multi-language environment is, how do we represent the overall architecture? There still must be a project-level architecture to define the interfaces and protocols between the subdomains. If part of the system is in C++, and part in C, and part in Smalltalk, and part in an AOL, what is the language of the architecture? Mary Shaw and her colleagues have been doing research on architectural definition languages that aspire to fill this need for a language [Shaw1994]. However, such languages have not yet achieved wide acceptance in the industry. It's dangerous to depend on a design notation alone, since notational artifacts are often limited in their expressive power and don't track product evolution well unless they are tied into the code-generation process. One can represent the overall architecture at the lowest common level of technology, close to C function bindings, but then most interesting system structure ceases to be explicit.

The most reasonable choice is to represent the architecture in the dominant programming language of the project. If the project is primarily in C++ and the project tools all support C++ linkage, then we capture the architecture in C++ header files. C++ can serve as the lingua franca for architectural dialogue, covering a multitude of paradigms—including procedures and templates.

Of course, this documentation is only one aspect of the architecture documentation. Notations have a place in system development; more on this shortly.

Another alternative is to generate architectural interfaces from a CASE tool, such as ObjecTime [Selic+1994]. CASE tools tend to suffer from poor linearity of change. That is, a small change to the architecture may ripple through many intermediate design artifacts, thus causing rework (or, at least, recompilation) of large volumes of code. With few exceptions, CASE tools don't express multiple paradigms well—most of them rally around a single paradigm. They often lead to a false sense of security, too. Few domains are regular enough to benefit from automatic code generation. When the designer does find such domains, it's wise to at least consider building an AOL for its benefits of formal analysis and efficiency [Weiss1999].

As a last resort, the C language or a language such as IDL can almost always be used to define interfaces between system parts, since most technologies and tools can interface with C. C is certainly not an ideal module definition language, and it lacks facilities to fluently capture architectural abstraction. But because it is portable and efficient and can be interfaced to many tools and environments, it is a practical and workable vehicle to formalize interfaces between system parts. Sometimes, we need to convert specific data types to a portable representation such as a character string; C language character strings can be directly accessed from many languages.

Notations

A designer sometimes must use multiple notations. Databases are particularly well-suited to tabular notations. Neither database notation nor object-oriented notation should be compromised in the interest of appeasing the other. Where possible, isolate different notations to their own subdomain.

There are other development notations such as use cases [Jacobson+1992], timing diagrams, natural language descriptions of nonfunctional requirements, and formal specifications that can serve a project well. Seminotational tools such as CRC cards [Beck1993] build on the team's domain expertise to converge on the best structures for object-oriented designs. When we use multiple tools and techniques, it's crucial to minimize the total number of tools, notations, and languages. Multiple languages help each part of a development team optimize their expressiveness, but multiple languages can also get in the way of effective communication between teams within a project. Training and cross-team membership provide classic attacks on these problems, but the most effective solution is to reduce the inventory of tools.

7.7.3 Beyond C++

While this book focuses on the paradigms supported by C++, the designer should carefully consider other solution domain tools, including the following, each of which addresses an important class of problems that are quite distant from the fundamental structures of C++:

- Database management systems
- GUI-builders
- Distributed processing frameworks
- Custom commercial languages such as Java Script
- AOLs crafted for the project
- ...

Designers who overlook these tools by forcing all aspects of design into a C++ implementation have the satisfaction of reducing their tool inventory, but they may miss substantial opportunities for design expressiveness, reduced development cost, and maintainability. Some of these alternatives are programming languages in their own right; there's nothing wrong with mixing multiple programming languages. Vendors are realizing the importance of multilanguage support more and more. Many C++ environments support linkages to Pascal and FORTRAN; some Eiffel environments support linkages to C++; and most C, Pascal, and FORTRAN programs can link to C++ using C language bindings (see [Coplien1992], Appendix A).

When using multiple programming languages or tool sets, it is best to map the languages closely to subdomains. Each language or tool set brings its own development culture, and it's important to keep the cultures logically separate.

7.7.4 Domain Expertise

A fool with a tool is still a fool. A classic shortfall of contemporary software development is to expect the object paradigm to make up for immature domain knowledge. This shortfall often builds on the naive view that objects are there just for the picking, that there is a strong isomorphism between the problem vocabulary and the classes of the solution. Multi-paradigm design goes beyond that naiveté by more thoroughly exploring the solution domain space. And while multi-paradigm design offers commonality and variability analyses as application domain tools, those alone cannot make up for immature domain experience. System architects and designers should understand the business thoroughly and should develop early consensus on the scope of the problem. Object-oriented expertise can't rescue you if the team lacks application domain expertise. Because multi-paradigm design focuses explicitly on the application domain (as well as the solution domain), it can make the designer aware of missing information, but it cannot compensate for poorly developed expertise.

Solution domain expertise is also important. The success of a project when using multi-paradigm design (indeed, *any* design) depends on competence with and perhaps mastery of the individual paradigms employed. The techniques in this book lay a foundation both for understanding those paradigms that are easily described using commonality and variability and for understanding the interaction between multiple paradigms in an implementation. But multi-paradigm design is not as mechanical as commonality and variability tables suggest. Good design always depends on taste, insight, and experience.

7.8 Summary

In this chapter, we went through an application domain analysis example, showing how to derive a C++ design and implementation from a commonality analysis. The first step of analysis was to generate a vocabulary. The next step was to divide the problem into subdomains, a process that drew heavily on the designer's experience and intuition. The last step was a special case of simple mixing, in which an individual subdomain offers a perfect fit for a single specialized paradigm and the tools that support it.

Design problems aren't always this easy. The examples in this chapter were a setup guaranteed to produce a design in which each domain could cleanly be implemented in a single paradigm. In such cases, the choice of subdomains and paradigms is trivial. In the next chapter, we look at the more general case of inextricably interwoven paradigms within a single domain.

CHAPTER 8

Weaving Paradigms Together

This chapter introduces notations and techniques to help combine paradigms within a domain and to carry design through to a C++ implementation. The chapter is based on a running text-editor example. It also develops analyses and solutions for a finite-state machine abstraction.

8.1 *Method and Design*

Frameworks usually capture the designs of multiple, tightly coupled subdomains (see the discussion of Section 4.3.1). Most design methods apply the principles of a single paradigm to minimize coupling between software modules. Conventional design techniques break down when coupling is inevitable or advantageous. Coupling and cohesion properties can sometimes be improved by using a distinct paradigm for each domain; Chapter 7 presented techniques that support that approach. But sometimes, we can build the most cohesive and decoupled abstractions by combining multiple paradigms *within* a domain. Some of the combinations are simple and almost idiomatic, such as this common combination of the procedural paradigm and templates:

```
template <class T>
bool sort(T elements[], int nElements) {
    . . . .
}
```

or this combination of templates and object-based abstraction:

```
template <class T> class List {
public:
    void put_tail(const T&);
    T get_head();
    . . . .
};
```

We want to know how to combine other C++ features to meet the needs of the application by using commonality and variability to point the way. Good analysis can suggest combinations of paradigms beyond those that are idiomatic.

Some designs defy clean modularization even with the partitioning techniques of multi-paradigm design described in Chapter 7. Intuitive business domains may exhibit mutual dependencies, thereby leading to coupling between the modules of the design. This chapter explores several attacks on circular dependencies between domains.

8.2 Commonality Analysis: What Dimension of Commonality?

We have now examined both commonality and variability, in both the application and solution domains. We use domain analysis to find commonality in application subdomains, broadening from the abstractions of the application at hand to the abstractions of the business in general. In the solution domain, we look for commonalities in the available technologies and paradigms. We have taken C++ and its paradigms as our solution technology. We can broaden the analysis to accommodate other solution domains if we wish.

Design is the process of aligning the application domain structures with suitable solution domain structures. Said another way, we must align the commonalities and variabilities of the problem with those that constrain the solution. Chapter 7 presented the simple case in which the mapping is one-to-one—a single paradigm dominated each of the subdomains chosen by the designer.

No single partitioning can capture all of the important structure of a complex system. Complexity is proportional to the number of distinct, meaningful partitionings (or views) of a system. In some systems, not only is the object paradigm a poor fit, but *any* single paradigm is a poor fit. It's difficult to motivate this point, since such a proof must demonstrate that a certain kind of architecture cannot exist. However, assume for a moment that the object paradigm might be a great fit for some system you know of. There are programmers—maybe yourself—who had probably built similar systems before the advent of the object paradigm. At the time, those programmers would have combined paradigms—perhaps data abstraction, data-function modularity, and function pointers—to solve the design problem. Such systems certainly exist today, and there are some systems for which no single paradigm will ever adequately express the commonalities and variabilities of the system structure.

Sometimes we are lucky enough that the paradigm partitioning falls along the same lines as the intuitive subdomain partitioning. In such cases, the techniques of Chapter 7 apply perfectly well—we apply paradigms at the individual subdomain or subsystem level instead of at the system level. But we sometimes find that we can't further subdivide the intuitive subdomain partitioning by using just one paradigm per subdomain. Several paradigms must be used together to capture and manage such complexity.

Consider the design of a general file abstraction. A system design may include indexed sequential files, blocked files, and other file types. These have common behaviors but different implementations, which suggests inheritance as an implementation technique. But individual file abstractions may also vary in the character sets they support: `char`, `unsigned char`, `wchar_t`, or a user-defined character set type. This variability shows up in the interfaces of the file family members. This is a different kind of variability, a variability in interface against a backdrop of a common implementation structure; this suggests templates. We could perhaps handle this using the techniques of Chapter 7 if the two application variabilities aligned with each other well. For example, the implementation is straightforward if all indexed sequential files use `wchar_t` and all others use `char`. But the character set partitioning doesn't fall along the same boundaries as the file type partitioning. Rather, the character set and file type can be mixed in any combination.

We must somehow weave these two paradigms together. Neither paradigm alone captures the variability necessary to generate all family members. The designer must generate family members from a genetic combination of the parameters of variation. We will explore this in Section 8.3 using the *TEXT BUFFER* subdomain from a text editor design. *TEXT BUFFERS* form a family, but the family members vary in complex ways that reflect complex dependencies on parameters of variation. We can't use the technique of Chapter 7 to find a single paradigm that captures its structure. Partitioning the subdomain into smaller parts doesn't help much either (though, because the lack of a counterexample is difficult to prove or demonstrate, the rationale is left as an exercise to the reader). We can identify the paradigms that make sense and can develop hints for applying them.

That accomplished, we will move on in Section 8.4 to a more advanced problem: multi-paradigm design for multiple, codependent subdomains. In that section, we will step back and study the relationship between two domains—*TEXT BUFFERS* and *OUTPUT MEDIUM*—that impinge on each others' designs. Ideal subdomains are decoupled from each other. We know that domains are never *completely* independent from each other—after all, their code works together to do the work of a system as a whole. The coupling between any pair of domains can vary widely even when we make the best use of partitioning techniques. Sometimes the coupling is so strong that further partitioning into subdomains would be arbitrary. We need a way to manage the relationship between tightly coupled subdomains when our intuition suggests that they should each retain their own identities so as to serve long-term maintenance, even when tightly coupled to other subdomains.

8.3 *Multiple Dimensions of Variability in One Set of Commonalities*

We can draw examples from the design of a text editor to illustrate the complexities of multi-paradigm design that go beyond the simplistic problem/solution pairs of Chapter 7. In this section, we will examine the *Text Buffer* subdomain in isolation to show how to use multiple paradigms within a single domain.

8.3.1 Variability Analysis

We form and describe abstractions according to their commonalities. Here, we look at *Text Buffers*, a family of abstractions in a text editor that maintain the logical copies of the file contents during editing. (Actually, *Text Buffers* are a generalization of *Text Editing Buffers* (Chapter 3), suitable to many applications beyond text editing.) A text file may reside on disk; the text buffer represents the state of the text file to the editing program. It caches changes until the user directs the editor to dump the text buffer into the disk file. A simple *Text Buffer* would maintain a primary storage copy of the entire file. A more sophisticated *Text Buffer* may implement a paging or swapping scheme to economize on primary memory while maintaining the illusion of a complete resident copy of the disk file's contents. Yet more sophisticated *Text Buffers* might support rollback, simple versioning schemes, or concurrent multiuser editing.

These abstractions form a family. What makes this a family, or subdomain, is that all of the variants share the same behaviors. That is, they can yield data from an editing image or replace data in an editing image on demand. All text buffers share some structure as well: a record of the number of lines and characters in the editing image, the current line number, and so on.

Family members are distinguished by their respective values for parameters of variation. We capture family variabilities with the variability table in Table 8.1. The first column in the table lists the parameters, or ranges, of the variabilities. The second column is explanatory. The third column lists the values that can be taken on over the range. The fourth column lists binding times, and the last column specifies the default.

As we move into multi-paradigm design, the overlap between the domains and ranges of the parameters of variation becomes increasingly important. The variability dependency graphs first introduced in Section 7.3.2 help us visualize such dependencies. We can build such a graph, shown in Figure 8.1, directly from information in the variability analysis table. The arrows originate at domain abstractions of interest and terminate on bubbles representing the parameters of variation.

TABLE 8.1   *Text Editor Variability Analysis for Commonality Domain:* TEXT BUFFER *(Commonality: Behavior and Structure)*

Parameters of Variation	Meaning	Domain	Binding	Default
Output medium	The formatting of text lines is sensitive to the output medium	Database, RCS file, TTY, UNIX file	Run time	UNIX file
Character set	Different buffer types should support different character sets	ASCII, EBCDIC, UNICODE, FIELDATA	Source time	ASCII
Working set management	Different applications need to cache different amounts of file in memory	Whole file, whole page, LRU fixed	Compile time	Whole file
Debugging code	Debugging traps should be present for in-house development and should remain permanently in the source	Debug, Production	Compile time	Production

The graph may look like a hobby horse at this point, but it will serve us well in a bit.

8.3.2   Expressing the Commonality and Variability in C++

We discussed variability in some detail in Chapter 3. Now that we understand how to express variability against a background of commonality, we can look at how to express the design commonality and variability by using C++ constructs. We do this by aligning the results of the TEXT BUFFER variability analysis with the abstractions that a designer can express in C++.

Commonalities characterize a family; variabilities differentiate family members. C++ can express several forms of commonality and variability. We can choose the appropriate C++ language constructs by

FIGURE 8.1   *Variability dependency graph for the* TEXT BUFFER *commonality analysis.*

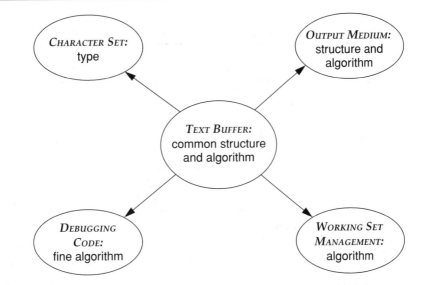

looking at the design commonalities and variabilities, as in Table 8.1, and matching them with the commonalities and variabilities of C++ as summarized in Table 6.2. That table maps the dimension of commonality, the dimension of variability, and the binding time onto a C++ language feature. Binding times express the earliest phase of the coding cycle in which the parameter of variability can be bound. The instantiation column tells whether multiple instances of the same abstraction are allowed; if so, variability in state is presumed. The final column denotes the best C++ construct for a given commonality, variability, and instantiation.

We can look at the structural needs captured in Table 8.1 and align them with the structural expressions captured in Table 6.2 to see what C++ language features are most suitable for different parts of the design. We capture these insights on an annotated version of the variability analysis table, resulting in Table 8.2. We have added three kinds of annotations (distingushed by italicized typeface). First, we remember that the commonality domain was TEXT BUFFERS. We recognize that text editing buffers are characterized by commonality of operations (behavior) and structure. Second, in the "Parameters of Variation"

TABLE 8.2   *Text Editor Transformational Analysis for Commonality Domain: TEXT EDITING BUFFERS*

Parameters of Variation	Meaning	Domain	Binding	Default Technique
Output medium *Structure, Algorithm*	The formatting of text lines is sensitive to the output medium	Database, RCS file, TTY, UNIX file	Run time	UNIX file *Virtual functions*
Character set *Nonstructural*	Different buffer types should support different character sets	ASCII, EBCDIC, UNICODE, FIELDATA	Source time	ASCII *Templates*
Working set management *Algorithm*	Different applications need to cache different amounts of file in memory	Whole file, whole page, LRU fixed	Compile time	Whole file *Inheritance*
Debugging code *Code fragments*	Debugging traps should be present for in-house development and should remain permanently in the source	Debug, production	Compile time	Production `#ifdef`

column, we characterize the range by the variability categories in the C++ commonality table. By looking at the variability of the range variable and reading the binding time directly from the table, we can select a suitable technique from the C++ commonality table. That technique is written as an annotation for the "Default" column of the table (not that it belongs there, but to save columns in the table).

The commonality analysis suggests that we use virtual functions for output (because we need different functions for different values of the parameter of variability *OUTPUT MEDIUM*). Inheritance is necessary for variability in the structure and gross algorithms, and templates are appropriate for the compile-time dependency on the character set.

We usually think of inheritance as an "is a kind of" relationship; inheritance differentiates between kinds of text buffers in this design. We may informally talk about "paged text buffers" and "LRU text buffers," thereby suggesting that we think of the memory management algorithms as the primary differentiators of family members. The row in Table 8.2 labeled "Working set management" might as well have been labeled "Text buffer type." This is often the case when inheritance is used. In fact, we probably use inheritance too often on the mistaken assumption that there is a "primary differentiator."

The resulting code might look like this:

```
template <class CharSet>
class OutputFile {
public:
    virtual void write(
        const class TextBuffer<CharSet> &);
    . . . .
};

template <class CharSet>
class TextBuffer {
public:
    TextBuffer(const OutputFile<CharSet> &);
    basic_string<CharSet> getLine(LineNumber) const { }
    void insertLine(LineNumber, const string&) { }
    void deleteLine(LineNumber) { }
    . . . .
};

template <class CharSet>
class WholeFileTextBuffer: public TextBuffer<CharSet> {
public:
    . . . .
    WholeFileTextBuffer(const OutputFile<CharSet> &);
    basic_string<CharSet> getLine(LineNumber 1) const
        { . . . . }
    void insertLine(LineNumber 1,
        const basic_string<CharSet>&s){
        . . . .
    }
    void deleteLine(LineNumber 1) { . . . . }
    . . . .
};

template <class CharSet>
class LRUTextBuffer: public TextBuffer<CharSet> {
public:
    . . . .
```

```
LRUTextBuffer(const OutputFile<CharSet> &);
basic_string<CharSet> getLine(LineNumber l) const
    { . . . . }
void insertLine(LineNumber l,
    const basic_string<CharSet>&s){
#ifndef NDEBUG
    . . . .
#endif
    . . . .
}
void deleteLine(LineNumber l) { . . . . }
. . . .
};
```

A cursory comparison of the code with the transformational analysis table should be enough to convince the experienced C++ designer that both represent the same design. However, we offer no mechanical transformation from the table to the code. While the coding is often straightforward, good designers often know when to express the transformation through design patterns or idioms that are difficult to codify. By not mechanizing the transformation, multi-paradigm design leaves room for this creative insight.

8.4 Codependent Domains

Section 7.1.2 discussed the MVC example, focusing on the dependencies between pairs of this classic human interface design. We found some circular dependencies, with CONTROLLER depending on the structure of VIEW for knowledge of the screen layout (is the mouse cursor over a button?) and VIEW depending on CONTROLLER to support functionality such as highlighting. We say that these domains are *codependent*. The techniques of Chapter 7 aren't powerful enough to handle such circularity. In fact, it is difficult to regularize solutions for circular dependencies. However, most solutions depend on our using one paradigm (for example, inheritance) for one direction of dependency and another paradigm (such as templates or run-time selection through pointers) in the other direction. We outline some attacks on this problem in the remainder of this chapter, further developing the text editing example.

The analysis of Section 8.3 applies to TEXT BUFFERS in isolation. For a broader system analysis, we must investigate TEXT BUFFERS in the context of other abstractions with which they interact. In our analysis of text editors, we found *Output Medium* to be another domain of text editing. We do a separate variability analysis for it and produce the variability graph of Figure 8.2. We use the C++ variability table to do transformational analysis, producing Table 8.3.

Figure 8.2 reflects a short-cut in the design process. Instead of making a separate variability diagram for *Encryption*, we use the diagram to capture its dependency on *Character Set* as a parameter of variation. To do this, we need first to realize that *Encryption* is not a "primitive" domain (in the sense that we think of *Character Set* as primitive) and then to realize that it depends on another domain in the same variability graph. Such shortcuts can be allowed as long as all such dependencies are captured in at least one variability graph. The final combination of all graphs will capture and optimize the dependencies.

The *Output Medium* table bears an important relationship to the variability analysis table for *Text Buffers*. Both have a run-time dependency on the same domain, that of the file/record type (the two are closely interdependent). The dependency is reciprocal. This problem is complicated by the dependence of the domain of the *Text Buffer* parameters of variation on the range of *Output Medium* and by the dependence of the domain of the *Output Medium* parameters of variation on *Text Buffers*.

FIGURE 8.2   *Dependency graph for the Output Medium commonality analysis.*

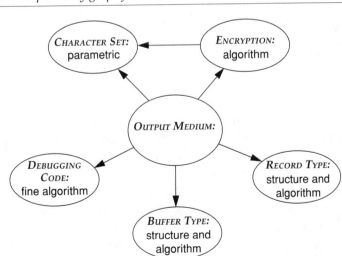

TABLE 8.3   *Text Editor Variability Analysis for Commonality Domain: Output Medium (Commonality: multiple behaviors; suggests inheritance)*

Parameters of Variation	Meaning	Domain	Binding	Default Technique
Buffer type *Structure, Algorithm*	The formatting and handling of text lines is sensitive to the Text Buffer type	Checkpoint, paged, versioned, full file...	Compile time	Full file *Inheritance*
Record type *Structure, Algorithm*	Differently formatted output for different record types	Database, RCS file, TTY, UNIX file	Run time	Character stream *Virtual functions*
Character set *Nonstructural*	Different file types should support different character sets	ASCII, EBCDIC, UNICODE, FIELDATA	Source time	ASCII *Templates*
Encryption *Algorithm*	Different markets require different encryption techniques	None, PGP (Pretty Good Privacy), NBS (National Bureau of Standards)	Compile time	None *Inheritance*
Debugging code *Code fragments*	Debugging traps should be present for in-house development	Debug, production	Compile time	Production *#ifdef*

That means that the selection of structure and algorithm, in several dimensions, depends on both the file/record type presented at run time *and* the buffer type. In general, there can be arbitrarily many dependencies in such a complex design. We can no longer choose paradigms on the basis of the structure of an individual subdomain. Instead, we must account for interference between subdomains as well.

We could partially solve this design problem by using multiple dispatch ("multimethods" in [Coplien1992]). Multiple dispatch is a feature of some object-oriented programming languages, such as CLOS, that causes run-time method lookup to use more than one method parameter. C++ member functions use only one parameter for method selection: the parameter whose address is implicitly passed to the member function as `this`. Even though C++ does not directly support multiple dispatch, a designer can simulate multimethods with suitable idioms [Coplien1992]. But multiple dispatch addresses only the variability in algorithm, not the variability in structure. Another solution must be explored for the buffer design.

The variability dependency graph for *Output Medium* in Figure 8.2 captures the parameters of variation within that subdomain alone (with the exception of capturing the obvious dependency between *Encryption* and *Character Set*). We constructed a similar graph for *Text Buffer*s in Figure 8.1.

When domain dependency diagrams were introduced in Section 7.3.2, we anticipated the usage under discussion here. That discussion mentioned that the parameters of variation in the figure can themselves be interpreted as domains, just as the central subdomain bubble can. That makes intuitive sense, if we believe that one setting's range can be another's domain. In fact, we talk about a "domain" for each parameter of variation in the variability table (as in Table 8.3). But parameters of variation need not be primitive domains such as `char` and `int`; they may be domains for which we have already done application domain analysis. In general, it is instructive to think of parameters of variation as being closely linked to their own domains.

Note that the graphs of Figures 8.1 and 8.2 share nodes. While each graph individually represents the structure of its subdomain, a *union* of the two graphs represents the two subdomains combined. The central domain bubble of each graph appear as a parameter of variation in the other. We combine the two subdomain variability dependency graphs into a single graph in Figure 8.3.

The graph of Figure 8.3 explicitly shows the duplication of nodes from the two subdomain graphs. Care must be taken to combine only compatible nodes of the graph. For example, we know that we can combine the two *Character Set* type nodes because the *Text Buffer* and *Output Medium* domains are covariant in the *Character Set* type. That is, both of the larger domains take the same type for this parameter of variation. They vary together with respect to this parameter of variation, and the binding time is the same in both domains for this parameter of variation. If the application needed to bind *Character*

FIGURE 8.3   *Combining two domains of the application.*

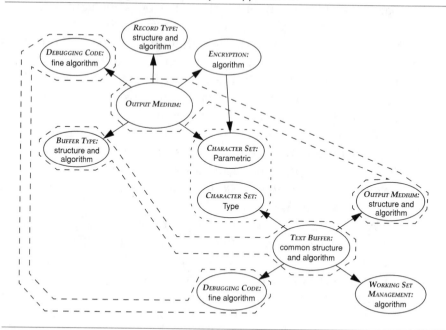

Set Type to *Output Medium* at run time and to *Text Buffer* at compile time, the two nodes could not be merged. The notation does not attempt to capture this level of detail; that is left to the insight of the designer. Projects wishing to use the variability dependency graphs for architecture documentation may wish to augment the notation to capture binding times and other notions of interest.

We enclose the redundant nodes in supernodes (the dotted lines) and then we reduce and reformat the graph in Figure 8.4. This graph represents the complete design (to this point), incorporating *Output Medium* and *Text Buffers*. While *Debugging Code* appears as an attribute of both output media and the text buffer, the two collections of code are likely to be unrelated (they are different domains), so we don't fold them together in this graph.

This new architecture represents a new design space with its own commonality and parameters of variation. You can think of it as a new beast that inherits a complex mixture of chromosomes from its parents. The new design space is distinct and different from each of its parents, yet it exhibits characteristics of both. We can use this graph as the archi-

FIGURE 8.4 *Reduced variability dependency graph.*

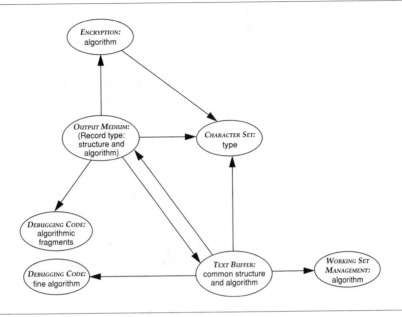

tecture of these two subdomains combined. Note that the individual subdomain architectures aren't explicit in the combined graph. The complex dependencies force us to derive a new structure from a broader perspective, a structure that has its own identity and "personality."

Some abstractions, such as the character set, factor out nicely. Some parameters are unique to their respective (original) subdomain, such as working set management and the encryption algorithm. But we find that the core abstractions of each domain take each other as a parameter of variation. The file type causes a type variation in *Text Buffers* against a backdrop of commonality in behavior and structure. Also, the *Text Buffer* type causes a structure and algorithm variability in *Output Medium*, for which behaviors (read, write, and so on) are common. We could use inheritance for each of the arrows in the cycle, but of course mutual derivation is absurd.

Assume for a moment that we need to defer all binding decisions until run time. We can implement that design in C++ if each abstraction has a type field and each modulates its behavior using case analysis on the other. Virtual functions aren't powerful enough for that. Even if C++ did have multiple dispatch, we needn't take on the complexities and inefficiencies of full-blown run-time flexibility unless the application demands it. When the primary abstractions of two domains are mutually dependent, we can use the binding times to choose an appropriate technique.

In the following sections, we look at three implementations of this architecture, as well as some minor variations within each one. Each one satisfies slightly different needs for binding time.

8.4.1   First Case: Compile-Time Binding

Presume that all design decisions can be bound at compile time and that we can use language features that support compile-time binding. These include templates, inheritance (without virtual functions), and overloading. Barton and Nackman [Barton+1994] often mix the first two of these to break circular dependency loops such as we find here. It's an important idiom to solve the problem of mutually dependent domains. The essence of the trick is to use code of this form:

```
template <class D> class Base {
public:
        . . . . D* . . . .    // a reference to D through
                              //            a pointer or
                              //            reference
      virtual D *base1() { . . . . }
      void base2() { . . . . }
};

class Derived: public Base<Derived> {
      . . . .
      Derived *base1() { . . . . base2() . . . . }
};
```

That is, Base takes its own Derived class as a template parameter. This makes it possible for Base to know more about Derived than it could deduce only from its role as Derived's base class. (In fact, base classes are usually oblivious to the existence of their derived classes; this is an important design feature of the C++ language.) In particular, the signature of the Base template foresees the type of the Derived class (namely, in the return type of member function base1).

This form bears careful study. I encourage the reader to try to diagram code of this form using a common notation, or to try coding examples that use this technique, to help developing intuition of its ramifications.

The code is structured roughly like this. Here is a generic `OutputMedium` template. We capture the dependency on `TextBuffer` as a template parameter:

```
template <class TextBuffer, class CharSet>
class OutputMedium {
public:
    void write() {
        . . . .
        subClass->getBuffer(writeBuf);
    }
    OutputMedium(TextBuffer *sc): subClass(sc) { }
protected:
    TextBuffer *subClass;
    CharSet writeBuf[128];
};
```

There may be several classes derived from this template. Here is one of them:

```
template <class TextBuffer, class Crypt, class CharSet>
class UnixFile: public OutputMedium<TextBuffer, CharSet>,
    protected Crypt {
    // inherited as a mix-in
public:
    UnixFile(TextBuffer *sc, basic_string<CharSet>
        key = ""):
        OutputMedium<TextBuffer, CharSet>(sc),
        Crypt(key) { }
    void read() {
        CharSet *buffer;
        . . . .
        Crypt::decrypt(buffer);
    }
};
```

Encryption is a mix-in class, incorporated with protected inheritance. We don't want clients of `UnixFile` to access the `Crypt` member functions directly, but we want to publish them to derived classes (if any) of `UnixFile`. Encryption might be provided in a simple mix-in class like this:

```
template<class CharSet>
class DES {
protected:
    void encrypt(basic_string<CharSet> &);
```

```
    void decrypt(basic_string<CharSet> &);
    DES(basic_string<CharSet> key);
};
```

We also have several `TextBuffer` base classes, one for each character set type, that expand from this template:

```
template <class CharSet>
class TextBuffer {
public:
    basic_string<CharSet> getLine() {
        basic_string<CharSet> retval;
        . . . .
        return retval;
    }
    void getBuffer(CharSet *) { . . . . }
    TextBuffer() { . . . . }
};
```

Here, we bind the combination in the `TextBuffer` derived class. We capture the dependency on `UnixFile` using derivation:

```
template <class Crypt, class CharSet>
class UnixFilePagedTextBuffer: public
    TextBuffer<CharSet>,
    protected UnixFile<UnixFilePagedTextBuffer<Crypt,
        CharSet>, Crypt, CharSet> {
public:
    UnixFilePagedTextBuffer():
        TextBuffer<CharSet>(),
        UnixFile<UnixFilePagedTextBuffer<Crypt,CharSet>,
            Crypt, CharSet>(this) {
        . . . .
    }
    basic_string<CharSet> getLine() {
        . . . .
        read();     // in UnixFile
        . . . .
    }
};


int main() {
    UnixFilePagedTextBuffer<DES<wchar_t>, wchar_t>
        buffer;
    basic_string<wchar_t> buf = buffer.getLine();
    . . . .
}
```

This solution exhibits strong coupling between the code for specific domains, particularly between the `UnixFilePagedTextBuffer` template and its parameters. Using run-time binding, we could more easily decouple the code for the specific domains.

We could also parameterize the `DES` encryption class to take `CharSet` as a parameter (omitted here for simplicity).

8.4.2   Second Case: *Buffer Type* depends on *Output Medium* Type at Run Time; *Output Medium* Type Depends on *Buffer Type* at Compile Time

In our example, the text buffer behavior varies according to the output medium type and the decision of which behavior to use must be deferred until run time. The output medium type depends on the buffer type, but it can bind its decisions at compile time. We address this using a multiple dispatch idiom. The text buffer notifies its associated output medium that it wants to perform an operation, and the output medium reciprocates. In addition to using the multiple dispatch idiom to manage variation in behavior, we can use inheritance to manage variability in structure. The selection of structure follows the selection of algorithm, so we gain the same flexibility in structure as we do for multiple dispatch of algorithm. Note that in this case, some of the structure (that of the output medium type) is compile-time bound, though the algorithm selection structure is the same as for the multiple dispatch idiom.

We note that the output medium type depends on the buffer type at compile time. The domain is *Output Medium*, the parameter of variation is the buffer type (variation in type), and the underlying commonality for *Output Medium* is structure and algorithm. Table 6.2 suggests that we use templates. Templates and inheritance can be used in powerful ways to break dependency cycles. Barton and Nackman [Barton+1994] have refined and catalogued many applications of these two language features in tandem. We can use templates for one of the arrows in the graph cycle and inheritance for the other. In this example, we handle encryption with inheritance, too (more about that later):

```
template <class CharSet, class ATextBuffer>
class OutputMedium {
public:
    virtual void write(const ATextBuffer *) = 0;
private:
```

```
virtual void encrypt(basic_string<CharSet> &s) {
// default encryption:  none
    . . . .
};
```

Output media (domain *OUTPUT MEDIUM*) also vary according to the record type, whether a UNIX file, database, RCS file, or other. This variation shows up in structure and algorithm. Requirements dictate that we track the variability at run time, so we use inheritance and virtual functions. The virtual declaration appears in the base class above. The write member function will be discussed later in the chapter.

```
template <class CharSet, class ATextBuffer>
class UnixFile: public OutputMedium<CharSet, ATextBuffer> {
public:
    // compile-time bound:
    void write(const ATextBuffer *buf)
        { buf->unixWrite(this); }
    UnixFile(string file): fileName(file) { /* . . . . */ }
    . . . .
private:
    string fileName;
    . . . .
};
```

The text buffer depends on the character set at compile time and on the output medium at run time. For example, the text buffer may take advantage of version information available in RCS files or it may use permanent tags or line identifiers available in a database medium. We may want to write buffer contents to several different output media as the program executes. The output medium causes variation both in algorithm and structure of text buffers. We handle this by using a variant of the multiple dispatch idiom [Coplien1992]. When the write member function of TextBuffer<CharSet> is invoked, it defers to its associated output medium (of unknown type) to dispatch to the proper write function. OutputMedium obliges (as in UnixFile::write above) by invoking the appropriate member function of TextBuffer<CharSet>:

```
template <class CharSet, class DerivedClass>
class TextBuffer {
    // DerivedClass is passed in just to support
    // casting, e.g., from
    // TextBuffer<char,PagedTextBuffer<char> >*
    // to PagedTextBuffer<char>*. Because the binding is
```

```
                // static, we know the downcast is safe
        public:
                void write(OutputMedium<CharSet, DerivedClass> *op)
                    const {
                        op->write(static_cast<DerivedClass*>(this));
                }
                void unixWrite(OutputMedium<CharSet, DerivedClass> *)
                    const;
                void databaseWrite(OutputMedium<CharSet,
                    DerivedClass> *)
                    const;
                . . . .
        };
```

The variability in output medium type also drives a variability in structure. This is captured in the output medium class, rather than in the text buffer class itself. The algorithm specific to each pair of buffer types and output media appears in the member function (named for the output medium) of the corresponding class (named for the buffer type):

```
        template <class CharSet>
        class PagedTextBuffer: public TextBuffer<CharSet,
                PagedTextBuffer<CharSet> > {
        public:
                void unixWrite(OutputMedium<CharSet,
                    PagedTextBuffer<CharSet> > *theMedium) const {
                        . . . .
                }
                void databaseWrite(OutputMedium<CharSet,
                    PagedTextBuffer<CharSet> > *theMedium) const {
                        . . . .
                }
                . . . .
        };
```

Each derived class of TextBuffer<CharSet> has its individual implementations of unixWrite, databaseWrite, and other functions specific to output media types:

```
        template <class CharSet>
        class FullFileTextBuffer: public TextBuffer<CharSet,
                FullFileTextBuffer<CharSet> > {
        public:
                void unixWrite(OutputMedium<CharSet,
```

```
            FullFileTextBuffer<CharSet> > *theMedium) const {
            . . . .
    }
    void databaseWrite(OutputMedium<CharSet,
        FullFileTextBuffer<CharSet> > *theMedium) const {
            . . . .
    }
    . . . .
};
```

As stipulated by the domain analysis, an output medium is associated with a text buffer type at compile time (and with a corresponding text buffer instance at run time). Note that for this `main` program, no object code for `FullFileTextBuffer` is incorporated in the executable, though object code for all output media is present:

```
int main() {
    PagedTextBuffer<char> textBuffer;
    UnixFile<char, PagedTextBuffer<char> > *file =
        new UnixFile<char,
            PagedTextBuffer<char> >("file");
    textBuffer.write(file);
    . . . .
}
```

We can handle encryption with inheritance. It would be straightforward to derive a new class from `UnixFile<char, PagedTextBuffer<char> >`, overriding the `encrypt` member function, to create a new family member that supported an encryption algorithm of our choice. If the number of encryption algorithms is limited, they can be stockpiled in a procedure library and suitably called from the overridden `encrypt` function in the derived class. As another alternative, we can do things in a more "object-oriented way" by using mix-ins. A mix-in is a lightweight class that is inherited to provide services to a derived class. Mix-ins are usually private (or protected) and often appear as one of several base classes:

```
template<class CharSet>
class DES {
protected:
    void encrypt(basic_string<CharSet> &cp) { . . . . }
    void decrypt(basic_string<CharSet> &cp) { . . . . }
    DES(basic_string<CharSet> key) { . . . . }
};
```

```
class DESUnixFile:
    public UnixFile<char, PagedTextBuffer<char> >,
    protected DES<char> {
public:
    void encrypt(string &s) { DES<char>::encrypt(s); }
    . . . .
};

int main() {
    PagedTextBuffer<char> textBuffer;
    DESUnixFile file("afile");
    . . . .
    textBuffer.write(file);
    . . . .
}
```

Of course, this approach works in C++ only if the application allows encryption to be compile-time or source-time bound. In languages with dynamic multiple inheritance (such as CLOS), it could be run-time bound.

Alternative Solutions

C++ offers multiple language features to express similar binding times and variability categories. Here, we investigate variants of the solution presented previously.

The domain analysis stipulates that encryption should be compile-time bound. Mix-ins are one way to do this, as shown previously. The inheritance hierarchy is compile-time bound and can capture variability in behavior (and structure as well, though that's not important to the ENCRYPTION parameter of variation).

Other C++ constructs express the same variability equally well; templates are one example of this. We can make the encryption algorithm available as a template parameter to the appropriate class (here, OutputMedium) and achieve the same end as we did previously with multiple inheritance. We might declare OutputMedium like this:

```
template <class CharSet, class TextBuffer, class Crypt>
class OutputMedium {
public:
    virtual void write(const TextBuffer &) = 0;
    . . . .
};
```

UnixFile, derived from an instantiation of OutputMedium, also takes the encryption parameter and just passes it along to its base class. (Another alternative would be to localize all encryption work to the UnixFile derived class, in which case the Crypt parameter could be removed from the OutputMedium template.)

```
template <class CharSet, class TextBuffer, class Crypt>
class UnixFile: public OutputMedium<CharSet, TextBuffer,
    Crypt> {
public:
    UnixFile(const string &filename);
    ~UnixFile();
    void write(const TextBuffer &buffer) {
        Crypt c = ::getKey();
        basic_string<CharSet> s;
        . . . .
        c.encrypt(s)
        . . . .
    }
    . . . .
};
```

The encryption algorithm itself is packaged either as a static function in a class or as a more conventional functor (the STRATEGY pattern of [Gamma1995]) for convenience:

```
class DES_char_Encryption {      // functor
public:
    void encrypt(string &);
    void decrypt(string &);
    DES_char_Encryption(const string &);
};
```

Some encryption algorithms such as stream ciphers have local state. This suggests the functor implementation over a static function.

PagedTextBuffer can be derived from a TextBuffer instantiation as before. The main code is similar to that of the previous example, except that the encryption variability appears as an explicit template parameter that captures the parameter of variation. This is aesthetically more pleasing than encoding the encryption algorithm in the name of the template itself. Yet we retain the same efficiency of compile-time binding:

```
int main() {
    UnixFile<char, PagedTextBuffer<char>,
        DES_char_Encryption>
```

```
        file("Christa");
    PagedTextBuffer<char> textBuffer;
    .  .  .  .
    textBuffer.write(file);
    .  .  .  .
    return 0;
}
```

There are many design alternatives for minor variations on binding time. For example, the file constructor might take a TextBuffer reference as a parameter to bind the type (and instance) of the text buffer to the file when the file is created, rather than rebinding each time write is called. Both this form and the above form use run-time binding. The constructor-based binding comes earlier than if we pass the buffer as a parameter to the write function; we would probably do the constructor-based binding only once for each file instance. This is a finer granularity of binding than that supported by the multi-paradigm notations, but it is well supported by C++ and is a valid and important design concern.

8.4.3   Third Case: *Buffer Type* Depends on *Output Medium* Type at Run Time; *Output Medium* Type Depends on *Buffer Type* at Run Time

We may want the text editor to be able to dynamically configure any buffer type with any file, looking at context (available memory, user preferences, and so on) to select among abstractions at the last microsecond. This case demands full run-time flexibility; both core abstractions depend on each other at run time. This is much like the previous example, except that the output medium can't depend on knowing the buffer type at coding time or template instantiation time. Figure 8.4 still applies as a domain dependency graph, except that the binding times have changed. Table 8.3 would change to look like Table 8.4.

All binding must be dynamic, so we use a full multiple-dispatch simulation. The code might look like this:

```
template<class CharSet>
class OutputMedium {
public:
    virtual void write(TextBuffer<CharSet> &) = 0;
private:
    virtual void encrypt(basic_string<CharSet> &s) = 0;
    .  .  .  .
};
```

TABLE 8.4 *Run-time handling of* Buffer *Parameter of Variability*

Parameters of Variability	Meaning	Domain	Binding	Default Technique
Buffer type *Structure, Algorithm*	The formatting and handling of text lines are sensitive to the Text Buffer type	Checkpoint, paged, versioned, full file...	Run time	Full file *Virtual Functions*

Here is yet another way of casting class DES, using operator() to elicit encryption:

```
template<class CharSet>
class DES {
private:
    void encrypt(basic_string<CharSet> &);
public:
    void decrypt(basic_string<CharSet> &);
    void operator()(basic_string<CharSet> &s) {
        encrypt(s); }
    DES(basic_string<CharSet> key);
};

template <class CharSet>
class TextBuffer {
public:
    void write(OutputMedium<CharSet> &op) {
        op.write(*this); }
    virtual void unixWrite(OutputMedium<CharSet> &) = 0;
    virtual void databaseWrite(OutputMedium<CharSet> &)
        = 0;
    . . . .
};

template <class CharSet>
class UnixFile: public OutputMedium<CharSet> {
public:
    void write(TextBuffer<CharSet> &buf) {
        buf.unixWrite(*this);
    }
    UnixFile(const string &fileName,
        const basic_string<CharSet> key = ""):
        cypher(key) { }
```

```
private:
    DES<CharSet> cypher;
    virtual void encrypt(basic_string<CharSet> &s) {
        cypher(s);
    }
    . . . .
};


template <class CharSet>
class PagedTextBuffer: public TextBuffer<CharSet> {
public:
    void unixWrite(OutputMedium<CharSet> &) { . . . . }
    void databaseWrite(OutputMedium<CharSet> &) { . . . . }
    . . . .
};


template <class CharSet>
class FullFileTextBuffer: public TextBuffer<CharSet> {
public:
    void unixWrite(OutputMedium<CharSet> &theMedium) {
        . . . .
    }
    void databaseWrite(OutputMedium<CharSet> &theMedium) {
        . . . .
    }
    . . . .
};


int main() {
    PagedTextBuffer<char> textBuffer;
    UnixFile<char> file("afile");
    textBuffer.write(file); // fully run-time bound
    . . . .
}
```

8.5 Design and Structure

Multi-paradigm design produces an architecture—a structure of components and relationships between them. The architecture is explicit in variability dependency graphs, such as Figure 8.2. It's important to understand that variability dependency graphs are not class diagrams or object diagrams. Class and object diagrams encode low-level design considerations, such as binding time, that go beyond the structure of the architecture.

The standard UML notation class diagrams for the designs of the preceding three sections are given in Figures 8.5, 8.6, and 8.7. We see from them that the architecture of Figure 8.4 shines through in all of them. The variability dependency graph captures the deep structure of the domain and is in some sense more abstract than a class diagram.

It should be obvious that all three figures have the same taxonomy as Figure 8.4. But they can't capture many important design dimensions. For example, variabilities handled with #ifdef (such as debugging code) don't surface to the class level, so they don't appear in the diagrams. The differences between virtual and nonvirtual functions don't appear, either. Nor do overloaded functions.

FIGURE 8.5 *Class diagram for the design of Section 8.4.1 (first design).*

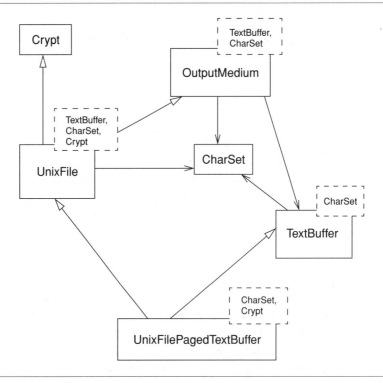

FIGURE 8.6   *Class diagram for the design of Section 8.4.2 (second design).*

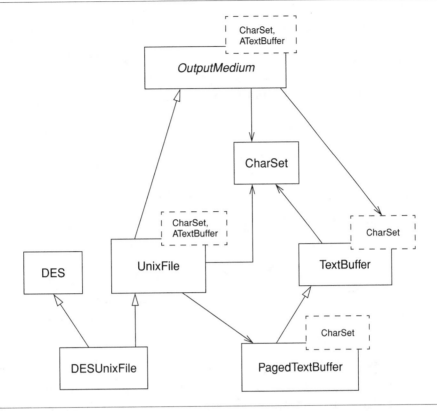

Figure 8.6 is similar to Figure 8.5. In Figure 8.6, the OutputMedium class doesn't take TextBuffer as a template parameter because it dynamically binds to a TextBuffer instance at run time through virtual functions.

8.5.1   A Note on Binding Time

The design diagrams for the three different binding times seem to emphasize the design stereotype that late or loose binding "cleans up" a design. It doesn't always work that way. Consider this classic problem in object-oriented programming with codependent domains: the output of polymorphic objects to a family of output abstractions.

FIGURE 8.7   *Class diagram for the design of Section 8.4.3 (third design).*

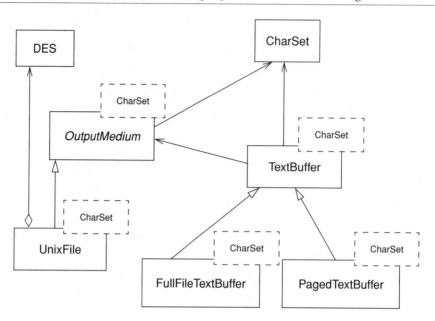

Let's pretend that we're designing a weather analysis and visualization system in which clouds are the major abstractions. There are cirrus clouds, cumulus clouds, nimbus clouds, tornado clouds, and a host of others:

```
class Cloud {
public:
     . . . .
};

class Cirrus: public Cloud {
     . . . .
};

class Tornado: public Cloud {
     . . . .
};
```

We may have several different types of output formatters, including a three-dimensional Phong shading renderer (which draws pretty pictures of the clouds), isobar and isotherm displays (which draw contour lines of constant pressure or temperature within the cloud), and wind vector displays (which draw little arrows indicating the wind velocity):

```
class Display {
public:
    . . . .
};

class Phong3D: public Display {
    . . . .
};

class IsoBar: public Display {
    . . . .
};
```

We can treat both the family of clouds and the family of output types as domains. We quickly find that the domains are codependent: each depends on the other. Each output formatter knows how to draw a particular kind of cloud for its medium, but it depends on knowing the type of each object it draws. Each cloud depends on the display device for its interface (such as drawing functions). In the worst case, some of these functions may not be generic, but they may be relevant only for a particular kind of cloud on a particular kind of output device (such as using a built-in Java applet for an animated tornado when using a Web browser for a renderer).

Assume that we can use compile-time binding to resolve the selection of member functions such as draw. The C++ solution is trivial:

```
void draw(const Tornado &t, IsoBar &d) { . . . . }
void draw(const Tornado &t, IsoTherm &d) { . . . . }
void draw(const Cumulus &fluffy, Phong3d &d) { . . . . }
void draw(const Cirrus &c, Phong3D &d) { . . . . }
    . . . .
```

The list gets a bit long and the friendship relationships get pretty messy—each class must declare friendships for each of the functions that access it—but the design is straightforward.

Now, presume that the dependencies must be run-time bound. That is, there must be a single function:

```
void draw(const Cloud &, const Display &);
```

that can accept any Cloud and any Display and do something reasonable. This is a challenging design to implement in C++, usually employing type fields to simulate multiple dispatch (see [Coplien1992], Section 9.7). This is at least one case in which deferred binding significantly complicates the implementation, rather than simplifying it.

In CLOS, a language construct that has a syntax analogous to C++ overloading has the semantics of run-time binding, complete with multiple dispatch. The selection of a suitable design technique for a given commonality analysis clearly depends on the implementation language of choice.

8.6 *Another Example: A Finite-State Machine*

In this example, we show that we can use multi-paradigm design even for low-level design. A finite-state machine (FSM) is usually thought of as a low-level abstraction that we could represent as a single class. But if we want to put a general FSM into a widely used library, we want to open up the parameters of variation to the many users of the library so that each can tune the design to a specific need.

We can look at FSMs in terms of the handful of abstractions that support a common implementation and external interface. An FSM is a collection of states, a finite set of values, each of which designates an interesting configuration of the system represented by the FSM. A state variable is often an integer or an enumerated type, but it might just as well be a string or any arbitrary class type. This will be one important parameter of variation. These subdomains are foreshadowed in the domain dictionary (you can find a discussion of the FSM domain dictionary in Section 2.2.2).

FSMs change state in response to "messages." We usually implement each "message" as a member function; to "send a message" to the FSM means to call a member function. Of course, we could also represent this interface with a single function that accepts more conventional messages as data structure arguments or enumerated message types. We'd like our implementation to support either of these.

FSMs also execute *actions* to produce outputs. In a fully general (Mealy) machine, the action executed is a function of the current state and the input message. (In a Moore machine, the output depends only on the current state; the discussion here describes a Mealy machine.) The programmer writes these actions to do the work of the system—this is where the meat is. These actions, taken together, are an important parameter of variation of FSMs.

Independent of all of these variations, there are two domains of commonality in FSMs. First, all FSMs share the same interface. The domain of *all* FSMs—call it ABSTRACTFSM—defines a generic interface. The parameters of variation include the type of user-defined transitions and the types for STATE and STIMULUS. We capture this domain in Table 8.5.

If we bind all of the parameters of variation of ABSTRACTFSM, we generate a family member that is still a high-level abstraction; it represents all possible state machines that respond to a given set of stimuli and that have a given range of states. The ABSTRACTFSM domain, then, provides a family of signatures or protocols that support the definition of a user-defined FSM. This isn't just a gratuitous design decision. We may define functions (for example, protocol handlers) with polymorphic interfaces to multiple, similar FSMs at the ABSTRACT FSM level. Such functions could handle multiple FSMs interchangeably.

Second, all FSMs might share the same implementation. We find a current state variable and a state mapping table inside the implementation of an FSM. The overall structure is common for

TABLE 8.5   *FSM Transformational Analysis for Commonality Domain: ABSTRACTFSM (Commonalities: Structure and Behavior)*

Parameters of Variation	Meaning	Domain	Binding	Default
User machine *Structure, Algorithm*	All generic FSMs understand how to add transitions in any UserFSM	Any class having member functions accepting a Stimulus argument (see bottom row)	Compile time	None *Templates*
State *Type*	How to represent the FSM state	Any discrete type	Compile time	None *Templates*
Stimulus *Algorithm*	The type of the message that sequences the machine between states	Any discrete type	Compile time	None *Templates*

all variants; the parameters of variation are similar to those for
ABSTRACTFSM. This is an interesting subdomain in its own right that
we'll call IMPLEMENTATIONFSM. Table 8.6 captures the variability analysis for this subdomain.

There is a third domain, which is the user-specified machine itself.
This subdomain captures most of the variability; the commonality has
been pushed into the two other subdomains. We'll call this the
USERFSM domain. It takes its protocol interface from one of the family
members of the ABSTRACTFSM subdomain. That makes it dependent
on the ABSTRACTFSM subdomain, which in turn depends on the
USERFSM subdomain—this is a circular dependency (Figure 8.8). The
IMPLEMENTATIONFSM subdomain in turn depends on the USERFSM subdomain for the definition of the state transition matrix and the implementations of the action semantics. The USERFSM variability table can
be found in Table 8.7.

Each FSM is unique enough that the variations can be hand-coded.
This uniqueness owes to the design factoring, which pushes the commonality into the IMPLEMENTATIONFSM and ABSTRACTFSM domains. For

TABLE 8.6 *FSM Transformational Analysis for Commonality Domain:
IMPLEMENTATIONFSM (Commonalities: Structure and Behavior)*

Parameters of Variation	Meaning	Domain	Binding	Default
UserFSM *Structure, Algorithm*	To implement the state/action map, the implementation must know the type of user-defined actions and transitions	See Table 8.5	Compile time	None *Templates*
State *Type*	How to represent the FSM state	Any discrete type	Compile time	None *Templates*
Stimulus *Algorithm*	The type of the message that sequences the machine between states	Any discrete type	Compile time	None *Templates*

FIGURE 8.8   *Domain diagram for the FSM example.*

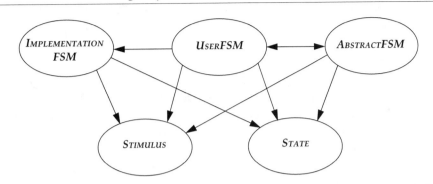

TABLE 8.7   *FSM Transformational Analysis for Commonality Domain:* **USERFSM**
(Commonalities: Aggregate Behavior)

Parameters of Variation	Meaning	Domain	Binding	Default
AbstractFSM *Structure, Algorithm*	The UserFSM uses the protocol from some family member of the AbstractFSM domain	See Figure 8.5	Compile time	None *Inheritance*
State *Type*	How to represent the FSM state	Any discrete type	Compile time	None *Hand-coded or typedef*
Stimulus *Algorithm*	The type of the message that sequences the machine between states	Any discrete type	Compile time	None *Hand-coded or typedef*
Actions *Algorithm*	Each UserFSM implements its own semantics in transition functions	Any number of functions that map a Stimulus parameter and the current state to a new state	Compile time	None *Inheritance*

notational convenience, recurring declarations for parameters such as *STIMULUS* and *STATE* can be expressed with typedef.

Note that this design also exhibits codependent domains; that is, *ABSTRACTFSM* and *USERFSM* depend on each other, as shown in Figure 8.8!

We start the implementation with a *class* AbstractFSM, which captures the semantics of the entire domain of FSMs. The subdomain defined by FSMs sharing the same protocol is represented in the ImplementationFSM class (below) that is (indirectly) derived from AbstractFSM:

```
template <class M, class State, class Stimulus>
class AbstractFSM {
public:
    virtual void addState(State) = 0;
    virtual void addTransition(Stimulus, State, State,
        void (M::*)(Stimulus));
};
```

We capture the variability of individual transition functions in the *USERFSM* simply by omitting these functions from the base class and adding them to the derived class for each machine:

```
class UserFSM: public AbstractFSM<UserFSM, char, char> {
public:
    void x1(char);
    void x2(char);
    void init() {
        addState(1);
        addState(2);
        addTransition(EOF,1,2,&UserFSM::x1);
        . . . .
    }
};
```

Notice the Barton and Nackman [Barton+1994] trick of passing the derived type as a parameter to the template that generates the base class.

The ImplementationFSM class captures the semantics of the *GENERICFSM* domain. This is where we bury the commonality that transcends all FSMs: the internal mapping table (using a common library abstraction called a map, which is an associative array), the current state, and the number of states. It also captures the behaviors common to all FSMs: construction, adding states, adding transitions between states, and a function called `fire` that causes the machine to cycle between states:

```
template <class UserMachine, class State, class Stimulus>
class ImplementationFSM: public UserMachine {
public:
    ImplementationFSM() { init(); }
    virtual void addState(State);
    virtual void addTransition(Stimulus, State from,
        State to,
        void (UserMachine::*)(Stimulus));
    virtual void fire(Stimulus);
private:
    unsigned nstates;
    State *states, currentState;
    map<Stimulus, void(UserMachine::*)(Stimulus)>
        *transitionMap;
};
```

This declaration captures the dependency of the *IMPLEMENTA-TIONFSM* domain on the *UserFSM* domain by using inheritance (`ImplementationFSM: public UserMachine`). It's now trivial to build the `ImplementationFSM` template from these declarations:

```
ImplementationFSM<UserFSM, char, char> myMachine;
. . . .
```

This declaration shows that the design has adequately shielded the user from the commonalities, while expressing the variabilities in the template parameters and in the functions of the `UserFSM` class. This code generates a rather elaborate design, one that is somewhat more involved than we would expect to find from a simple-minded FSM or from an object-oriented analysis that goes to the same depth as this solution. Yet the user interface to the library is clean and minimal and expresses the desired design variations suitably well, as shown in Figure 8.9.

This figure stretches the UML notation to its limits. `ImplementationFSM` and `AbstractFSM` are templates. The classes

```
AbstractFSM< UserFSM, char, char >
```

and

```
ImplementationFSM< UserFSM, char, char >
```

are instantiations of those templates for which `UserFSM` (and `State` and `Stimulus` as well, shown as `char` arguments in the diagram) has

FIGURE 8.9   *Class diagram of the solution.*

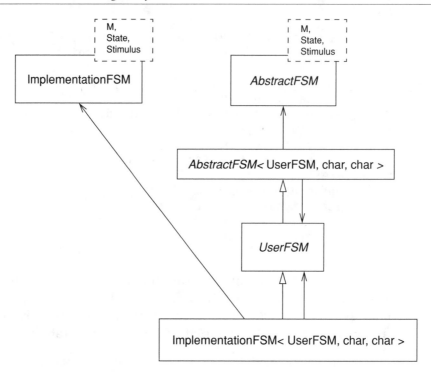

been supplied as a parameter of variation. Class UserFSM takes the AbstractFSM instantiation as a base class, while serving as a base class for the ImplementationFSM instantiation. UserFSM uses both of its neighboring classes for both its interface and implementation.

This is an unconventional but powerful design. The presentation here has left out many details that would make this an "industrial strength" FSM. However, it still serves as an example that is small enough to understand, yet large enough to stretch the imagination. The example illustrates that designers can use multi-paradigm design even at the lowest levels of design. Or maybe this *isn't* such a low level of design, since many of these decisions relate to the fundamental structure of systems based on state machine paradigms.

"State machine paradigm" is an eye-catching phrase. Are state machines themselves a paradigm, and if so, can we capture its dimensions of commonality by using C++ and multi-paradigm design? I believe state machines are a paradigm,[1] but I don't believe C++ *naturally* captures its important parameters of variation, except for the simplest state machines. SDL [Turner1993] is an example of a language whose goal is to more naturally capture state machine semantics. Many projects have built their own state machine languages suitable to their domains. The designer is faced with a decision: to use the state machine architecture here or to use an AOL tuned for state machines. Section 7.2 explores the trade-offs in this design decision.

8.7 Pattern-Based Solution Strategies

Design patterns can be used as an advanced technique to break circular dependencies. For example, consider a behavior, such as `write`, whose implementation depends on two different abstractions such as the FILE type and the TEXT BUFFER type. Instead of burying the behavior in either FILE or TEXT BUFFER—which would lead to one directly violating the encapsulation of the other—we can objectify the codependent behavior and factor it into a STRATEGY object. If the behavior depends on both the FILE and TEXT BUFFER types at run time, then it can be treated as a multiple dispatch problem, by using the multiple dispatch idiom [Coplien1992] or the VISITOR pattern [Gamma1995]. The STRATEGY pattern would also serve well to implement different forms of encryption.

Pattern solutions are covered in depth in [Gamma1995], while Chapter 9 explores the relationship of multi-paradigm design to patterns. Multi-paradigm design can often provide clues about which patterns to use for given commonality, variability, binding time, and instantiation. Other problems beg pattern solutions that go beyond conventional commonality and variability analysis; see the discussion in [Coplien1996a].

8.8 Summary

This chapter has taken multi-paradigm design to its limits: capturing the interaction between multiple paradigms. Multi-paradigm design

---

[1]   For the record, my colleague Tim Budd, also a pioneer in multi-paradigm design [Budd1995], disputes this point.

can help the designer find the paradigms that apply to a given domain, while leaving the designer free to weave those paradigms using individual or project-wide styles and conventions. Multi-paradigm design can also identify recursive design dependencies between "independent" domains. Such designs are difficult to regularize and depend on experience with the implementation technology and potentially with the domain of application.

Up to this point, this book has focused on abstraction techniques that C++ can express naturally. Sometimes, a higher-level perspective illuminates an even more powerful system partitioning. These partitionings sometimes solve problems by using indirect techniques that often don't succumb to methodical attacks or even intuition. Designers have captured these historically successful partitionings as software design patterns. Some of these patterns go beyond multi-paradigm design, but some are closely related to the material covered so far in this book. Chapter 9 explores the relationship between multi-paradigm design and the emerging discipline of design patterns.

Augmenting the Solution Domain with Patterns

This chapter introduces patterns into the solution domain vocabulary. Patterns extend C++ to reflect rich combinations of commonality and variability that C++ constructs cannot express directly. Patterns commonly solve problems that arise from negative variabilities.

9.1 The Value of Idioms and Patterns

A credible methodologist can no longer discuss software design without also covering patterns. Patterns provide a vocabulary for mature, proven design structures and techniques known to expert programmers. Some of these techniques were first captured as *idioms*[1] [Coplien1992] and have become crystallized in the work of Gamma, et al. [Gamma1995].

Software patterns solve recurring software problems. Patterns are a useful companion to most formal design methods, filling in holes that some methods leave unfilled. No common design method would lead

---

[1] Andrew Koenig calls these *cliches*. Idioms and cliches are the same thing, but, according to Koenig, the term *idiom* is a less pejorative, idiomatic term than *cliche*.

directly to all of the patterns described in the *Design Patterns* book by [Gamma+1995]. They provide key structures used by experienced designers to supplement the structures produced by object-oriented design methods. Some of these structures supplement the structures created by multi-paradigm design, and some of them are closely related to the structures produced by multi-paradigm design. This chapter explores the intersection between design patterns and multi-paradigm design.

Patterns are not just an interesting adjunct to multi-paradigm design but are intrinsically linked to commonality and variability analysis. Patterns themselves are recurring units of design that are common to many programs, so it pays to add them to the commonalities we expect to find in the solution domain. Many patterns factor the variability out of commonly recurring design structures to accommodate frequently recurring changes. For example, the BRIDGE pattern of [Gamma+1995] factors changing representations from a common interface. Gamma et al. use design variabilities to tabulate design patterns early in the *Design Patterns* book ([Gamma+1995], p. 30); we return to that table frequently in this chapter. Wolfgang Pree calls these loci of change "hot spots" [Pree1995], which are similar to parameters of variation in multi-paradigm design.

9.1.1   Patterns Beyond Language

Patterns often express what programming languages cannot directly express. Whereas multi-paradigm design builds solutions only at the level of language features, patterns are much more explicit about how to solve problems and are rich in design insight. Good patterns instruct the reader what to do, why to do it, and what the consequences might be. Patterns come in many forms, but all patterns describe a problem and a solution. Most good patterns discuss design trade-offs commonly called *forces*. A pattern should discuss how it transforms a design and what complementary patterns should be considered, as well as the benefits and liabilities of the pattern. A pattern is a much richer solution than a simple language technique, and we'd like to take advantage of patterns where we can.

Many patterns capture commonalities and parameterize variabilities, but we shouldn't interpret all software patterns as commonality/variability encodings. A pattern is just a documented solution to a problem in a context. There is no reason to believe that, by such a broad definition, any pattern should fit any commonality category of multi-paradigm design. Patterns are much more general. For example, the pattern LEAKY BUCKET COUNTER [PLoP1996] tells how to manage an error counter that is periodically decremented to offset error count increments. The counter can reach a threshold only if the error frequency is sufficiently high. This is a pattern we surely can implement in C++, but it isn't really a structural pattern. Further, it is difficult to talk about it in terms of commonalities and variabilities (except within the domain of leaky bucket counters themselves, where leak rates and frequencies become the "hot spots" of design).

More generally, multi-paradigm design tends to overlap with patterns that lie in the middle of the software abstraction spectrum. We can casually divide patterns into three categories: framework patterns, design patterns, and idioms. Framework patterns, such as CLIENT/SERVER, are usually distant from programming language considerations. At the opposite end of the spectrum, idioms are closely tied to programming language constructs that the designer must face in implementation. Design patterns live in that middle ground, where we align application structure with solution structures—the same transformation addressed by multi-paradigm design.

9.1.2 Patterns and Multi-Paradigm Design

So if patterns address these issues, why bother with multi-paradigm design? Patterns solve recurring problems that are specific to a domain—either application or solution. Multi-paradigm design, on the other hand, doesn't rely on previous solutions and is indifferent to the application domain. Most patterns don't deal with the mapping between these domains.[2] Multi-paradigm design beats the application and solution domains against each other to converge on a structure that balances the forces of each. Patterns provide a large (but fixed) number of solutions that we can combine in infinitely many ways; multi-paradigm design builds its solutions from a small set of programming language constructs. In one sense, multi-paradigm design

---

2. There are technically some exceptions, notably the CATERPILLAR'S FATE pattern language of Norm Kerth (Chapter 16 in [PLoP1995]). However, Norm's work is different in focus and level than the multi-paradigm design work presented here.

is more general than any collection of patterns can be. To be as general as multi-paradigm design, a pattern catalog would have to be very large and thus would be difficult to search.

If we can recognize commonalities and variabilities well-served by a specific pattern, then the design can benefit from the supporting material in the pattern description: the rationale, suggested implementation structures, alternative solutions, performance ramifications, and other trade-offs. Just as we used commonality analysis in early design to justify the use of the object paradigm in an example in Chapter 5, here we use commonality analysis to point to general patterns. The pattern descriptions offer insights into more specialized design and implementation details.

So how do patterns and multi-paradigm design relate to each other? We can view their relationship from three perspectives of how patterns are used:

1. As aliases for commonality/variability pairs that emerge from the solution domain analysis (Section 9.1.3)

2. As abstractions that are more abstract than the C++ constructs beneath them (Section 9.1.4)

3. As a powerful mechanism to deal with negative variability (Section 9.1.5)

Beyond these relationships, patterns cover many design structures that have little to do with multi-paradigm design. We don't explore such patterns here. More broadly, patterns complement multi-paradigm design. In this chapter, we discuss only the intersection of these two design techniques.

9.1.3 Nicknames for Solution Domain Constructs

Commonality and variability are a staple of most design methods and tools. Many recurring patterns of commonality and variability make it into programming languages so as to support design styles we call paradigms. Some combinations of commonality and variability are not common enough to make their way into a programming language, but they are common enough to be in our design vocabulary. These constructs become patterns that complement the dominant abstractions of common application domains and solution domains.

TEMPLATE METHOD [Gamma1995] is one such pattern. We find the roots of this pattern in the private virtual function idiom ([Coplien1992], Section 11.1) and in other early C++ practice. A template method is an algorithm (function) that has a common overall structure with specific steps that vary across applications. Most programming languages can't easily express fine-grain run-time variations in algorithms (particularly those variations smaller than a function). The trick is to express the main algorithm in terms of finer algorithms that are called from the main algorithm and that can be dynamically dispatched. The main algorithm encodes the commonality. The variation in algorithm can be factored into inheritance hierarchies by using virtual functions—something most object-oriented programming languages support well.

Pree [Pree1995] explicitly recognizes TEMPLATE METHOD as a case of commonality and variability analysis. *Hot spots* is a term he uses to describe the sites of variation, such as the algorithmic variation of TEMPLATE METHOD, that we want to parameterize in a robust design. Pree's HOOK pattern is closely related to TEMPLATE METHOD. Both of these patterns capture algorithmic structure as a commonality and variability category.

Not all combinations of commonality and variability merit nicknames. What is the name for a technique that overloads the same function in the same way in each class of an inheritance hierarchy? We'd generate an encyclopedic vocabulary if we enumerated all of these combinations. And not all patterns build on commonalities and variabilities in the sense that we use the terms in multi-paradigm design.

9.1.4   Higher-Level Than Programming Language Constructs

Consider the ITERATOR pattern [Gamma1995]. This is another pattern that captures design commonality and variability. What is common is the need to iterate over a collection no matter how it is represented. What varies is the implementation of the collection's structure and the types of the elements it contains. Most object-oriented programming languages have aggregate types, and iterators are a common and convenient way of interacting with aggregates. A few languages (such as Lisp) have built-in iteration constructs, but most languages build iteration into library abstractions using a common pattern.

In most cases, we think of list iteration as a more general concept than the concepts expressed in the syntax of a particular programming language. Patterns provide a "standard" for the semantics of iterators and other high-level design constructs that is abstract enough to port across programming languages.

Note that many of these "high-level" patterns can be thought of as nicknames for constructs that are part of a programming language culture but not part of the language itself, as in the previous section.

9.1.5   Negative Variability

Section 5.1.4 discussed a common commonality/variability pair that leads to a special kind of negative variability. Many classes may share common behavior, but they may have different structures. A special case of this problem appears in this code:

```
class Complex { // size = 16 bytes
private:
    double realPart, imaginaryPart; // 16 bytes of space
public:
    Complex &operator+=(const Complex &);
    friend Complex operator+(const Complex &, const
        Complex &);
    . . . .
};

class Real: public Complex { // size should be 8 bytes
private:                     // (presuming implementation
                             //  as a double)
    // ??? add a real part and waste base class data?
    // make base class data protected, and waste
    // imaginaryPart?
    . . . .
};
```

Not only are the implementations of Real and Complex different, but it isn't possible to construct the implementation of Real in terms of Complex. The external behaviors of these two classes are nonetheless the same and obey all reasonable laws of subtyping. The C++ language uses a single language construct—inheritance—for both of these; here, the coincidence does not serve us well. This shows up in multi-paradigm design as a negative variability because the derived class Real must violate the commonality of the ostensibly more abstract `Complex` base class. Looking back to Table 6.2, we see that multi-paradigm design provides no C++ language solution to this pairing. So, we turn to patterns.

One solution is to break implementation and interface into separate hierarchies tied together by pointers: the BRIDGE pattern of [Gamma1995]. The solution looks like this:

```
Complex operator+(const Complex &n1, const Complex &n2) {
    // machinery to orchestrate multiple dispatch
    // see [Coplien1992], sec. 9.7
    . . . .
}

class NumberRep { };

class ImaginaryRep: public NumberRep {
friend class Complex;
friend class Imaginary;
    double imaginaryPart;
    ImaginaryRep &operator+=(const ImaginaryRep&);
    . . . .
};

class ComplexRep: public NumberRep {
friend class Complex
    double realPart;
    ComplexRep &operator+=(const ComplexRep&);
    . . . .
};

class Complex {
public:
    Complex(): rep(new ComplexRep()) { . . . . }
    ~Complex() { delete rep; rep = 0; }
    Complex &operator+=(const Complex &c) {
        (static_cast<ComplexRep *>
            rep)->operator+=(c.rep);
        return *this;
    }
    . . . .
protected:
    Complex(NumberRep *);    // for use by derived
                             // classes
    NumberRep *rep;          // the Bridge pointer
};
```

```
class Imaginary: public Complex {
public:
    Imaginary(): Complex(new ImaginaryRep()) {
        . . . .
    }
    ~Imaginary() { }
    . . . .
};
```

This brings to closure the problem presented in Section 6.7, and elucidates the solution structure of Figure 6.4. Also, see "An Example of Data Cancellation" in Section 6.11.1, for an analogous example.

Clearly, pattern solutions are related to multi-paradigm design—they solve similar problems, at least in some cases. In fact, some design patterns can more formally be linked to multi-paradigm design as specific configurations of commonality and variability. Said another way, we can use multi-paradigm design to regularize a subset of commonly used design patterns.

9.2 Commonality and Variability in Common Patterns

Chapter 6 tabulated the C++ solution domain structure in Table 6.2. To the C++ solution domain, we add the "pattern solution domain," which can represent rich, new combinations of commonality and variability to support the back end of multi-paradigm design. A summary is found in Table 9.1. Think of this table as an extension of the C++ solution domain table, so both are considered as one when aligning the application domain structure with the solution structure.

9.2.1 Patterns Beyond Domain Engineering Techniques

Table 9.1 does not, of course, encode all useful patterns. Many patterns go beyond the commonality and variability structure of multi-paradigm design to address problems ranging from implementation efficiency (as in the FLYWEIGHT pattern) to common system-level architectures (such as CLIENT/SERVER patterns). Such patterns can be used as adjuncts to multi-paradigm design, just as they can be an adjunct to any design method. Even the design patterns of [Gamma1995] can be thought of as adjuncts to object-oriented methods.

TABLE 9.1   *Factoring Commonalities and Positive Variabilities into Patterns*

Commonality	Variability	Binding	Instantiation	Pattern
Function name and semantics	Fine algorithm	Run time	N/A	Template Method (Section 9.2.3)
	Algorithm	Run time with compile time default	N/A	Unification (Section 9.2.6) + Template Method
	Algorithm: Parameter of variation is some state	Run time	Yes	State (Section 9.2.5)
Related operations and some structure (positive variability)	Gross algorithm	Run time	N/A	Strategy (Section 9.2.4)
	Value of state	Source time	Once	Singleton (Section 9.2.7)
	Gross algorithm	Source time (or compile time)	N/A	Strategy (using templates, Section 9.2.4) or Unification (Section 9.2.6)
Related operations but *not* structure	Incompatible data structure	Any	Yes	Bridge or Envelope/Letter (Section 9.2.2)

The following sections explain each of the patterns and their commonalities, variabilities, and implementation considerations in more detail.

9.2.2   The BRIDGE Pattern

BRIDGE of Figure 9.1 breaks the "binding between an abstraction and its implementation" ([Gamma1995], 153). This hides the implementation from clients, both by removing details from the class that represents

FIGURE 9.1 *Structure of the* BRIDGE *pattern (adapted from [Gamma1995], p. 153).*

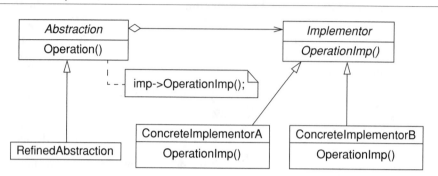

the abstraction and by breaking compilation dependencies through the pointer in the client-visible abstraction. This is also known as the *handle/body idiom* [Coplien1992]. The *Design Patterns* book [Gamma1995] relates that the variability captured by BRIDGE is "the implementation of an object" but, as for all of the book's patterns, the commonality isn't explicitly tabulated.

One way to think of BRIDGE is that it presumes no commonality in structure across family members. Each family member brings its own structure that builds on an empty foundation. That means that family members can exhibit structures that are completely unrelated to each other and that we need not worry about the problems of negative variability. Commonality comes from the broader context of the related signatures of family members (the base class interface).

9.2.3 The TEMPLATE METHOD Pattern

TEMPLATE METHOD (Figure 9.2; [Gamma1995], p. 325) captures the predominant commonality of a family of algorithms. It highlights the fragments of the algorithm that vary across applications and factors those variations into a derived class. Gamma et al. [Gamma1995] tell us that TEMPLATE METHOD captures "steps of an algorithm" as a variability. The commonality is the surrounding algorithm skeleton.

9.2.4 The STRATEGY Pattern

STRATEGY ([Gamma1995], p. 315) is like TEMPLATE METHOD, except for the granularity of variability. TEMPLATE METHOD deals with fragments,

FIGURE 9.2 *Structure of* TEMPLATE METHOD *(adapted from [Gamma+1995], p. 327).*

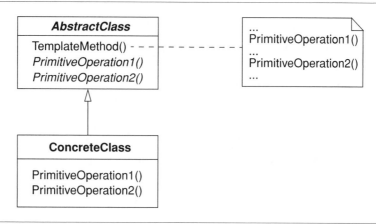

while STRATEGY presumes no common structure between algorithms (in Table 9.1, compare the "Variability" entries for these two patterns). In the *Design Patterns* book [Gamma+1995], STRATEGY's variabilities are "an algorithm." The only commonality is the contract between the family of algorithms and their client. The *Design Patterns* book suggests two implementations for STRATEGY. Though they both share the same intent, multi-paradigm design treats them differently because they have different binding times. That is why STRATEGY appears twice in Table 9.1.

The first implementation of STRATEGY is a variant of TEMPLATE METHOD, except that each class bears only a single function, as shown in Figure 9.3. Virtual functions make run-time binding convenient and integrate it into the language and its type system. STRATEGY goes one step further and pushes the variability out to run time.

In the second implementation (as in [Gamma+1995], p. 319), we bind the STRATEGY to the client at compile time by using templates. The code might look like this:

```
class MyEncryptionAlgorithm {
public:
    string crypt(const string &);
};

template <class AnEncryptionAlgorithm> class TextBuffer {
    /* static */ AnEncryptionAlgorithm encryptor;
```

FIGURE 9.3   *Structure of* STRATEGY: *First implementation (adapted from [Gamma1995], p. 315–6).*

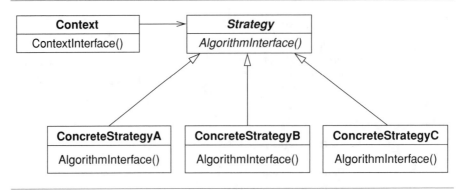

```
public:
    void someMemberFunction() {
        string c, s;
        .  .  .  .
            c = encryptor.crypt(s);
        .  .  .  .
    }
};

TextBuffer<MyEncryptionAlgorithm> aBuffer;
```

Or we can be fancier and use functors:

```
class MyEncryptionAlgorithm {
public:
    string crypt(const string &);
    string operator()(const string &s) { return crypt(s); }
};

template <class AnEncryptionAlgorithm> class TextBuffer {
    /* static */ AnEncryptionAlgorithm encryptor;
public:
    void someMemberFunction() {
        string c, s;
        .  .  .  .
        c = encryptor(s);
        .  .  .  .
    }
};

TextBuffer<MyEncryptionAlgorithm> aBuffer;
```

Note that C++ overloading is a special or degenerate version of STRATEGY, where the parameter of variation reduces to the types in the function signature. In the template and virtual function examples, the parameter of variation lives in the application domain (it is the algorithm itself).

This is similar to the entry in the C++ solution domain analysis table (Table 6.2) that stipulates inheritance for a commonality of related operations, variability in algorithm, bound at compile time, with optional instantiation. There is a subtle difference in binding. When the template implementation of STRATEGY is used, the parameter of variation is explicit and clear at the point of template instantiation; with inheritance, the variability must be encoded in the name of the class. The code that implements the template version is compact and expressive. The inheritance technique generates a new derived class for each combination of base class and parameter of variation—this is administratively clumsy and pollutes the global name space.

Returning to our running text-editor example of Chapter 3, the declarations

```
TextBuffer<DESEncryption> myTextBuffer;
TextBuffer<NoEncryption> tempFileBuffer;
```

both use the single source abstraction `TextBuffer`. Compare that with this:

```
TextBufferForDESEncryption myTextBuffer;
TextBufferWithoutEncryption tempFileBuffer;
```

where the underlying class declarations are left to the imagination of the reader. The template version is closer to source-time binding; the inheritance version is more reminiscent of compile-time binding (see Section 3.5.4).

There is also a difference in granularity. A programmer can use inheritance to conveniently express how several algorithms vary together against the commonality of a base class. We can do this with STRATEGY, but inheritance is much more expressive and convenient. These two factors, simplicity and granularity, are the pragmatics that distinguish these two techniques.

9.2.5   The STATE Pattern

The implementation of STATE builds on STRATEGY with minor variations; a change in the state of the `Context` object causes it to select a different `Strategy` object. The difference between STATE and STRATEGY is in the intent. With STATE, the change in algorithm follows a change in object state. The parameter of variation for STATE is the state of the `Con-text` object. The first implementation of STRATEGY is almost indistinguishable from STATE. The second implementation of STRATEGY treats the function itself as a parameter of variation. STATE supports later binding than does the second STRATEGY implementation: For STATE, the behavior is designed to change during the object's lifetime, whereas it's more common to bind STRATEGY behavior at instantiation time.

9.2.6   The UNIFICATION Pattern

Pree's UNIFICATION pattern suggests a combination of the two implementations of the STRATEGY pattern with an implementation that puts an interesting spin on ordinary inheritance and virtual functions. Start with the TEMPLATE METHOD pattern, as indicated by a domain analysis that suggests large commonality of algorithm, with minor variations:

```
class Base {
public:
    void commonCodeFunction() {
        . . . .
        this->hookFunction();
        . . . .
    }
private:
    virtual void hookFunction() = 0;
};
```

Now presume that the same domain analysis suggests a predominant, or *default*, algorithm for the parameter of variation that corresponds to `hookFunction`. We'd find this in the "Default" column of the application domain commonality table.

```
class Base {
public:
    void commonCodeFunction() {
        . . . .
        this->hookFunction();
        . . . .
    }
private:
    virtual void hookFunction() {
```

```
         . . . .
         // code for the default case
         . . . .
     }
};

class Derived: public Base {
    void hookFunction() {              // specialized hook
                                       // function

         . . . .
     }
};

Base commonCase;
Derived specialCase;
```

This is reminiscent of Pree's SMALL CAPS UNIFICATION pattern, which integrates the hook function and template function in a single class called TH (template hook) ([Pree1995], Section 4.3.2). We can use this same class as the basis for the more general TEMPLATE METHOD pattern as in Section 9.2.3.

9.2.7   The SINGLETON Pattern

SINGLETON (Figure 9.4, [Gamma1995], p. 127) is a pattern that forces a one-to-one mapping between a class and its instances. The GOF book notes that the "sole instance of a class" is the sole item that can vary, and the variation field in the Gamma pattern characterization is a bit weak. Singleton has a simple variability in instantiation—zero or one—and its state can vary. Everything else is constant.

FIGURE 9.4   *Structure of* SINGLETON *(adapted from [Gamma1995], p. 127).*

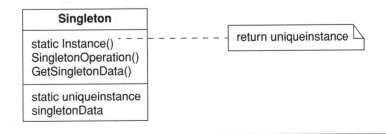

9.3 *Patterns of Negative Variability*

Table 9.1 captures the patterns for positive variability against some backdrop of commonality. Just as we developed a similar taxonomy for language features that capture negative variabilities, so we can develop an analogous table for patterns of negative variability. Table 9.2 captures a couple of interesting cases in which patterns express negative variability well.

Notice that the format of Table 9.1 is similar to that of the C++ solution domain variability table, Table 6.2. Binding, instantiation, and commonality categories are important to both. In one case, we can capture the structure with language features; in the other, we can capture the structure with a pattern. Table 9.1 takes more liberty with the variability description because the commonality categories—or those of the C++ language alone—aren't powerful enough to capture the semantics.

9.3.1 The BRIDGE Pattern

We use BRIDGE to handle implementation variations that violate prevailing commonality. This is similar to the positive variability case. In fact, it is best to think of BRIDGE as a negative variability pattern for which positive variability is a special case. Positive variability is the total cancellation of *common* structure, followed by the addition of new structure.

BRIDGE can be used to factor out function membership as well as data membership. Consider a family of `Message` abstractions that

TABLE 9.2 *Factoring Commonalities and Negative Variabilities into Patterns*

Kind of Commonality	Kind of Variability	Binding	Instantiation	Pattern
Some structure and algorithm	Function name or semantics	Compile or run time	Optional	Adapter (Section 9.3.2)
Related operations but *not* structure	Cancellation of class membership	Any	Yes	Bridge or Envelope/ Letter (Section 9.3.1)

usually require checksums, with the exception of single-byte ACK and NAK messages. We could use BRIDGE to factor this variability into an implementation "helper" class, MessageBody. Here, we use private multiple inheritance (a mix-in) to factor the checksum function; we could have factored this function into another level of the class hierarchy:

```
class CheckSummedMessageBody: public MessageBody {
    . . . .
};
```

Here is the implementation side of the BRIDGE hierarchy:

```
class MessageBody {
public:
    virtual void dispatch() = 0;
};

class CheckSummable {        // mix-in class
public:
    long checksum(const unsigned char*);
};

class FilePacketBody: public MessageBody,
    private CheckSummable {
    // CheckSummable is a mix-in
public:
    . . . .
private:
    using CheckSummable::checksum;
};

class AckBody: public MessageBody {
public:
    . . . .
    // no checksum member
    void dispatch() { . . . . }
private:
    . . . .
};
```

There is a parallel structure on the application interface side:

```
class Message {
public:
    Message(const unsigned char *);
```

```
        void send() {
            . . . .
            implementation->dispatch();
            . . . .
        }
        . . . .
protected:
    MessageBody *implementation;      // the bridge
};


class AckMessage: public Message {
public:
    AckMessage(const unsigned char *c): Message(c) {
        . . . .
        implementation = new AckBody. . .
    }
};


    . . . .
```

9.3.2   The ADAPTER Pattern

The designer can use ADAPTER to remove part of an abstraction's interface, while leaving its implementation untouched. The commonality includes all of the base algorithms and data structures, while the variability is in the interface. This is the opposite of STRATEGY. ADAPTER also differs from STRATEGY in scale because STRATEGY applies to a single function, while ADAPTER applies to an entire class.

As an example, consider this attack on the well-known problem of List and Set ([Coplien1992], Section 6.5):

```
template <class T> class List {
public:
    List();
    bool has(const T&) const;
    T head() const;
    T tail() const;
    void insert(const T&);
    void sort();
    unsigned size() const;
    . . . .
};
```

```
template <class T> class Set {
public:
    Set(): rep(new List<T>) { }
    void insert(const T &t) {
        if (!has(t)) rep->insert(t);
    }
    bool has(const T &t) { return rep->has(t); }
    unsigned size() const { return rep->size(); }
    // no sort, because there's no sense of ordering
private:
    List<T> *rep;
};
```

Is this adaptation or containment? Both have the same semantics (at least for the one-to-one case), so it's a matter of how the designer views it.

9.3.3   Other Patterns

Section 9.2 and the preceding subsections of Section 9.3 showed how patterns from the popular literature dovetail with the principles of multi-paradigm design. However, this was not a thorough analysis, even for the work of Gamma et al. Furthermore, the *Design Patterns* book [Gamma1995] is just the beginning of an ever-growing collection of design patterns. Readers should carefully explore other patterns and add them to Table 9.1 and Table 9.2 as their experience grows.

More importantly, many patterns capture exotic design concerns beyond the expressive power of multi-paradigm design. Such patterns are powerful design aids, especially for application-specific design problems further removed from programming language than the design patterns of [Gamma1995].

9.4 *Multi-Paradigm Tools as a Patterns Adjunct*

Most of this chapter has portrayed patterns as an adjunct to multi-para-digm design. Turnabout is fair play, and patterns might benefit from multi-paradigm design principles. Gamma et al. take a step in this direc-tion when they tabulate design pattern variabilities ([Gamma1995], p. 30), but their taxonomy falls short of the broader design space of multi-paradigm design. Commonality/variability pairs might serve as a good organizing principle for patterns, thus complementing taxonomies like those of Buschmann, Meunier, et al. ([PLoP1995], pp. 134–135, 428–430).

Consider TEMPLATE METHOD, STATE, and STRATEGY. TEMPLATE METHOD and STRATEGY vary in their granularity of variability but otherwise are similar. The first implementation of STRATEGY is similar to STATE, with a subtle difference in binding times. (STRATEGY is usually a bind-once pattern, whereas STATE is more dynamic.) From the perspective of multi-paradigm design, there is probably more variation between the two implementations of STRATEGY than between STRATEGY and STATE because of the stark contrast in binding times. Patterns don't emphasize that distinction; multi-paradigm design makes it explicit.

Multi-paradigm design helps the designer look at these patterns as points on a spectrum, rather than as specific points in the design space that solve specific problems. Commonality and variability help elicit the design principles that underlie many (but not all) patterns. Just as patterns help orient multi-paradigm design in the larger context of codified design experience, multi-paradigm design helps orient the software designer by exposing the commonality and variability categories that form the heart of design patterns.

9.5 Summary

Some software design patterns are just shorthand names for design techniques we find in multi-paradigm design. Patterns can raise the level of design dialogue above specific commonality and variability categories to recurring constellations of classes and other language features. Many of these combinations support negative variability. But multi-paradigm design alone can't do justice to the full spectrum of patterns that have been catalogued.

References

[Barton+1994]   Barton, John, and Lee Nackman. *Scientific and Engineering C++*. Reading, MA: Addison-Wesley. 1994.

[Beck1993]   Beck, Kent. "Think Like an Object." *UNIX Review* 9, 10. September 1993. pp. 39–4.

[Bentley1988]   Bentley, J. L. *More Programming Pearls: Confessions of a Coder*. Reading, MA: Addison-Wesley. 1988.

[Booch1994]   Booch, Grady. *Object-Oriented Design with Applications, 2d ed.* Redwood City, CA: Benjamin/Cummings. 1994.

[Budd1995]   Budd, Timothy. *Multi-Paradigm Programming in Leda*. Reading, MA: Addison-Wesley. 1995.

[Cain+1996]   Cain, Brendan, James O. Coplien, and Neil Harrison. "Social patterns in productive software development organizations." *Annals of Software Engineering,* 2. December 1996. pp. 259–286. See http://www.baltzer.nl/ansoft/articles/2/ase004.pdf.

[Campbell+1990]   Campbell, G. H., S. R. Faulk, and D. M. Weiss. "Introduction to Synthesis." Software Productivity Consortium, INTRO_SYNTHESIS-90019-N, Version 01.00.01. June 1990.

[Cockburn1998]   Cockburn, Alistair. *Surviving Object-Oriented Projects: A Manager's Guide*. Reading, MA: Addison Wesley Longman. 1998.

[Constantine1995]   Constantine, Larry. "Objects in your Face." In *Constantine on Peopleware*. Englewood Cliffs, NJ: Prentice-Hall. 1995. pp. 185–190.

[Coplien1992] Coplien, J. O. *Advanced C++ Programming Styles and Idioms*. Reading, MA: Addison-Wesley. 1992.

[Coplien1995a] Coplien, J. O. "A Generative Development-Process Pattern Language." *Pattern Languages of Program Design*. J. O. Coplien and D. Schmidt, eds. Reading, MA: Addison-Wesley, 1995. pp. 183-238.

[Coplien1996a] Coplien, J. O. "A Professional Dilemma." *C++ Report* 8, 3. New York: SIGS Publications. March 1996. pp. 80–89.

[Date1986] Date, C. J. *Introduction to Database Systems, 4th ed*. Reading, MA: Addison-Wesley. 1986.

[DeChampeaux+1993] DeChampeaux, Dennis, Doug Lea, and Penelope Faure. *Object-Oriented System Development*. Reading, MA: Addison-Wesley. 1993.

[Dijkstra1968] Dijkstra, E. W. "Notes on Structured Programming." *Structured Programming*. O. J. Dahl, W. Dijkstra, C. A. R. Hoare, eds. London: Academic Press. 1968.

[Flanagan1997] Flanagan, David. *Java in a Nutshell*. Bonn, Germany: O'Reilly and Associates. 1997.

[Fowler+1997] Fowler, Martin, and Scott Kendall. *UML Distilled: Applying the Standard Object Modeling Language*. Reading, MA: Addison Wesley Longman. 1997.

[Fusion1993] Coleman, Derek, et al. *Object-Oriented Development: The Fusion Method*. Englewood Cliffs, NJ: Prentice-Hall. 1993.

[Gamma+1995] Gamma, Erich, Richard Helm, Ralph Johnson, and John Vlissides. *Design Patterns: Elements of Reusable Object-Oriented Software*. Reading, MA: Addison-Wesley. 1995.

[GoldbergRubin1995] Goldberg, Adele, and Kenneth S. Rubin. *Succeeding with Objects: Decision Frameworks for Project Management*. Reading, MA: Addison-Wesley. 1995.

[Jerrell1989] Jerrell, Max E. "Function Minimization and Automatic Differentiation Using C++." *Proceedings of OOPSLA '89, SIGPLAN Notices*, 24, 10. October 1989. pp. 169–173.

[Jacobson+1992] Jacobson, Ivar, et al. *Object-Oriented Software Engineering: A Use Case Driven Approach*. Reading, MA: Addison-Wesley. 1992.

[Kiczales1994] Kiczales, Gregor. Keynote address at the 1994 ACM Conference on Object-Oriented Programs, Systems, Languages, and Applications. Portland, OR. Oct. 23–27, 1994.

[Kiczales1997] Kiczales, Gregor. "Aspect-Oriented Programming." *Computing Surveys* 28(4es). 1996. p. 154.

[Kuhn1970]   Kuhn, Thomas. *Structure of Scientific Revolutions*. Chicago: University of Chicago Press. 1970.

[Liskov1988]   Liskov, Barbara. "Data Abstraction and Hierarchy." *SIGPLAN Notices* 23, 5. May 1988.

[McConnell1997]   McConnell, Steve M. *Software Project Survival Guide: How to be Sure Your First Important Project Isn't Your Last*. Microsoft Press. 1997.

[Meyer1992]   Meyer, Bertrand. *Eiffel: The Language*. New York: Prentice-Hall. 1992.

[Meyers1992]   Meyers, Scott. *Effective C++: 50 Specific Ways to Improve Your Programs and Designs*. Reading, MA: Addison-Wesley. 1992. Note: 2nd Edition published 1998.

[Neighbors1980]   Neighbors, J. M. "Software Construction Using Components." Tech Report 160. Department of Information and Computer Sciences, University of California. Irvine, CA. 1980.

[Palsberg+1994]   Palsberg, Jens, and Michael I. Schwartzbach. *Object-Oriented Type Systems*. Chichester, England: John Wiley & Sons. 1994.

[Parnas1976]   Parnas, D. L. "On the Design and Development of Program Families." *IEEE Transactions on Software Engineering*, SE-2: March 1976. pp. 1–9.

[Parnas1978]   Parnas, D. L. "Designing Software for Ease of Extension and Contraction." *Proc. 3rd Int. Conf. Soft. Eng.* Atlanta, GA. May 1978. pp. 264–277.

[PLoP1995]   Coplien, J. O., and D. C. Schmidt, eds. *Pattern Languages of Program Design*. Reading, MA: Addison-Wesley. 1995.

[PLoP1996]   Vlissides, J., J. O. Coplien, and N. Kerth, eds. *Pattern Languages of Program Design — II*. Reading, MA: Addison-Wesley. 1996.

[PLoP1998]   Martin, R., Dirk Riehle, and Frank Buschmann. *Pattern Languages of Program Design—3*. Reading, MA: Addison Wesley Longman. 1998.

[Pree1995]   Pree, Wolfgang. *Design Patterns for Object-Oriented Software Development*. Reading, MA: Addison-Wesley. 1995.

[Reenskaug1996]   Reenskaug, Trygve. *Working with Objects: The OOram Software Engineering Method*. Greenwich: Manning Publications. 1996.

[Rumbaugh1991]   Rumbaugh, James. *Object-Oriented Modeling and Design*. Englewood Cliffs, NJ: Prentice-Hall. 1991.

[Selic+1994]   Selic, Bran, Garth Gullekson, and Paul T. Ward. *Real-Time Object-Oriented Modeling*. New York, NY: John Wiley & Sons, 1994.

[Shaw1994]   Shaw, Mary. "Formalizing Architectural Connection." *Proceedings of the 16th International Conference on Software Engineering*. 1994.

[Snyder1986]   Snyder, Alan. "Encapsulation and Inheritance in Object-Oriented Programming Languages." *SIGPLAN Notices* 21,11. November 1986.

[Stevens+1974]   Stevens, Myers, Constantine. "Structured Design." *IBM Systems Journal*. 1974.

[Stroustrup1986]   Stroustrup, B. *The C++ Programming Language*. Reading, MA: Addison Wesley Longman. 1997. p. 123. Note: 3rd Edition published in 1998.

[Tracz1995]   Tracz, Will. *Confessions of a Used Program Salesman: Institutionalizing Software Reuse*. Reading, MA: Addison-Wesley. 1995.

[Turner1993]   Turner, Kenneth J. *Using Formal Description Techniques: An Introduction to Esterel, Lotos, and SDL*. Chichester, England: John Wiley & Sons. 1993.

[Ungar+1987]   Ungar, David, and R. B. Smith. "Self: The Power of Simplicity." *Proceedings of OOPSLA 1987 (SIGPLAN Notices* 22(12)). New York: ACM Press, December 1987. pp. 227–241.

[Wegner1987]   Wegner, Peter. "Dimensions of Object-Based Language Design." *SIGPLAN Notices* 22, 12. December 1987. pp. 168–182

[Weinberg1971]   Weinberg, Gerald M. *Psychology of Computer Programming*. Van Nostrand. 1971.

[Weiss1999]   Weiss, David M., and Chi Tau Robert Lai. *Family Based Domain Engineering*. Reading, MA: Addison Wesley Longman. 1999.

[Whorf1986]   Whorf, B. J. Cited in *The C++ Programming Language*, by Bjarne Stroustrup. Reading, MA: Addison-Wesley. 1986. p. iii.

[Winograd1987]   Winnograd, Terry. *Understanding Computers and Cognition: A New Foundation for Design*. Reading, MA: Addison-Wesley. 1987.

[Wirfs-Brock+1990]   Wirfs-Brock, Rebecca, Brian Wilkerson, and Lauren Wiener. *Designing Object-Oriented Software*. Englewood Cliffs, NJ: Prentice-Hall. 1990.

[Yourdon1979]   Yourdon, Ed. *Structured Design: Fundamentals of a Discipline of Computer Program and Systems Design*. Englewood Cliffs, NJ: Prentice-Hall. 1979.

Index